PRACTICAL S
SECOND EDIT

PRACTICAL SGML
SECOND EDITION

by

Eric van Herwijnen

NICE Technologies
Veraz, France

KLUWER ACADEMIC PUBLISHERS
Boston / Dordrecht / London

Distributors for North America:
Kluwer Academic Publishers
101 Philip Drive
Assinippi Park
Norwell, Massachusetts 02061 USA

Distributors for all other countries:
Kluwer Academic Publishers Group
Distribution Centre
Post Office Box 322
3300 AH Dordrecht, THE NETHERLANDS

Library of Congress Cataloging-in-Publication Data

Van Herwijnen.
   Practical SGML / by Eric van Herwijnen. --2nd ed.
      p.   cm.
   Includes bibliographical references and index.
   ISBN 0-7923-9434-8
   1. SGML (Computer program language)   I. Title.
   QA76.73.S44V36   1994
   005-dc20   93-47579
                                                        CIP

Printed on acid-free paper.

Printed in the United States of America

Since my wife's patience ran out during the first edition, I dedicate this second edition to my son, Théo...

Contents

Foreword

In the past three years since the initial publication of *Practical SGML* by Eric van Herwijnen, the computer industry has seen a dramatic increase in the use and acceptance of SGML and many of the concepts derived from it. Much of this growth can be attributed to the work of Eric and a small army of other experts and professionals who have educated end-users, application programmers, managers, and others on SGML and the inherent benefits of those who work with it.

This latest version of *Practical SGML* is another step in this process, with greater emphasis and focus on helping the novice work his way through the vast amounts of information required to become proficient in SGML:

• the tools currently on the market that enable the easy creation of SGML data and the use and distribution of that data in a variety of forms;

• the minimum amount of information needed by people who wish to understand and use ISO 8879;

• aids and information on how to stay current with the volumes of material written on SGML in publications throughout the world;

• practical examples of the many SGML constructs and guidelines on their appropriate uses;

• other helpful hints and insights based on years of working with the standard and integrating it into a complex and challenging computer environment.

This book is both practical and vital for anyone who needs an introduction to the many facets of SGML and how it fits into an organization, either in the government, corporate enterprises, or industry groups. Organizations throughout the world are recognizing the need for international standards and open systems as they build computer systems and networks employing applications, hardware, network protocols, operating systems from a multitude of computer software and hardware manufacturers. In addition, the requirement to develop, access, and reuse corporate information as a key corporate asset has become a predominant motivating factor in the industry. SGML has played a central role in this development in the past several years and will continue to play a more central role in the years to come.   The emergence of on-line information and information by-products (including multi-media applications) requires the diversity and exchange of content identification that SGML enables.

With the second edition of *Practical SGML* Eric will be training the new generation of SGML experts who are needed to help their organizations improve their productivity and competitiveness. These days no one can ignore the SGML standard for who knows what your competitors are doing!

Sharon Adler and *Anders Berglund*
Boulder, Colorado

Preface to the second edition

During the past 30-40 years we have seen an enormous growth in all areas of computer applications. Initially, computers were mainly used by scientists to do numerically intensive calculations ("number crunching"). Now they have found their way into homes and offices. Companies equip all staff, managers, and secretaries with powerful personal computers instead of typewriters.

Computers are applied more and more in areas of human communications, particularly those concerned with text processing. This is a natural evolution, encouraged by the availability of cheap and user-friendly micro computers. Despite the obvious benefits there are some frustrating problems associated with the use of text processing systems. Partly for competitive reasons, partly for functional reasons, the formats used by computer manufacturers are often incompatible. Data which are processed by one system cannot be used on another. Storing text in a machine-readable form raises expectations that cannot always be met. It is hard to explain to an author that text, which exists on a computer, needs to be retyped in a different format. Another problem with electronically stored information is that it is difficult to understand and retrieve.

In areas of professional computer use — for example, programming languages — the emphasis on portability through standardization has existed for a relatively long time. Only quite recently, in October 1986, the International Organization for Standardization (ISO) issued a standard for document representation: **SGML**, the Standard Generalized Markup Language (International Standard 8879) which immediately attracted much attention. This ISO standard explains how documents may be split into a part containing the text and a part describing its *structure* without reference to a particular word- or text-processing system. SGML conforming documents can be interchanged and processed on many different systems in many different ways. Programs can analyze SGML texts because their structure is clearly indicated. Hence computers can manage large amounts of complex data and provide easier access to these data.

Traditionally, the only dimension of text is the paper it is printed on. Perhaps the most important property of SGML is its ability to add a new dimension to information, since the latter becomes independent of the medium. This permits new kinds of processing. Storage is no longer restricted to paper, but could be in different forms such as in a database or on optical media. Retrieval facilities may be used that cannot be applied to unstructured text. If there ever will be "paperless offices," SGML will play an important role in them.

During the lifetime of the first edition of this book, SGML has become widely accepted and is becoming more widely used. Since it is becoming so important, I felt it was worthwhile to do a major revision. A complete re-write should enable *Practical SGML* to withstand the test of time and make it *the* definitive introductory book about SGML.

Two major points of criticism of the first edition were that the book was not yet simple enough to be given to complete novices, and that for detailed points it was not precise enough. I have therefore tried to present the minimum information about SGML as directly as possible. The book was also criticized as being a "book for programmers," and although it has been simplified in many places, I should point out that document analysis and writing DTDs are very akin to programming.

There are four parts to this book. Part I, Getting Started with SGML, explains what SGML is, how to use it, and what kind of software is needed. It is written for beginners and does not touch on any programming aspects of SGML.

Part II, Writing DTDs, explains document analysis, DTD design, markup declarations, an overview of available DTDs, and tips for writing DTDs. I have introduced structure diagrams as an intermediate step which should make writing DTDs easier for non-programmers. Parts I and II contain the minimum information that is required for using standard SGML.

Part III, Customizing SGML, explains advanced concepts such as the SGML declaration, minimization, notation, short references, marked sections and ambiguities. It is intended for anyone who is interested in the more subtle features of SGML, or who needs to customize SGML because its default functionality is not adequate.

Part IV, Special Applications, contains some examples of the application of SGML to EDI (Electronic Document Interchange), mathematics, and graphics. SGML is part of a suite of ISO standards called "Information Processing - Text and Office Systems." This suite includes related standards such as the Hypermedia/Time-based Structuring Language (HyTime), the Document Style Specification and Semantics Language (DSSSL), the Standard Document Interchange Format (SDIF), the Standard Page Description Language (SPDL), and the Fonts standard. The final chapter contains an introduction to these standards.

Exercises throughout the text allow you to test your understanding. The answers are given in Appendix A. In Appendix B I explain how to interpret the output of the public domain sgmls parser.

I do not address the LINK, CONCUR, and SUBDOCument features. The first edition contained descriptions of a number of SGML products, which I have removed to avoid a too rapid outdating of the book. Wherever appropriate, I included the output of the public domain sgmls parser. I choose this parser to remain independent of any commercial bias. It should not be seen as a value judgment on behalf of this or other parsers.

Acknowledgments

Many people have contributed to this book by their constant encouragement or by discussing text processing and SGML with me. The second edition of Practical SGML evolved during the SGML courses that I was invited to give for TEXcel by Bruce Wolman (TEXcel). Without these courses, this second edition would never have appeared.

I thank Paula Angerstein (TEXcel), for allowing me to use her document ISO/IEC JTC1/SC18/WG8 N1427 as the basis for the section on DSSSL. I thank Wayne Wohler (IBM) for many helpful comments after a careful reading of the manuscript. I also thank him for allowing me to use his figures (5 and 15) and his articles which were published in <TAG> (Volume 5, 10, 1992; Volume 6, 1 and 2, 1993) as a basis for chapter 15 on the SGML declaration. Permission from SGML Associates, the publisher of <TAG>, is gratefully acknowleged. I thank my co-authors Nico Poppelier (Elsevier Science Publishers) and Chris Rowley (Open University) for allowing me to use parts of the article "Standard DTD's and Scientific Publishing" in the chapter on mathematics and SGML. This article appeared in EPSIG News (September 1992).

The SGML Tutorial, an electronic book produced by Electronic Book Technologies Inc. was an intermediate step in between the first and second editions of Practical SGML. I thank Lou Reynolds (EBT) for making this happen and Paul Kahn (Dynamic Diagrams) for many helpful suggestions concerning the content.

The book was prepared with the ADEPT 5.0 software and I am grateful to ArborText Inc. for providing me with an advance release of their software and expert help teaching me how to use it. I thank Nick van Heist (TEXcel) for writing the first version of the FOSI. This FOSI was converted to 5.0 and debugged by Jim Salois (ArborText), to whom I would like to express my gratitude. A first draft of the material was tested during a course at ArborText.

I would like to thank my friend David Foster (CERN) for many NICE remarks.

I have tried to minimize the use of any specific trademark or product name in the text. Wherever such a term appears, I ask the relevant vendor to accept this paragraph as an acknowledgment.

Finally I thank all past participants to my courses for their patience with the imperfect, fast evolving material.

Conventions and definitions

The following conventions and definitions are used in this book:

- When new terms are introduced, they appear in **bold** typeface and a definition follows in the text. For example: **SGML**, the Standard Generalized Markup Language, became an ISO standard in 1986.

- The glossary at the end of the book groups all definitions given in the text and contains an explanation of some typesetting concepts.

- Examples are printed in a monospaced font and are preceded and followed by a blank line, such as:

```
This is an example.
```

- Markup and names of elements are given in a monospaced, bold characters, such as **<MEMO>**.

- Whenever a special character or symbol is referenced in the text, it is shown within quotes between parentheses. For example, a reference to the exclamation mark character is written as:

```
("!")
```

- Unless mentioned otherwise, the notation, reserved names and definitions described in this book all refer to the **reference concrete syntax** (see section 15.5).

- At the end of each chapter I have included a bibliography that will help you to understand the text better.

When I speak about **text** in this book, I assume that it is part of a **document** and that it is available in electronic form on a computer or on any of its peripherals such as magnetic tape, hard disk, diskette, or memory. An electronic document is stored in a **file** on a computer. By text and document **interchange** I mean the transfer of texts or documents to a different computer system (via a network, diskette, or tape). Interchange can also mean moving a document to a different processor, such as from a text formatter to a database. The text formatter and the database need not be on the same computer.

---

[1] The difference between word processing and text processing systems is that the former display the results on the screen and allow interaction with the user while the latter are non-interactive. In this book, however, I use these terms without making the distinction.

Text processing is the set of processes that are carried out on documents such as document preparation, edition, formatting, and publication. **Text formatters** and **word processors** are computer programs that group words into paragraphs, choose fonts, calculate the position of words on a page, and so on.[1] **Desktop publishing** systems enable professional results to be obtained.

This book is a very personal view of SGML, containing opinions, advice, and warnings. An "SGML guide" shows where the material is subjective via three icons, "Your SGML guide thinks", "Your SGML guide advises" and "Your SGML guide warns" that are displayed in the margin next to the text:

The disadvantages of this approach are: ...

This is a feature that I have never needed. Should you nevertheless decide to use it, do it in the way described here.

You should avoid doing this to keep out of trouble.

Part I. Getting started

This part of the book is for authors, document managers, programmers and everyone who needs an introduction to SGML. At the end you should know:

- why you need SGML;
- something about the history of SGML;
- the basic ideas of SGML;
- the components of an SGML system;
- how to create an SGML document;
- how to read a DTD;
- some selection criteria for SGML editors;
- how to keep up to date with SGML developments.

1. Introduction

The Standard Generalized Markup Language (**SGML**) is the International Organization for Standardization (**ISO**) standard for document description (ISO 8879:1986 [1]). It is designed to enable text interchange and is intended for use in the publishing field, but can also be applied in the office and engineering areas. SGML documents have a rigorously described structure that may be analyzed by computers and easily understood by humans.

1.1 The problem with today's word processors

Today, computers are frequently used in homes and offices (PCs, Macintoshes, workstations like Sparc, HP, RISC/6000). These user-friendly machines are entering the domain of administrative applications including word- and text-processing.

The choice of products for processing documents is large: Microsoft (MS) Word, WordPerfect, Displaywrite, Wordstar, FrameMaker, ADEPT•Publisher, Interleaf, PageMaker and Quark Xpress are just a small selection of what is available on the market. Each product has its own user interface, its own purpose, and its own advantages. Indeed, it is common for an organization to use a number of different programs. Problems arise when moving a document between systems.

1.1.1 A simple document (memorandum)

As an example, consider the simple office memorandum in Figure 1.

This memo could have been written with a typewriter or with a word processor. There are no text formatter commands in this memo, which is a straight ASCII [2] text file. There are no special characters. You can, however, distinguish the different parts of this memo since they are separated by blank lines. Alignment is achieved by some extra blank spaces. These are **visual** properties of a document.

1.1.2 Exercise

Make a list of the visual properties of the memo.

---

[2] ASCII is the character set which is used by most PCs.

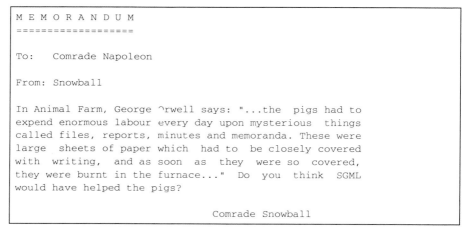

Figure 1. An Example of an Office Memorandum (ASCII)

1.1.3 Using MS Word to make the memo

You could have created this memo with a WYSIWYG word processor such as MS Word [2] on a Macintosh, as shown in Figure 2.

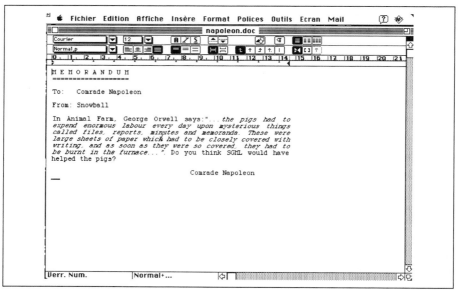

Figure 2. Making the Memo in MS Word

In addition to the visual properties of the memo above, I put the text between the quotation marks in italic (slanted) letters to make the quotation stand out.

When you save your MS Word document, you give it a name. You have to remember this name if you want to find this document back later. In addition to saving the document as a standard MS Word file, you can use the "exchange" format recommended by Microsoft, the so-called Rich Text Format (RTF[3]).

Figure 3 shows the RTF form of the memo. RTF can be read by the PC version of MS Word and some other products.

```
{\rtf1\mac\deff2 {\fonttbl{\f20\froman Times}{\f22\fmodern Courier;}}
\paperw11880\paperh16820\widowctrl\ftnbj \sectd\pgnx720\pgny720
\linemod0\linex0\cols1\endnhere \pard\plain \qj\fi360 \f20
{M E M O R A N D U M\par}\pard \qj\fi20 {\f22 ===================\par
\par
To:    Comrade Napoleon\par
\par
From: Snowball\par
\par
}\pard \qj\fi20 {\f22 In Animal Farm, George Orwell says:"...}{\i\f22
the pigs had to expend enormous labour every day upon mysterious
things called files, reports, minutes and memoranda. These were large
sheets of paper which had to be closely covered with writing, and as
soon as they were so covered, they had to be burnt in the furnace..."}
{\f22 Do you think SGML would have helped the pigs?
\par }\pard \qj\fi360 {\f22 \par
                              Comrade Napoleon}\par

}
```

Figure 3. The RTF Form of the Memo

The RTF file contains commands that are interpreted as formatting instructions by Word. Even without understanding the RTF language, you can recognize commands for fonts ({\f22\fmodern Courier}), paper width (\paperw), etc.

The first problem with RTF and other internal formats is that there is no indication who, for example, is the author of the memo, or who the memo was sent to. This makes it difficult to retrieve the document later, when you have forgotten how its filename relates to its content. In traditional systems, the only indication of the content of a file is its name.

Your SGML guide thinks...

Another problem arises because the RTF commands are mixed up with the data and they contain explicit instructions about the visual properties of the document. You'll understand why this causes a problem by looking at the same memo in a different system.

1.1.4 Using T_EX to create the memo

The next figure shows the memo in a form that can be used as input for the T_EX [4] program:

```
%
\noindent
M E M O R A N D U M
\noindent
==============

\noindent
\settabs 6 \columns
\+TO: &Comrade Napoleon\cr
\+\cr
\+FROM: &Snowball\cr
\noindent


In Animal Farm, George Orwell says: { \it "...the pigs
had to expend enormous labour every day upon mysterious
things called files, reports, minutes and memoranda.
These were large sheets of paper which had to be closely
covered with writing, and as soon as they were so
covered, they were burnt in the furnace..."}
Do you think SGML would have helped the pigs?
\noindent

\+&Comrade Snowball\cr
\bye
```

Figure 4. The TEX Form of the Memorandum

TEX commands all start with the symbol '\' (backslash).

The percent symbol is a comment, meaning that TEX ignores that line. If you don't give TEX any commands, it assumes that a blank line starts a new paragraph. Since paragraphs are indented, the effect of the command `\noindent` is to leave a blank line and to start the next line without an indent. The command `\settabs 6 \columns` tells TEX to place a tab stop at columns which are 6 characters wide (the & positions text at a tab stop), and `\cr` is a carriage-return. A change to an italic typeface is achieved by {`\it ''...the pigs...''`}.

1.1.5 Exercise

Make a list of the TEX commands that influence the visual properties of the memo.

1.1.6 Proprietary formats: closed systems

Now imagine you want to send your memo in MS Word to a colleague who uses TEX. As you can see from the example above, the backslash is about the only thing that RTF and TEX systems have in common.

To make the MS Word file processable by TeX, all RTF commands for MS Word have to be taken out and replaced by equivalent TeX commands. This requires a detailed knowledge of both systems. Some commands may not have an equivalent in the other system; how, for example, would you tell TeX that the MS Word document uses the font "modern Courier"? [3]

The lack of interchangeability of documents is frustrating. In a multivendor environment, it is almost impossible to create an integrated database of documents.

To summarize, the two major problems with unstructured use of word processors are:

Your SGML guide thinks...

1. Mixing commands that affect visual properties with the data makes it difficult to transport documents to other software. Of course, you need to add visual properties to give some indication of the information content — but it's subjective. That is why you need a formal approach.

2. Concentrating on the visual properties without concern for a document's structure causes important information to be hidden. Information that is hidden is, in fact, lost.

Proprietary formats only allow exchange within themselves. A proprietary format encourages a proprietary view of the information content. In other words, they can be considered *closed.*

1.2 The solution: SGML

1.2.1 Separating form and structure

When you are working with a word processor, such as MS Word in Figure 2, you are thinking about the choice of font, the weight of the letters, the size of the margins, columns, and so on. You worry how to place the text on the page. Should it be centered? Should the text be left adjusted or surrounded by blank lines? These visual properties of a document define its *form.*

Each document also has *content* (the name of the person who the memo is for, who it is from, the main text, etc.) while the content has a *logical structure.* For example, a book has a title, followed by a nested collection of chapters, sections, and paragraphs. Figure 5 shows how a document's logical structure relates to its form.

As you are typing in the content of your document, the system adds the commands that affect the document's form. When the visual information is mixed up with the data of a document, it becomes difficult to export to other systems. SGML solves the problem by isolating any visual information in a document because the information is declared explicitly.

---

[3] TeX uses its own fonts, called Computer Modern fonts.

1.2.2 Exercises

1. Describe the logical structure of the memo in Figure 1.

2. Represent the memo in a way that is independent of its appearance and permits the recognition of its logical parts.

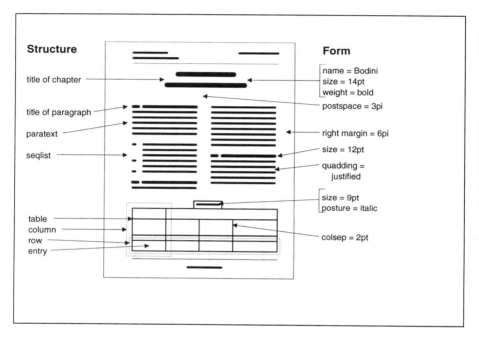

Figure 5. Structure vs. Appearance

1.2.3 SGML: an open solution

Now look at the SGML representation of the memo in Figure 6. There are no formatting instructions nor any special characters in the SGML memo, although some characters, such as the "<" and ">", have a special meaning. Documents in SGML can be sent from one system to another without loss of information or misinterpretation. The transferred document, which is independent of application-specific information, can be processed as required. The SGML document is also completely vendor independent, which is a significant advantage for data that must survive many years, perhaps outliving several systems.

```
<!DOCTYPE MEMO SYSTEM "memo.dtd">
<MEMO>
<TO>Comrade Napoleon
<FROM>Snowball
<BODY>
<P>In Animal Farm, George Orwell says: <Q>...the pigs  had
to expend enormous labour every day upon mysterious things
called files, reports, minutes and  memoranda.  These were
large sheets of paper which had to be closely covered with
writing, and as soon as they were so  covered,  they  were
burnt in the furnace...</Q> Do you think SGML  would  have
helped the pigs?</P></BODY>
</CLOSE>
</MEMO>
```

Figure 6. Memorandum (SGML)

The logical parts (for example, the person the memo is sent *to*, the person the memo came *from*) are clearly marked (by <TO>, </TO>, <FROM>, </FROM>, etc.). In contrast to other formats (such as RTF), a document can be read, understood, and edited with little effort. Databases of SGML documents with intelligent searching facilities become possible.

The strong points of SGML can be summarized as follows:

- hardware independence, meaning easy interchange of texts;

- separation of structure and layout;

- software independence, giving an open-endedness to data;

- unambiguous format, enabling database storage and retrieval.

SGML makes a document portable because it contains an unambiguous description of its logical structure, independent of its visual form. SGML is not vendor specific and it is controlled under ISO rules which generate and modify standards in a process that is open to the public through participation in national standards bodies. This makes SGML an *open* standard.

1.3 When should you use SGML?

Making the choice for SGML should be a strategic decision that is taken at a high management level in a company. SGML can be used in the following situations:

1. For publishing in its broadest definition, ranging from single medium conventional publishing to multimedia database publishing.

2. In office document processing when the benefits of human readability and interchange with publishing systems are required.

In other words, when you want to:

- give your document *multiple* purposes;

- *interchange* a document through a network;

- *add* a document to a database or document filing system;

- *revise* a document later in its lifetime;

- exploit the *full* lifetime of a document;

- make use of the *structure* in a document;

- *present* a document in different ways;

- *retrieve* information in a document;

- make *CALS* compliant documents (see section 1.5).

SGML will help your organization to have a well-defined and logical information structure. SGML is not quite the same as other standards. Committing yourself to use SGML is not the same as using a local area network standard such as Ethernet. Using Ethernet is a question of buying a board, placing it in your PC, installing some software and plugging a cable into a socket. SGML requires an effort to install and has particularly long term benefits.

1.4 Some myths about SGML

Your SGML guide warns...

Ever since SGML has been accepted as an ISO standard, false statements about it appear in the literature and elsewhere. Be aware of the following misconceptions:

1. *SGML is a text formatting system.* SGML describes the structure of information *independent* of any text formatter or use of the data. To obtain a formatted output from an SGML document, however, text formatter commands must be added for formatting and printing.

2. *SGML is unnecessary since there are de facto standards such as* TEX *and PostScript* [5]. SGML is designed to be a standard for interchanging information in textual form. TEX is a text formatter and PostScript is a page description language. A publishing system can use SGML as text interchange format, TEX as text formatter, and PostScript as page description language.

3. *The G in SGML stands for Graphics.* The G in SGML stands for Generalized, and it is a standard for text interchange, not for graphics interchange. It is possible to include graphics in SGML documents.

4. *SGML defines a standard set of document types.* SGML defines neither a standard document structure nor a standard language that uses it. Any type of document may be described by SGML, from simple

office documents (business letters, memos) to complicated scientific or technical documents which include graphics and mathematics.

5. *SGML is an IBM proprietary standard for mainframes.* SGML is an ISO standard, developed by a working group of technical experts with representatives from leading computer manufacturers and the typesetting industry. SGML data are independent of software and hardware. Products are available for large and small computers. Charles Goldfarb from IBM is the editor of the SGML standard.

6. *SGML is a definition of character sets or coding schemes for special symbols. SGML is an extension of ASCII.* SGML is not a character set although it does define which character sets are used in a document.

7. *SGML is user-unfriendly.* SGML says nothing about the user interface of SGML systems and therefore it cannot be considered user-unfriendly. There are several WYSIWYG SGML systems, such as SoftQuad Author/Editor [6], available for PC, Macintosh, and UNIX.

1.5 CALS

1.5.1 Replacing paper flow

"Computer-aided Acquisition and Logistics Support" is an initiative of the U.S. Department of Defense (DoD) to electronically receive, store and distribute technical product documentation with its suppliers. Figure 7 shows the problem that CALS tries to solve.

The subcontractors to the DoD use their own automated, but incompatible, systems. These islands of automation are associated with a paper-intensive administration of weapon systems and therefore carry a heavy overhead. A B-1B bomber, for example, has one million pages of documentation, and a U.S. Navy ship carries 15 to 25 tons of manuals. The major problem preventing automation is this incompatibility.

To coordinate the information that is generated during the lifetime of weapon systems, e.g., design, manufacturing, support, and mainte-nance, between suppliers and government, the DoD imposed a number of standards for exchanging and archiving technical information. By implementing these standards, the current flow of paper should be re-placed by electronic data interchange.

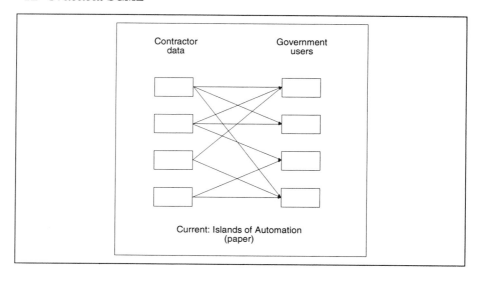

Figure 7. Current Islands of Automation for DoD Suppliers

The four CALS standards are shown in Table 1:

Table 1. The CALS standards

Standard	Description	Use
CALS MILS-STD-1840A	Automated Interchange of Technical Information	Overall standard for exchanging and archiving technical information. Specifies the standards below.
IGES MIL-D-28000	Initial Graphic Exchange Specification	A graphics standard for representing sophisticated 3-D CAD drawings. CALS specifies the 2-D subset for technical illustrations in manuals.
SGML MIL-M-28001	Standard Generalized Markup Language	CALS specifies that technical documents should be marked up with SGML, using the guidelines established in MIL-M-28001. A description of the printed output uses the guidelines established in Appendix B, the Output Specification, and is expected to be superseded by DSSSL.

Standard	Description	Use
CCITT G4MIL-R-28002	Group 4 Facsimile Standard	A standard for describing raster (bit-mapped) data.
CGM MIL-D-28003	Computer Graphics Metafile	CGM is a standard format for describing 2-D illustrations with geometric graphics objects.

Once these standards are in place, contractors can exchange information with the DoD electronically. The "paper" flow will be replaced by a "digital" flow in an automated and integrated system. Figure 8 shows phase I of CALS, to be completed in the nineties.

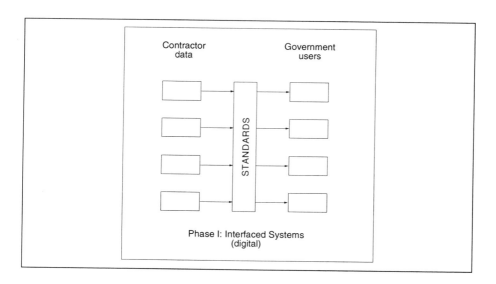

Figure 8. CALS Phase I: Interfaced Systems

The benefits of CALS are:

- increased productivity in creation of technical manuals;
- online access to maintenance information;
- cheaper updating of technical manuals;
- better support through an integrated database;
- savings in weapons-systems life cycle cost.

In the second phase of CALS (see Figure 9), contractors will share data with the DoD and among themselves.

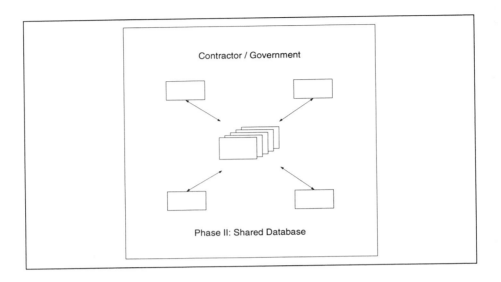

Contractor / Government

Phase II: Shared Database

Figure 9. CALS Phase II: Shared Database

The ultimate aim is a shared (between government and suppliers) database for the entire weapon acquisition, design, manufacture, support and maintenance process. Figure 9 shows a CALS database shared between suppliers and government.

1.5.2 CALS compliance

Information or products that comply with CALS must satisfy the following four conditions:

1. Text and data files must exist in a single package in the format specified by MIL-M-1840.

2. The text files must be marked up with SGML using the guidelines established in MIL-M-28001.

3. The graphics files must conform to CGM, IGES or FAX IV.

4. The composed document satisfies the formatting guidelines from MIL-M-28001.

1.5.3 How useful is CALS for the non-defense industry?

The problems that the DoD set out to solve with CALS appear in all sectors of industry. The CALS strategy can therefore be adopted perfectly well to, say, the acquisition of chemicals by a pharmaceutical company. CALS software packages, however, are specifically intended for the creation of DoD documents (military specifications). To use them for general purposes usually requires extensive modifications.

For a more complete description of CALS than these pages will allow, see [7].

1.6 Exercises

Try to answer the following questions to check whether you understood the material presented in this chapter.

1. Is SGML a text formatting system?

2. Are SGML and WYSIWYG incompatible?

3. Mention some processes that are performed on documents in a text processing application.

4. What is the difference between SGML and PostScript?

5. How does SGML achieve the separation of the structure and the appearance of a document?

1.7 Bibliography for Chapter 1

[1] ISO
ISO 8879:1986 Information processing — Text and office systems — Standard Generalized Markup Language (SGML)
Geneva, 15 October 1986
[2] Microsoft Corporation
Using Microsoft Word, Word Processing Program Version 5.0
Redmond, 1991
[3] Microsoft Corporation
Rich Text Format Specification
Redmond, 1987 and 1990
[4] Donald E. Knuth
The TEX book, Addison-Wesley
Reading, 1986
[5] Adobe Systems Incorporated
PostScript Language Reference Manual, Addison-Wesley
Reading, 1986

[6]   SoftQuad
      Author/Editor Advanced version Users' Guide
      Toronto, 1988
[7]   Joan Smith
      An Introduction to CALS: The Strategy and the Standards, Tech-
      nology Appraisals Ltd
      London, 1990

2. A brief history of SGML

2.1 Traditional markup

SGML is short for "Standard Generalized Markup Language." To get a feeling for what **markup** is, consider the traditional processing of texts arriving at a publisher, ready to be printed. The copy editor annotates manuscripts with instructions to the typesetter concerning layout, fonts, spacing, indentation, and so on:

```
Set this header in 12-point Helvetica Medium Italic on a
14-point text body, justified on a 22-Pica slug with
indents of 1 en on left and none on the right.
```

These traditionally hand-written instructions are called markup. It is the first step in the conversion process of the different formats arriving at the editor's desk (hand-written, double-spaced type, etc.) to the single style that is characteristic of a particular publisher. Notice that in the process of transforming a manuscript to a printed document many different professionals are involved. Also, there is a complete separation of structure and appearance.

The document's structure, i.e., the number of chapters, the order of the paragraphs and sections, are designed by the author. The copy editor and the person responsible for the page make-up design the document's appearance. This separation lies at the heart of SGML.

2.2 Electronic markup

With the introduction of computers into the printing industry, the copy editor's remarks were coded electronically using a special coding system. Each phototypesetter had its own proprietary "language," called a markup language by analogy to the manual system. An example written in the Nortext language [1] looks as follows:

```
<CC 15,5,12>Here we set text with typeface no. 5, point
size 12 and a line length of 15 basic units.
<SS><QL><CC 20,8>Now we have changed to typeface no. 8
and a line length of 20 basic units.
<QL><RS>Here we are back to the typographical
specifications we started with.
```

Figure 10 shows the typeset result of this sequence.

Here we set text with typeface no.
5, point size 12 and a line length
of 15 basic units.
Now we have changed to typeface no. 8
and a line length of 20 basic units.
Here we are back to the typographical specifications we started
with.

Figure 10. Typeset Nortext Example

Typesetting companies or groups inside organizations provided
"keyboarding" services. The source of documents to typeset was always
the same, namely a hand- or type-written manuscript, and a lack of
compatibility did not arise. When authors and clients of typesetting
companies started to do their own typing on a computer, this created
problems: it was only useful if the authors knew the format of their
typesetting vendor in advance. The electronic format of the author's
system was likely to be incompatible with that of the typesetter.

2.3 Specific markup

As computers became more widely available, general purpose programs were written for processing text. Text formatting languages like
IBM Script [2](or DCF), Waterloo Script [3], and the UNIX[4] based nroff
[4] date from the late sixties and the early seventies. TeX came along
a little later. These systems take as input a complete data file that is
processed without interaction with the user.

Like in the case of phototypesetting systems, documents were
marked up with low level formatting "commands" such as "carriage
return," "center the following commands," "go to the next page." The
text is interspersed with **specific markup** commands that tell the
formatter what action to take at that point. In other words, these
commands tell the formatting language *how* to do its work. The
following specific markup commands (Script) could be found at the
beginning of a chapter:

```
.cm skip one line
.sp
```

___
4 UNIX commands are case sensitive and must therefore be given in the case showed.

```
.cm start font roman times 12 points
.bf roman12
.cm center and print in bold
.bd .ce Chapter 1. Introduction
```

Script processes the data (skips one line, changes font size, centers "Chapter 1. Introduction" and prints it in bold) so that it may be sent to a device such as a printer. Comments (lines starting with `.cm`) are ignored. Documents containing this type of markup can only be converted to other typesetting systems at great cost.

Formatting languages such as Script and TEX are powerful; TEX in particular is still in heavy use today. They have the disadvantage that their syntax is complicated, and they don't offer the interactive facilities of most modern systems.

2.3.1 Desktop publishing

The real push toward electronic text processing came with the introduction of small and cheap personal computers for the desktop. User friendly interactive **WYSIWYG** (What You See Is What You Get) word processing systems such as Wordstar [5], MacWrite [6], Microsoft Word and WordPerfect [7] quickly gained in popularity. WYSIWYG means that the results of user instructions are instantaneously visible on the screen approximately like the printed result.

These programs are inexpensive and provide a powerful layout and composition environment with a graphical user interface. The result is that professional-looking documents are at everybody's fingertips.

Desktop publishing goes a level beyond WYSIWYG word processing and provides many powerful features (e.g., text flowing around arbitrarily shaped illlustrations) which enable a completely electronic page layout. Newsletters, magazines, and publicity pamphlets are ideally suited to this technology since they are small and require a flexible page layout. Frequently these documents are soon obsolete and do not need to be reused.

When any kind of automation is required, a desk top publishing system does not suffice. Strangely enough, WYSIWYG word processors do not seem to have taken advantage of the experience gained by batch formatters in the late sixties. As we have seen in section 1.1, WYSIWYG editors mix specific markup with the data in such a way that structure and appearance become inextricably intertwined.

Another problem with the flexibility and ease of use of WYSIWYG word processors is that even with a standard "company" word processor it is almost impossible to obtain a uniform style.

Authors are subject matter experts for whom it is a waste of time to be concerned with typography or document layout. Some call it creativity, but inside organizations where the author has free reign over format, the result is usually an incoherent collection of documents which are not aesthetically pleasing.

2.4 Generic markup

Generic markup can help us to reintroduce the important separation between structure and appearance. This was realized at the time of the confusion over specific markup with photo-typesetting systems. A movement was started to create a standard markup language, which all typesetting vendors would be persuaded to accept as input. It would be the typesetting houses' problem to translate this language into the language of their own photocomposer machines.

To be able to do this, a **generic** markup language was needed. Generic markup means adding information to the text indicating the logical components of a document, such as paragraphs, headers, footnotes. This initial generic markup effort was lead by the GCA [8], an industry group who owns the trademark "GenCode" which is the name of the generic markup language intended for typesetters. The memo example from above, marked up with a fictitious generic TeX like language, is shown in Figure 11.

```
\begin{document}
\documentstyle{memo}
\begin{fm}
\to{Comrade Napoleon}
\from{Snowball}
\end{fm}
\begin{body}
\para{
In Animal Farm, George Orwell says: \quote{... the pigs had to
expend enormous labour every day upon mysterious
things called files, reports, minutes and memoranda. These were
large sheets of paper which had to be closely covered with writing,
and as soon as they were so covered, they had to be burnt in the
furnace...}}
\para{Do you think SGML would have helped the pigs?}
\end{body}
\close{Comrade Napoleon}
\end{document}
```

Figure 11. Generic TeX Markup

Technically, this generic markup is achieved by grouping specific markup commands together as **macros**. For example, in the TeX language above, \to{Comrade Napoleon} stands for the three commands:

```
\noindent
\settabs 6 \columns
\+TO:&Comrade Napoleon\cr
```

This causes the formatting associated with the logical component to be decoupled from the structure of the text. Any information concerning the style of the document is kept separate, i.e., it is not imbedded in the source of the document as with specific markup. Each logical part of a document maps onto a macro call.

Since a few macro calls do the job of many specific commands, a macro package is easier to learn and use. Besides, macros may be called over and over for different documents. They may be stored in a separate file, where they are easier to change, and included when needed. By sharing them between different users, a "corporate" style can be enforced. Macro calls can also be context sensitive. Identical calls may have different properties depending on where they are in a document. A paragraph macro call, for example, will produce an indented line everywhere except for the first time it is called in a chapter or section.

The names of the macro calls corresponding to these parts are also called **tags** (such as \to in the example above).

By using generic markup an author can show the purpose of a textual element without considering its physical appearance. In the example of the \to tag, the author need not worry about questions of presentation such as "Do I leave one or two blank lines after the name of the memo's recipient?" The document is less device dependent, since the title may appear in bold-faced type on one system and in italics on another. Computer programs can analyze texts with rigorously defined markup.

Examples of generic macro systems that were available in the midseventies for the formatters mentioned above are GML (based on IBM Script), Syspub (based on Waterloo Script) and ms (based on nroff/troff) [9]. Later LaTeX [10], [11] was written for TeX.

The WYSIWYG equivalent of generic markup are **stylesheets**. A stylesheet is a way of grouping formatting instructions. These can be applied to a text element, or to a group of text elements, by giving a single code. By attaching a stylesheet to a document its structure is separated from its appearance as with macro calls.

To summarize, the properties and advantages of generic markup are:

Your SGML
guide thinks...

• it indicates the *logical structure* of the document (who is the author of the memo? what is its subject? where are the paragraphs?);

• it separates form and content (the form is hidden in macros or stylesheets);

• it is processable (provided these languages describe the same generic structure, the differences between commands are often trivial: e.g., <FN>, .footnote, .fs, \footnote, and <FOOTNOTE> are used to mark up footnotes in SGML (with the AAP DTD, see section 14.1, BookMaster [12], ms/mm macros of nroff, LaTeX and VAX Document [13], respectively);

- does not require knowledge of typography or pagelayout.

 Please note however, that generic markup in the form of macro collections or stylesheets is not always portable, since the source codes still depend on the formatter.

2.4.1 SGML and generic markup

In 1978 an ANSI (American National Standards Institute) working group (X3 J6) was formed to provide an unambiguous format for text interchange and a markup language that would be sufficiently rich to permit any (future) processing. In the early eighties this work was moved to ISO under a working group which is part of SC18 (ISO/IEC JTC1/SC18/WG8) whose work later resulted in the SGML standard.

SGML is a natural evolution of generic markup and goes a step further by formalizing the document representation and enabling text interchange. Generic markup is combined with the observation that the logical parts of a document can be expressed in a *tree structure*.

The tree structure of the memo from Figure 1 is shown in Figure 12.

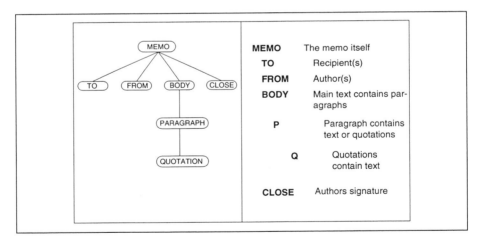

Figure 12. Tree Structure of the Memo

This tree structure shows the logical elements of memos and their nesting. A *structural* markup language for memos contains codes for the logical parts MEMO, TO, FROM, BODY, P, Q, and CLOSE. This markup language defines a class of documents with the "memo" structure.

SGML has the flexibility to define an infinite set of generic markup languages (one for memos, one for articles, one for books, etc.). An SGML markup language defines the possible hierarchical structures of documents in this class. The memo language above, for example, could permit the order of the TO and FROM elements to be interchanged. Defining a markup language is called "creating an SGML application" or "creating a **document type definition** (DTD)" (see section 4.2).

SGML is not a "markup language" in the sense of troff, TEX, or LaTeX: it contains the rules for creating an unlimited variety of markup languages but does not concern itself with the formatting of marked-up documents. Figure 13 shows the SGML form of the memo again.

```
<!DOCTYPE MEMO SYSTEM "memo.dtd">
<MEMO>
<TO>Comrade Napoleon
<FROM>Snowball
<BODY>
<P>In Animal Farm, George Orwell says: <Q>...the pigs  had
to expend enormous labour every day upon mysterious things
called files, reports, minutes and  memoranda.  These were
large sheets of paper which had to be closely covered with
writing, and as soon as they were so  covered,  they  were
burnt in the furnace...</Q> Do you think SGML  would  have
helped the pigs?</P></BODY>
</CLOSE>
</MEMO>
```

Figure 13. Memorandum (SGML)

The symbols "<",">","<!" and "</" are called **delimiters** since they delimit the markup. These delimiters are used to construct **tags** (such as <MEMO>) which mark-up the documents logical parts, or **elements**.

To format or further process an SGML document, additional information is required. How this is done will be discussed later.

2.5 Exercises

1. What is the difference between specific and generic markup?

2. Why does specific markup make a document less portable?

2.6 Bibliography for Chapter 2

[1]   Norsk Data
      Nortext-1 typographic function codes, ND-61.029.1 EN
      1986

[2]   S.E.Madnick, A.Moulton
      SCRIPT: An on-line manuscript processing system, IEEE Trans-
      actions on Engineering Writing and Speech, 11(2), Pages 92-100
      1968
[3]   B. Uttley
      Waterloo Script
      1973
[4]   J.F. Osanna
      NROFF Users' Book — Second Edition
      1974
[5]   Micropro
      WordStar 20 Reference Guide
      San Rafael, 1986
[6]   Claris
      MacWrite II User's Guide
      Mountain View, 1989
[7]   WordPerfect Corporation
      WordPerfect (PC version 5.0)
      Orem, 1988
[8]   100 Daingerfield Road
      Graphical Communication Association
      Alexandria, VA 22314–2888,
[9]   M.E.Lesk
      Typing documents on the UNIX system: Using the —ms macros
      with TROFF and NROFF, Bell Laboratories
      1976
[10] L. Lamport
      LaTeX User's Guide and Reference Manual
      Addison-Wesley, Reading, 1986
[11] M. Goossens , F. Mittelbach and A. Samarin
      The LaTeX companion
      Addison-Wesley, Reading, 1994
[12] IBM Corporation
      Document Composition Facility BookMaster - Version 3
      (SC34-5009-03)
      Boulder, 1990
[13] Digital Corporation
      VAX Document User's Guide — Using Global Tags. Ref. No.
      AA-JT84C-TE
      1991

3. Components of an SGML system

An SGML system consists of SGML documents and SGML software. This chapter offers a first orientation in the land of SGML systems.

3.1 The three parts of an SGML document

In addition to the marked-up data, an SGML document has two formal parts of whose existence you should be aware: the **SGML declaration** and the **document type definition (DTD)**.

3.1.1 The SGML declaration

The SGML declaration is a formal part of each SGML document, specifying which characters and delimiters are used. It:

• is usually common to all documents in an SGML installation;

• may or may not be part of the document (a default will be used in its absence);

• gives the precise details on how SGML was applied to this document;

• defines which characters should be used as delimiters (e.g. `<`, `>`, `/ >`);

• defines which character set (ASCII or other) is used.

An example of an SGML declaration is shown in Figure 70. For Part I of this book you do not need to know about the SGML declaration, except that it exists.

3.1.2 The document type definition (DTD)

The **DTD** defines the rules for marking up a class of documents. It:

• it defines the structure of a document;

• is different for each set of documents with a different structure (memo's, articles, books);

• is written in SGML;

- may be stored externally to the document.

The DTD for the memo is shown in Figure 14. As an author, you need to know that the DTD exists and what DTDs are available on your system. Before you can use SGML, you have to select a DTD. As a manager, you need to know that the creation and maintenance of DTDs is of crucial importance to the success of SGML in your organization.

```
<!-- DTD for simple office memoranda                        -->
<!--          ELEMENTS    MIN   CONTENT            (EXCEPTIONS) -->
<!ELEMENT MEMO          - -   ((TO & FROM), BODY, CLOSE?)     >
<!ELEMENT TO            - O   (#PCDATA)                       >
<!ELEMENT FROM          - O   (#PCDATA)                       >
<!ELEMENT BODY          - O   (P)*                            >
<!ELEMENT P             - O   (#PCDATA | Q )*                 >
<!ELEMENT PREF          - O   EMPTY                           >
<!ELEMENT Q             - -   (#PCDATA)                       >
<!ELEMENT CLOSE         - O   (#PCDATA)                       >
<!--          ELEMENTS    NAME    VALUE                DEFAULT   -->
<!ATTLIST MEMO          STATUS  (CONFIDEN|PUBLIC) PUBLIC        >
<!ATTLIST P             id      ID               #IMPLIED      >
<!ATTLIST PREF          refid   IDREF            #IMPLIED      >
```

Figure 14. Memorandum (DTD)

I'll come back to why you need DTDs and what the symbols in Figure 14 mean in Chapter 4.

3.1.3 *The document instance*

The document **instance** is the document itself which:

- contains data (contents);
- contains markup;
- includes a reference to the DTD (if it is not present in the document).

The word instance is used because it is one concrete realization of a class of documents that have the structure defined by a DTD. The instance of the memo was shown in Figure 13.

3.2 The parts of an SGML installation

See Figure 15 for a schematic presentation of the parts of an SGML installation, including its system software.

Notice that SGML only describes the SGML data, the DTD and what the role is of the SGML parser. These parts are usually hidden inside the software that you interact with as a user such as the editor, the text formatter, or the database.

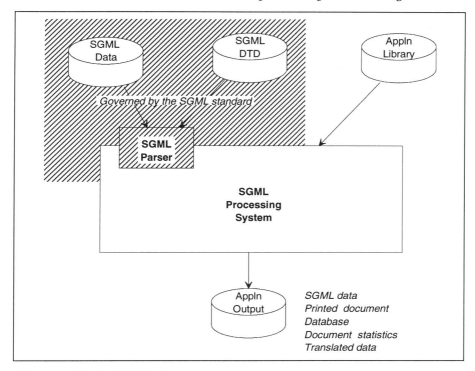

Figure 15. An SGML System

3.2.1 The SGML data

This is the file containing the text plus the SGML markup (that is, the document instance). In case you are worried how the markup between brackets will appear in the data, rest assured that this is taken care of automatically by a program called an SGML editor (see section 5.1). As an author, it is helpful to know what SGML files look like, but hopefully you will never need to create one by marking up the data "by hand."

SGML does not describe how the SGML editor should operate. In Figure 15 it would typically be situated in the box marked "SGML Processing System". There is much software available to get your data into SGML.

3.2.2 One or more DTDs

The DTD is the hub of any SGML system. You can not use SGML without thinking about a DTD.

DTDs should be carefully designed by a specialist. This process is explained in detail in Part II.

3.2.3 A parser

To ensure that the markup of an SGML document is consistent, error free, and correctly interpreted, each SGML system contains a program that recognizes markup in SGML documents. This program is called a **parser**. The parser checks:

- if the document's DTD conforms to SGML;

- if the document instance conforms to the DTD.

Often parsers are included in an SGML editor, but they can also be used independently. Parsers help prevent making mistakes and the misuse of markup. For the memo example, paragraphs are only allowed in the main body part. If you add a paragraph after the main text of the memorandum:

```
</BODY>
<P>Text in a place where it is not allowed</P>
<CLOSE>
```

the SGML parser will complain about the incorrect markup. You will learn later why the markup in this example is wrong. Parsers shuold verify very document before translating it for processing, or before exporting it to a different computer.

A variety of parsers are commercially available (for example from Exoterica[1] or Sema-Metra[2]) and in the public domain (the Amsterdam SGML parser [3]). A free parser also exists in the public domain (arcsgml[4]). This parser, which is distributed by the SGML User's Group, may be obtained (among others) via anonymous FTP from the University of Oslo: FTP.IFI.UIO.NO, or [129.240.64.2].

The files are:

```
-rw-r--r-- 1 enag wheel   60957 Jul 19 17:41 arcrexx.exe
-rw-r--r-- 1 enag wheel  113776 Jul 19 17:41 arcsgmlc.exe
-rw-r--r-- 1 enag wheel   72136 Jul 19 17:41 arcsgmlh.exe
-rw-r--r-- 1 enag wheel   58041 Jul 19 17:41 arctest.exe
-rw-r--r-- 1 enag wheel   50460 Jul 19 17:41 arcvm2.exe
-rw-r--r-- 1 enag wheel  140124 Jul 19 17:41 pkz110ex.exe
-rw-r--r-- 1 enag wheel    2274 Jul 19 17:41 readme
```

To retrieve them, do the following:

1. Connect to ftp.ifi.uio.no [129.240.64.2] via ftp.

2. Log in as anonymous and use your e-mail address as your password.

3. Type *cd SIGhyper/SGMLUG/distrib.*

4. Set *type image.*

5. Retrieve the files with *get* or *mget* **.

For more information about the network, see section 6.4.

3.2.4 A processing system

An SGML document by itself only has structure (in addition to its contents), since it was dissociated from any machine or process-specific information. Once an SGML document has been verified by a parser, it has to be processed. The structure has to be translated into, for example, word processor-, formatter- or database loader-commands. The processing of SGML documents is not under the control of the SGML standard. DSSSL [5] is an attempt to standardize text formatting applications.

As I remarked before, an SGML editor is also part of a processing system; the editor looks at the DTD to determine the structure of the document that is being created or modified; a parser checks the validity of the data whenever this is required.

3.2.5 The output of a processing system

The output of the processing system could be, for example, the translated document, in a form that is suitable for input to a word processor. It could also be statistics about the document or the printed document.

Note that an SGML parser should only inform you of SGML errors in your document. In this case it is called a **validating SGML parser**. It is not obliged to give you any other output, and when it does, this output is not standardized in any form.

If the parser only recognizes markup, but does not do any checking, in can not be called a validating SGML parser, and is simply called an SGML parser. This definition of a parser is not quite the same as the one used in compiler terminology. The word SGML "scanner" would be more appropriate, whereas a validating parser would simply be called a parser.

3.3 Bibliography for Chapter 3

[1]   Exoterica
      The XGML Kernel
      Ottawa, 1992
[2]   Sema-Metra
      Mark-it
      Brussels, 1992

[3]   J. Warmer, S. van Egmond
The Implementation of the Amsterdam SGML Parser, Electronic
Publishing, Origination Dissemination and Design, vol 2 (2),
Pages 65–90
July 1989

[4]   SGML User's Group
Arcsgml SGML parser material
Exeter, 1991

[5]   ISO
ISO DIS 10179 :1993 Information Technology — Text and office systems — Document Style Semantics and Specification Language (DSSSL)
Geneva, 1993.

4. Document type components

4.1 Exercises

To get focused, let's start this chapter with some exercises:

1. Look at the document in Figure 16.

```
<!DOCTYPE MEMO SYSTEM "memo.dtd">
<MEMO>
<TO>Comrade Napoleon
<FROM>Snowball
<BODY>
<P>In Animal Farm, George Orwell says: <Q>...the pigs  had to expend
enormous labour every day upon mysterious things called files,
reports, minutes and  memoranda.  These were large sheets of paper
which had to be closely covered with writing, and as soon as they
were so  covered,  they  were burnt in the furnace...</Q>
Do you think SGML  would  have helped the pigs?</P></BODY>
<CLOSE>Comrade Snowball</CLOSE>
</MEMO>
```

Figure 16. A Memorandum (SGML)

2. Now look at the document in Figure 17:

```
<!DOCTYPE LETTER SYSTEM "letter.dtd">
<LETTER>
<TO>
<NAME>Henry Ford</NAME>
<ADDRESS>Motor way, Detroit, U.S.A</ADDRESS></TO>
<FROM>
<NAME>Eric van Herwijnen</NAME>
<ADDRESS>Geneva, Switzerland</ADDRESS></FROM>
<SUBJECT>thief-proof cars</SUBJECT>
<SALUT>Dear Henry,</SALUT>
<BODY>
<P>Wouldn't it be nice if you could design me a thief-proof car?</P>
</BODY>
<CLOSE>Sincerely yours,</CLOSE>
</LETTER>
```

Figure 17. A Letter

3. Are both documents SGML documents?

4. What is the difference between the two?

5. How would you design a single system that can describe both documents?

4.2 The document type definition

4.2.1 Why do we need DTDs?

In the exercise above, the markup language for memo's consists of the tags <MEMO>, <TO>, <FROM>, <BODY>, <P>, <Q>, and <CLOSE>. The markup language for letters has the tags <LETTER>, <TO>, <NAME>, <ADDRESS>, <SUBJECT>, <SALUT>, <BODY>, <P>, and <CLOSE>. Each tag is used to delimit a logical element. The example above describes two distinct languages, each defined by their own **document type definition** (DTD) and applicable to two distinct classes of documents, i.e., memos and letters. SGML lays down the rules for constructing these markup languages.

This example shows that it would not be practical to standardize on a single set of element definitions for all documents. The concept of the DTD supports *any* element definition. The choice of element names can be different for each DTD, but a DTD exists for any document class. A DTD is also called an SGML **application**.

The users of an application (for example, the exchange of documents between authors and one or more publishers) get together to analyze their *joint* requirements. For example, a group of publishers may get together with a group of authors to design a DTD for articles in journals. This should result in commonly supported document types and structures through a specific set of tags. Both parties may agree on common elements like chapter, paragraph, footnote, etc.

The invention of the DTD means that the problems of standard tag names and structures are skirted, since everyone can invent their own markup language and still benefit from SGML tools and products. A lot of thinking and analysis, however, has to be done before documents can be freely exchanged between systems.

4.2.2 What does a DTD do?

More precisely, a DTD defines:

- the *names* of elements that are permissible;

- how *often* an element may appear;

- the *order* in which elements must appear;

- whether markup, such as the start- or end-tag (see section 4.4), may be *omitted*;

- the *contents* of elements (see section 4.4), i.e., the names of other elements that are allowed to appear inside them, down to the character data level;

- tag *attributes* (see section 4.6) and their default values;

- the names of all *entities* (see section 4.8) that may be used;

- any *typewriter conventions* that can be exploited to ease adding markup. For example, a blank line followed by a line indented by three spaces can be interpreted as a paragraph start-tag. This is achieved by **short references** that are described in Part III, section 19.1.

A DTD does not contain information on how to process a document or what it should look like. Whenever one is talking about SGML, it is very important to specify which DTD is being used. An example of a DTD that was developed for books is the DTD by the Association of American Publishers (AAP)[1].

A DTD defines three types of markup commands: **elements**, **attributes**, and **entities**. Marking up an SGML document is done by classifying its elements, attributes, and entities according to the general tree-like structure which is formally described by the DTD. The following sections describe how to use these three types of markup.

4.2.3 Example of a DTD

Figure 18 contains the DTD for the memo example.

```
<!-- DTD for simple office memoranda                          -->
<!ENTITY % doctype "MEMO"   -- document type generic identifier -->
<!--          ELEMENTS    MIN   CONTENT           (EXCEPTIONS) -->
<!ELEMENT  %doctype;    - -   ((TO & FROM), BODY, CLOSE?)      >
<!ELEMENT  TO           - O   (#PCDATA)                        >
<!ELEMENT  FROM         - O   (#PCDATA)                        >
<!ELEMENT  BODY         - O   (P)*                             >
<!ELEMENT  P            - O   (#PCDATA | Q )*                  >
<!ELEMENT  PREF         - O   EMPTY                            >
<!ELEMENT  Q            - -   (#PCDATA)                        >
<!ELEMENT  CLOSE        - O   (#PCDATA)                        >
<!--          ELEMENTS    NAME    VALUE              DEFAULT   -->
<!ATTLIST  %doctype;    STATUS  (CONFIDEN|PUBLIC) PUBLIC       >
<!ATTLIST  P            id      ID               #IMPLIED      >
<!ATTLIST  PREF         refid   IDREF            #IMPLIED      >
```

Figure 18. Memorandum (DTD)

I'll use this example to explain the components of a DTD.

4.3 Exercises

1. How can you recognize the definitions for elements, attributes, and entities in the memo DTD in Figure 18?

2. List the types of information in the letter shown in Figure 19.

```
Henry Ford
Motor Way
Detroit
U.S.A.

subject: thief-proof cars

Dear Henry,

Wouldn't it be nice if you could design me a thief-proof car?

                        Sincerely yours,

                        Eric van Herwijnen
                        Geneva, Switzerland
```

Figure 19. A Letter

3. Compare your list to the formal SGML description in Figure 20.

```
<!DOCTYPE LETTER SYSTEM "letter.dtd">
<LETTER>
<TO>
<NAME>Henry Ford</NAME>
<ADDRESS>Motor way, Detroit, U.S.A</ADDRESS>
<FROM>
<NAME>Eric van Herwijnen</NAME>
<ADDRESS>Geneva, Switzerland</ADDRESS>
<SUBJECT>thief-proof cars</SUBJECT>
<SALUT>Dear Henry,</SALUT>
<BODY>
<P>Wouldn't it be nice if you could design me a thief-proof car?</P>
</BODY>
<CLOSE>Sincerely yours,</CLOSE>
</LETTER>
```

Figure 20. A Letter (SGML)

4.4 Markup defined in the DTD: elements

An element is marked up with symbols called a **start-tag** and an **end-tag**. In its simplest form, an SGML start-tag consists of the start-tag open delimiter (<) followed by the **generic identifier** (or **tag-name**, i.e., the name of the element defined by the DTD), followed by the tag close delimiter (>); for example

```
<FROM>
```

In this example **FROM** is the generic identifier, and this start-tag indicates the start of the FROM element.

4.4.1 *The parts of elements*

The parts of an element are shown in Table 2. In many tables in this book you will see the Abstract Name in the fourth column. I include it for reference purposes. To SGML, all delimiters and many keywords are known by these names and not by their characters.

Table 2. The parts of an element

Example: <FROM>Snowball</FROM>			
Order	**Part**	**Description**	**Abstract Name**
1	<FROM>	The opening tag	START-TAG
2	Snowball	The element's content	CONTENT
3	</FROM>	The closing tag	END-TAG

Element names are not case sensitive. An element may have empty content (for example, a **<DATE>** tag could indicate that the processing system should use today's date), or delimit a logical entity in the text (e.g., **<P>** to delimit a paragraph) with character data (with or without markup) as contents.

If their presence can be deduced from the context, tags may be omitted. See Part III, section 16.1 for a discussion of tag minimization.

4.4.2 *The parts of a tag*

The parts of a tag are shown in Table 3.

Table 3. The parts of a tag

Example: <FROM> or </FROM>			
Order	**Part**	**Description**	**Abstract Name**
1	<	start-tag open delimiter	STAGO
	</	end-tag open delimiter	ETAGO
2	FROM	generic identifier	GI
3	>	tag close delimiter	TAGC

A generic identifier is, by default, not case sensitive. It may be in uppercase (**FROM**), lowercase (**from**), or a mixture (**From**). A tag can appear anywhere on a line; it does not have to start at the beginning. An end-tag has the same generic identifier as the start-tag but is preceded by the end-tag open delimiter (**</**):**</FROM>** (the end of the **FROM** element.) Figure 21 shows the parts of tags and elements.

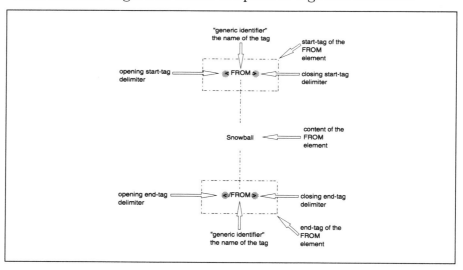

Figure 21. Anatomy of an Element

4.5 Exercise

How would you indicate in the SGML letter example, whether a letter is a personal or business letter?

4.6 Markup defined in the DTD: attributes

Elements can have one or more optional or mandatory **attributes** that provide further information about the element that are specified for. In programming languages, the specification of attributes can be compared to the specification of parameters.

Imagine, for example, a program called "DAY," which prints the name of the day upon receipt of a "DATE" parameter:

```
DAY DATE="20 june 1993"      ----->      "Tuesday"
```

The "DATE" parameter can be compared to an attribute.

As another comparison, look at the English language, where nouns can be compared to elements:

```
This is a car:                   <CAR>
```

Here, adjectives can be compared to attributes:

```
This is a red car:                   <CAR COLOR="red">
```

Attributes *must* be given on the start-tag. Attributes and the set of their possible values and defaults for a particular element are defined in the DTD.

In their fullest form, SGML start-tags can consist of the start-tag delimiter, the generic identifier, an **attribute list**, a tag close delimiter, and tagtext; for example:

```
<TITLEP FORMAT="standard" STATUS="public">This document ...
```

An attribute consists of an attribute name (**FORMAT**, **STATUS**), an "=," and a value (standard, public). An attribute's value may contain letters, digits, and other characters provided they are delimited by quotes or apostrophes:

```
<TITLEP FORMAT="not standard" STATUS="eric's" SCALE="1.5">
```

Attribute names are, by default, not case sensitive, although their values may be.

4.6.1 The parts of attributes

The parts of attributes are shown in Table 4. Note that:

1. what appears within quotes is a **literal string**;

2. quotes must match;

Table 4. Markup for specifying attributes

Ex.: <Element-Name Attribute-Name = "Attribute-Value">			
Order	**Part**	**Description**	**Abstract Name**
1	<	start-tag open delimiter	STAGO
2	Element-Name	name of the element	
3	Attribute-Name	name of the attribute	
4	=	value indicator	VI
5	"	literal string delimiter to delimit attributes value	LIT
	'	alternative literal string delimiter	LITA
6	Attribute-Value	attribute's value	
7	"	literal string delimiter	LIT
	'	alternative literal string delimiter	LITA
8	>	start-tag close delimiter	STAGC

3. under certain circumstances attribute names (if the attribute value is one of a finite set) and literal string delimiters (if there are no blanks in the attribute value) may be omitted. For example:

```
<TITLEP standard public>This document ...
```

is the same as:

```
<TITLEP FORMAT="standard" STATUS="public">This document ...
```

4.6.2 Examples of using attributes

In addition to simple character strings, attributes can have values that have a special meaning. An attribute can be declared, for example, to have a value which is unique. This is called a **unique identifier** attribute, and it allows you to single out individual elements in a document instance. A unique identifier attribute sets a marker at a particular point in your document. This point can be used by other elements for reference, or for hypertext systems as start or end points of links (see section 24.5 for a discussion of hypertext).

Other types of value are: a reference to a unique identifier, a value consisting only of numbers, names of a certain length and composed of certain characters. Here are some examples of attributes:

1. In a list of bibliography items (`<BIBLIST>`), for example:

```
<BIBLIST>
<BIBITEM ID=Orwell>
<AUTHOR>George Orwell<TITLE>Animal Farm
```

The bibliography item (`<BIBITEM>`) is given a unique identifier attribute "`ID`" that can be referred to in other places.

2. A reference to the bibliography item with attribute `ID=Orwell` can be done by using a reference tag (for example, `<BIBREF>`):

```
In Animal Farm <BIBREF RID=Orwell>, ...
```

The attribute `RID` is a reference attribute to a unique identifier.

3. The example

```
<MEMO STATUS="secret">
```

shows how attributes can be used to indicate a closed readership.

4. The example

```
<LETTER TYPE="business">
```

allows you to identify the information that is required to store the letter in a database of business letters.

Other attribute value types are shown in Table 15 and discussed in Part II, chapter 11.

4.7 Exercise

The é (e acute accent) character does not appear on the keyboard, nor is it part of ASCII. Think of a way to describe it using only ASCII characters.

4.8 Markup defined in the DTD: entities

After elements and attributes, **entities** are the third important SGML markup construct. Documents may contain characters such as Greek letters and mathematical symbols that cannot be directly entered on the keyboard. You may also wish to include illustrations such as scanned images, output from drawing programs, photos or text from another document. In all these cases, SGML uses an **entity reference** which is represented by a character string that is entered in the text at the location where the external material has to be placed.

Entities are used:

- as a shorthand notation for text strings (**general entities**);

- as a common way of coding special characters, accents, symbols (general and **character entities**);

- for including external files (**external entities**);

- as variables in a DTD (**parameter entities**; their discussion takes place later, see section 12.6).

Figure 22 shows several types of entities.

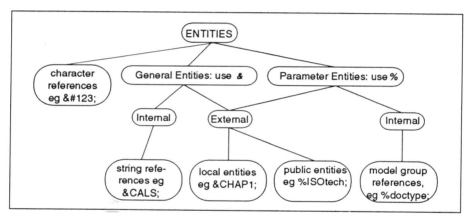

Figure 22. General and Parameter Entities

4.8.1 Parts of general entity references

An general entity reference indicates where the entity should be placed in the document; for example, &SGML;. Contrary to element names and attribute names, entity names are, by default, case sensitive (for example, &SGML;, &sgml;, and &SgMl; refer to three different entities.)

The parts of general entity references are shown in Table 5; this example shows a reference to an entity with the name "CALS" ("Computer-aided Acquisition and Logistics Support.")

Table 5. Construction of general entity references

Ex.: &CALS;			
Order	**Part**	**Description**	**Abstract Name**
1	&	entity reference open delimiter	ERO
2	CALS	entity name	NAME
3	;	entity reference close delimiter	ERC

The SGML parser replaces the entity reference &CALS; by its replacement text as if this text had been entered directly.

4.8.2 General entity definitions

Like elements and attributes, entities are defined in the DTD. Entity definitions, however, can also be included by users in their documents. For example, the string "Standard Generalized Markup Language" can be defined as the replacement text for an entity "SGML" as follows:

```
<!ENTITY SGML "Standard Generalized Markup Language">
```

If this declaration has not been made in the DTD, it must be placed at the top of the document in an area called the **document type declaration subset**, i.e. within the square brackets ([]) that follow the reference to the DTD. See section 13.3 for more information about the document type declaration subset.

Figure 23 shows how to include a general entity definition in the doctype declaration subset and how to refer to it in the text.

```
<!DOCTYPE book SYSTEM "/home/eric/book.dtd"  [
<!ENTITY SGML "Standard Generalised Markup Language">]>
<book>
<preface>
<p>This book explains the &SGML;</p>
</preface>
<body>
<chapter><title>The first chapter</title></book>
```

Figure 23. General Entity Definition and Reference

How would you go about defining an entity for a symbol (for example, an Ω) , or an accented character (for example, a ê) which does not exist on the keyboard? As you learned from exercise 4.7, you can define an entity name without too much difficulty (for example, Omega and eacute), and you can refer to them in the usual way. What however, should their replacement text be? The replacement text can not be the special character, since you cannot type it in.

Your SGML guide thinks...

Without going into the technicalities of this problem (that are discussed in the context of data text in section 12.4), remember that the important thing is to identify the information. Representing a symbol on paper or on the screen is not SGML's problem.

4.8.3 Character entities

Sometimes it is necessary to include a character which is invisible on the screen (for example, one of the control characters in positions 0–31 of the ISO646:1983[5] characterset in Table 45), or does not occur on your keyboard (for example, the square brackets on the IBM 3179 terminal family), or it has a special function (for example, the space character or a record start/end character).

Character entity references allow you to refer to any character in the character set used by your document.

The entities are the decimal numbers of the characters in the character set. Instead of a decimal number, you can also give the name of a character with a special function (**RE**, **RS**, or **SPACE**, see Table 31).

The parts of a character entity reference are shown in Table 6.

Table 6. The parts of a character entity reference

Ex.: [or &#RE;			
Order	**Part**	**Description**	**Abstract Name**
1	&#	character reference open delimiter	CRO
2	91	decimal character in the document's characterset	NUMBER
	RE	a function character (e.g. RE, RS or SPACE)	FUNCTION NAME
3	;	reference close delimiter	REFC

---

[5] ISO 646:1983 is to all extents and purposes equivalent to ASCII.

If the document's character set is ISO 646:1983 you can refer to an opening square bracket ([) by giving the character reference [where 91 is the bracket's position in the set.

Although this unambiguously determines the reference with respect to the original character set, the number may need changing if the document is transferred over a heterogeneous network. The document's character set may have changed and the square bracket may be at position **BA** (decimal 172), for example. Because the square bracket is often defined in different positions and can be translated incorrectly, a general entity reference (e.g.[) is better for this purpose. The characters of a general entity reference will never be wrongly translated.

Table 45 in Appendix C contains the ISO 646:1983 character set.

4.8.4 External entities

Since smaller units are easier to manage, it is convenient to split a document into several parts. You can include parts of a document by defining external entities. In its definition, the entity name is followed by a **system identifier**, as shown in Figure 24. The system identifier contains the pathname of the entity, which in this case, is an SGML file. The parser replaces the entity reference by the external document and parses it as if it were included directly.

```
<!DOCTYPE book SYSTEM "/home/eric/book.dtd" [
<!ENTITY SGML "Standard Generalised Markup Language">
<!ENTITY chap1 SYSTEM "/home/eric/chap1.sgm">
<!ENTITY chap2 SYSTEM "/home/eric/chap2.sgm">
]>
<book>
<preface>
<p>This book explains the &SGML;</p>
</preface>
<body>
&chap1;
&chap2;
</book>
```

Figure 24. External Entity Definitions and References

External entity definitions for files containing special data (mathematical or graphical) can also be defined and are explained later, under data entities (see section 12.3).

4.9 How to refer to a DTD?

An SGML document refers to its DTD in the **DOCTYPE declaration** in the first line. Figure 25 contains the DOCTYPE declaration of the memo example.

```
<!DOCTYPE MEMO SYSTEM "memo.dtd">
```

Figure 25. The DOCTYPE declaration

Remember that:

1. every document must have or refer to a DTD;

2. every document must contain a DOCTYPE declaration;

3. the DOCTYPE declaration does *not* belong to the DTD;

The parts of the DOCTYPE declaration are shown in Table 7.

Table 7. The parts of the DOCTYPE declaration

Ex.: <!DOCTYPE MEMO SYSTEM "/home/eric/memo.dtd">			
Order	**Part**	**Description**	**Abstract Name**
1	<!	markup declaration open delimiter	MDO
2	DOCTYPE	DOCTYPE keyword	
3	MEMO	document type name	NAME
4	SYSTEM	DTD is external, but on the system	
5	"	literal string delimiter to delimit attributes value	LIT
	,	alternative literal string delimiter	LITA
6	system or public identifier	the pathname or public name of the DTD	SYSTEM DATA or MINIMUM LITERAL
7	"	literal string delimiter	LIT
	,	alternative literal string delimiter	LITA
8	>	markup declaration close delimiter	MDC

4.10 Processing Instructions

Besides elements, attributes, and entities, which are defined in the DTD, SGML also offers an author the possibility of directly giving instructions to a processing system. There are various occasions when including processing dependent commands can be necessary. This can be done with a **processing instruction**.

In an environment where the most important application of SGML is text processing, users may try to use SGML as a word-processing system. They will want to make documents without structure or with a structure that is forbidden by the DTD. In that case the DTD may be too restrictive, and processing instructions can be added to achieve the desired effect. The correct way to handle this situation, however, is to modify the DTD, add a new one, or contemplate the use of a word processor.

Another reason for user frustration may be that the text formatter has faults. A common problem is the appearance of a page break between the title of a chapter and the text that belongs with it. This problem, which is a typical disadvantage of some macro packages, may be solved by adding a specific formatting instruction to force a page break in the correct place. This is a more legitimate use of a processing instruction, although it makes your document system dependent.

To enable easy modification when moving data from system to system, you are recommended to define processing instructions in general entities (see section 12.4).

Your SGML guide advises...

4.10.1 The parts of a processing instruction

Table 8 shows the parts of a processing instruction.

Table 8. The parts of a processing instruction

Example: <?.cc 5>			
Order	**Part**	**Description**	**Abstract Name**
1	<?	processing instruction open delimiter	PRO
2	.cc 5	system specific processing instruction	CHARACTER DATA
3	>	processing instruction close delimiter	PRC

4.11 Bibliography for Chapter 4

[1]   American National Standards Institute
ANSI/NISO Z39.59-1988, American National Standard for Elec
tronic Manuscript Prepation and Markup. This standard has be
come ISO DIS 12083 and passed the ISO voting procedure in
November 1992. The full ISO standard is scheduled to appear
by the end of 1993.
Bethesda, 1988
[2]   ISO
ISO 12083:1993 Electronic Manuscript Prepation and Markup
Geneva, 1993

5. Creating SGML documents

5.1 Why use an SGML editor?

To be able to profit from SGML, you need a way to put your data into SGML using the DTD of your choice. Four options enable the creation of SGML documents, as shown in Figure 26.

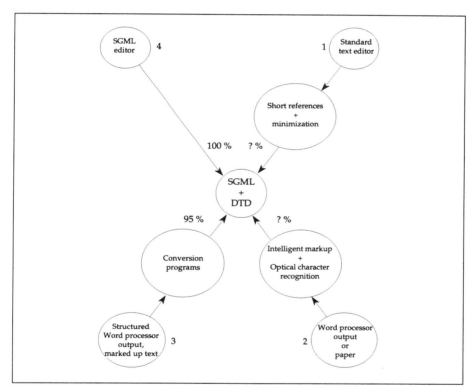

Figure 26. Four Options for Making SGML

1. Use a standard, nonstructured text editor (e.g., the vi editor, textedit, Xedit, NOTEPAD) and type in the tags by hand. To ease the pain of adding the markup by hand, tags can be omitted in certain circumstances. This is called **minimization** and is described in section 16.1.

The use of typewriter short cuts (i.e., replace a blank line by the start of a paragraph tag) via short references is described section 19.2.

The parser will complete the markup as required. The problem with this method is that some systems are unable to handle minimized markup or short references. The typewriter conventions also need to be known and used consistently by the people creating the document.

The success rate for conversion to SGML is uncertain, and even if it is more than zero, your users are unlikely to survive for long in such a hostile environment.

2. If you have a database of existing (paper) documents, use an intelligent markup or auto-tagging system (e.g., Avalanche's FastTAG[1]).

Combined with an **optical character recognition** (OCR) system (such as Xerox's Textbridge [2]) you can transfer your documents into a machine readable form, and provided they follow a clear visual structure, intelligent markup can be done for a fair amount of cases.

The success rate of this approach is uncertain, but probably between 40-60%. This can already be a significant saving if the alternative is to retype all the documents.

For an excellent overview of the pros and cons of the various methods for data conversion, see [3].

3. Have your authors use their favorite system and convert (e.g. LaTeX or MS Word into SGML), by writing a conversion filter. An example of a good tool to write these filters with is Exoterica's OmniMark [4].

This approach will only work if some structured environment which follows the structure of the DTD can be created (e.g., through stylesheets) in the favorite system. In this case, the success rate for conversion to SGML is around 95%, which may not be enough to reliably automate certain processes. It also crucially depends on the willingness of the authors to use the stylesheet, which can be an important drawback.

There is some overlap between methods 2 and 3. Conversion programs usually work by recognizing and substituting codes, whereas intelligent markup recognizes visual structures.

4. The best approach is to create your documents directly in an SGML editor. Your documents are automatically compatible with SGML. It may require some time to customize the editor to the structure of your DTD, particularly if this has formatting capabilities. An example is ArborText's ADEPT•Publisher [5], which was used for the preparation of this book.

5.2 SGML editor checklist

The following points are useful to consider when you are selecting an SGML editor (general requirements of text preparation systems such as speed, mouse, icon, and window support are taken for granted):

1. The editor should be able to recognize generic identifiers, attributes and entities defined in **any** DTD.

2. The editor should prevent you from making markup errors, display available tags and attributes, and indicate where you are in the document's structure. You should be able to view all instances of elements upon request, such as all heading titles to produce a table of contents.

3. You should be able to move through the text by going from tag to tag.

4. The editor should give informative and user-friendly error messages which can be understood by users that are not SGML experts.

5. You should be able to indicate how the contents of elements is formatted on the screen in a user-friendly way, e.g., via a menu or stylesheets.

6. The editor should conform to the SGML standard, including amendment 1, but need not necessarily include any optional features.

7. You should be able to use the editor in a mode where it does not check if a document conforms to the DTD. This gives you more flexibility.

8. The editor should be able to add tags to the document without displaying them on the screen. You should be able to enter them either through commands, through menus, or by the editor's recognizing typewriter conventions. You should be able to see the tags whenever you want.

9. Tags entered on the command line or typed into the text should be recognized as tags, not as data. Sometimes it is quicker to add markup by hand than to select it from a menu.

10. Editors and other processing programs should support a general notation processing mechanism to allow use of user notations such as graphics and mathematics.

11. You should be able to work on a subset of a document — for example, a chapter — although according to the DTD this could be an invalid document.

12. The editor should be programmable.

A wide selection of editors with a large amount of these characteristics is now available. For more information see the SGML source guide [6].

ML*

5.3 Bibliography for Chapter 5

[1] M.Whiteside
IMSYS, the Intelligent Markup System
Boulder, 1986
[2] Xerox Imaging Systems
Textbridge User's Guide
Peabody, 1993
[3] D.Waldt
Strategies for Data Conversion, <TAG>, vol 6, no.4, Pages 1–7
april 1993
[4] Exoterica Corporation
OmniMark User's Guide
Ottawa, 1992
[5] ArborText Incorporated
ADEPT User's Guide version 5.0
Ann Arbor, 1993
[6] Graphics Communication Association
The SGML Source Guide
Arlington, 1992

6. How to keep up to date with SGML

There are several ways to find out more about SGML and to keep up to date with any SGML developments, new products, and so on. The following sections describe some of the channels that you can use.

6.1 The SGML Users' Group

The objectives of the SGML Users' Group are to promote the use of the Standard Generalized Markup Language and to provide a forum for the exchange of information about SGML.

A large number of active regional chapters now exists. They organize frequent meetings.

Membership of the SGML Users' Group includes up-to-date information about SGML and related standards, reduced rates at events organized by the Users' Group, a subscription to the SGML Users' Group's Bulletin and Newsletter. For more information, contact them at the following address:

```
SGML Users' Group
PO Box 361, Great Western Way
Swindon, Wiltshire SN5 7BF, United Kingdom
(phone +44 793 512 515; fax +44 793 512 516)
```

6.2 The GCA

The Graphic Communications Association is a nonprofit organization, affiliated to the Printing Industries of America, Inc. The have sponsored the development of SGML right from the start, and continue to support and stimulate its acceptance and use. They are the organizers of the most important SGML conferences, they also sell books and standards and organize courses. Their address is:

```
Graphic Communications Association
100 Daingerfield Road
Alexandria, VA 22314-2888, USA
```

6.3 Books, magazines

The classic books on SGML are: Martin Bryan's pioneering work [1], Joan Smith and Robert Stutely's useful index and guide to the SGML standard [2], and Charles Goldfarb's monumental reference work [3]. The bibliography lists in Practical SGML contain a selection of the SGML literature that I have studied, which in turn, will point you to other references you may find helpful.

<TAG>, *The SGML Newsletter*, is published monthly by SGML Associates, Inc. and the Graphic Communications Association. This magazine is a reliable source of information on SGML ideas, tips, literature, products, and conferences. Subscriptions may be obtained from:

```
SGML Associates, Inc.,
<TAG> The SGML Newsletter,
6360 S. Gibraltar Circle,
Aurora, CO 80016-1212, USA
```

The Department of Computing and Information Science at Queen's University at Kingston, Ontario, publishes a bibliography on structured text. This is an excellent comprehensive database of all literature published on SGML and related topics. It is compiled and kept up to date by Robin Cover [4]. An up-to-date copy may be obtained from:

```
N. Duncan
Department of Computing and Information Science
Queen's University
Kingston, Canada
K7L 3N6
```

6.4 The network

Your SGML guide advises...

The academic world has used international computer networks for a number of years to distribute and discuss information electronically. Industries are now also gaining access to these facilities. The network is an excellent way to learn, test new ideas, and keep up to date with anything going on (not only SGML).

If your computer has access to the Internet network, most of these activities will be accessible to you. See [5] for an excellent initiation to the fun that networks can give you.

The following services, which survive thanks to an enormous effort on behalf of a few voluntary enthusiasts, exist.

6.4.1 Servers

These contain public domain software, parser materials, documents, and DTDs. Here are two servers:

1. The University of Exeter provide an anonymous ftp server for their "SGML project." It contains information on SGML (in the ISO8879.info subdirectory), the SGML User's Group parser materials (in the arcsgml subdirectory), SGML bibliographies (bibliog), information on the SGML project (sgml.project), and SGML User's Group UK regional chapter information (sgml.uk). The address of the server is:

```
sgml1.ex.ac.uk [144.173.6.61]
login: anonymous
pwd: your-email-address
```

2. The University of Oslo provide a similar service, with additional information and a complete archive of the messages posted on the comp.text.sgml Newsgroup (see below). The address of the server is:

```
ftp.ifi.uio.no [129.240.64.2]
login: anonymous
pwd: your-email-address
```

6.4.2 Discussion groups

Experts and nonexperts discuss their problems in a general way in discussion groups. Don't be put off by the style of some of the correspondents — the net doesn't always increase people's patience nor their politeness. Here are two discussion groups:

1. The most important SGML discussion group is the Usenet News-group `comp.text.sgml`. A large number of expert users and developers of SGML systems discuss their ideas on this list. It is most conveniently accessed from Unix systems in the standard way. See your systems programmer for details about your local installation.

2. The Text Encoding Initiative (TEI), which is a major international academic effort to establish guidelines for the encoding and interchange of electronic texts using SGML, has an electronic list called `TEI-L`. To subscribe to this list, send an electronic mail to `LIST-SERV@UICVM.BITNET` with the following line:

```
subscribe TEI-L Your Name
```

Its committees for various text types are numerous and substantial, and the resulting DTDs have an important influence on current thinking on DTD design.

Robin Cover's SGML Bibliography and List of Resources contains a complete list of all servers and discussion groups relevant to SGML.

6.5 Bibliography for Chapter 6

[1]   M. Bryan
      SGML An Author's Guide to the Standard Generalized Markup Language
      Addison-Wesley, Wokingham, 1988
[2]   J.M. Smith, R. Stutely
      SGML: The user's guide to ISO 8879
      Ellis Horwood, Chichester, 1988
[3]   C.F. Goldfarb
      The SGML Handbook
      Clarendon Press, Oxford, 1990
[4]   R. Cover
      The SGML Bibliography
      Queen's University, Kingston, 1992
[5]   E. Krol
      The Whole Internet User's Guide and Catalog
      O'Reilly & Associates, Sebastopol, 1993

Part II. Writing a DTD

The aim of this part is to explain document analysis, structure diagrams, and markup declarations. It is intended for everyone who needs to write or modify a DTD. At the end you should have learned:

1. how to carry out a document analysis;
2. how to draw structure diagrams;
3. how to use structure diagrams to generate markup declarations;
4. how to write element declarations;
5. how to write attribute declarations;
6. how to write entity declarations;
7. which pitfalls to avoid when writing a DTD.

7. Document analysis

Document analysis is like data modeling, i.e. an abstraction of reality that is easier to handle than the real world. There is, however, no unique hidden document structure waiting to be discovered. Everyone sees what they need for their applications. Consider for example:

```
A paragraph which does not contain a list of points.
```

```
1. First item in the list.
2. Second item in the list.
```

The list of numbered points (**list**) can be on the same hierarchical level as a paragraph (**paragraph**, see Figure 27). In other words, lists and paragraphs both occur inside sections. A list, however, can not occur inside a paragraph, nor can a paragraph occur inside a list:

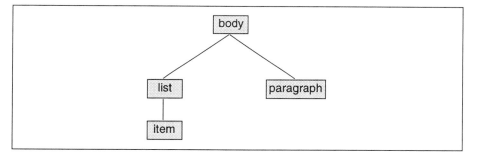

Figure 27. List not inside Paragraph

Nothing in the example above indicates that the paragraph is closed when the list of points begins. The list could equally well be a sub-element of a paragraph, and occur only inside paragraphs (see Figure 28). SGML can accommodate widely varying perceptions of the same data.

Bear in mind that the results of the data modeling activity will be better if everyone who will be involved with the use of the application, is represented in the team that is responsible for the analysis of documents. Each person brings something different to the table. Technical documentation writers, for example, have other requirements than database programmers.

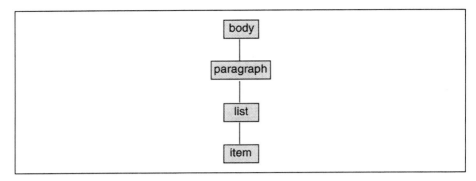

Figure 28. List inside Paragraph

Designing a DTD while leaving out a group of users can result in the omission of elements that are important for that group.

Common sense is an indispensable ingredient to ensure the quality of a DTD. The more people that are exposed to the design of the DTD, the lesser the chance of omissions will be.

Document analysis consists of the following points:

- delimit the area of applicability;

- define a strategy for the DTD;

- determine who the users are;

- choose a name;

- recognize the logical elements in the document class;

- choose between elements and attributes;

- determine the tree structure of the document class and structure diagrams for the contents of the elements.

7.1 The area of applicability of the DTD

The number of different types of text that circulate in business and personal environments is bewildering. To apply SGML, order must be brought into this chaos. Group documents with similar properties and purposes into *classes*.

For example, bound documents which are found on bookshelves in libraries are *books*; texts that are sent from one person to another by post are *letters*; magazines contain *articles*. Office documents with instructions or remarks between colleagues are *memo's*. Be clear which types of documents are included for each class.

Go to the highest level possible when defining these classes. Having recognized a book as a document class, an encyclopaedia which consists of different books should nevertheless be defined as a separate class.

7.2 A strategy for the DTD

Before deciding on its structure, you need to define a strategy for the DTD. To do this, ask yourself the following questions:

- *Why* do we want to write this DTD? *How* will it be applied? *What* are the *priorities* of its functions?

- *What* objectives do we want to achieve? What are the short- and longer term *goals*? What *problem* are you trying to solve?

- Is there a previous version? Should it be *backwards compatible?*

A DTD for converting existing documents to SGML will differ from a DTD for new documents. If markup is done by hand, you may want to use tag minimization (see section 16.1) or short references (see section 19.1), features which must be foreseen in the DTD.

7.3 The name

Suppose you have identified the document classes: business letters, memoranda, technical manuals and scientific reports. Decide to which classes you want to apply SGML and choose a descriptive name of up to eight characters for each class (e.g. letter, memo, manual, report). The DTD name must follow the rules for SGML names (see section 15.5).

7.4 The logical elements in the document class

One of the results of the document analysis is a list of elements, attributes and entities. Attributes and entities are not part of a document's tree structure; they are discussed later (see chapters 11 and 12).

To describe a document's structure, make a list of all possible logical elements that you want to distinguish. For example, in the case of the memo shown in Figure 29, the logical elements are:

1. The element MEMO, containing the entire memo.

2. The element TO, containing the name of the person the memo is addressed to.

3. The element **FROM**, containing the name of the person who sent the memo.

4. The element **BODY**, containing the text part of the memo. This element contains the subelements **P** (paragraph) and **Q** (quotation).

```
<!DOCTYPE MEMO SYSTEM "memo.dtd">
<MEMO>
<TO>Comrade Napoleon
<FROM>Snowball
<BODY>
<P>In Animal Farm, George Orwell says: <Q>...the pigs  had
to expend enormous labour every day upon mysterious things
called files, reports, minutes and  memoranda.  These were
large sheets of paper which had to be closely covered with
writing, and as soon as they were so  covered,  they  were
burnt in the furnace...</Q> Do you think SGML  would  have
helped the pigs?</P></BODY>
</CLOSE>
</MEMO>
```

Figure 29. Memorandum (SGML)

5. The element **P**, containing the text of a paragraph.

6. The element **Q**, containing the text of a quotation.

7. The element **CLOSE**, containing the name of the person who signed the memo.

During this process, ask yourself the questions "Do I need to distinguish this element?" and "What do I want to do with it?". In the memo class you may want to add an element containing the subject of the memo (in addition to the elements in the example).

Your SGML guide advises...

Think of all possible applications of your documents. For example, if you want to create a database in which you want to store author, date, title and keywords, the DTD must guarantee that elements corresponding to these items are marked up. Find out what type of information needs to be made available to the processing system that will use your SGML data. This will frequently require that you review the needs together with specialists in othear areas. If you want to make a CD-ROM version, and you are unsure what elements are required for the search software on the disk, make sure a CD-ROM specialist is in on the design.

Another example are tabular data. The correctly tagged data should allow a text formatting application to present them in graphical form (a histogram for example), while a different application can present them as a spreadsheet.

Any application can have implications on the structure. The final set of elements should meet the demands of all possible applications.

7.5 Elements or attributes?

When making the list of elements, you may come across some cases where you hesitate between elements and attributes. An interesting discussion of whether to describe data with an element or an attribute is given in [1]. Here are a few questions that can help you decide.

- Is the data structural? An object whose presence is required (e.g. the name of the sender of a memo) or excluded (a quotation inside the name of the sender of a memo), is a good candidate for an element.

- Does the data describe the content? A letter being a business letter applies to its complete content. Attributes are used for data which is described by a list of discrete values (business, private).

- Is the data presentational? Attributes should not be used to describe the way the data looks. For example, a poetry element should be formatted differently from the text. To describe computer output, don't use an attribute on the poetry tag, but create a special element .

- Repetitive patterns should be described by an attribute. A property that is one out of a finite list (green, yellow, etc.) usually has nothing to do with the subject (car), and should be an attribute.

- Does the data require special processing? A mathematical formula in a subtitle may require a separate element, for example,

```
<head subtitle="The <f>sqrt x</f> for <f>x lt 0</f>?">
<ht>Square roots of negative numbers
```

does not achieve the desired effect, since the data inside the attribute is not parsed. Figure 30 shows how the parser ignores the content of the attribute (see Appendix B to interpret the output of the parser).

```
ASUBTITLE CDATA The <f>sqrt x</f> for <f>x lt 0</f>
(HEAD
(HT
-The square root of negative numbers
)HT
)HEAD
```

Figure 30. Parsing Markup inside an Attribute Value

It is better to use an element to contain the formula:

```
<head><ht>Square roots of negative numbers
<subtitle>What is <f>sqrt x for <f>x lt 0?
```

In figure 31 the parser recognizes the two formulas.

```
(HEAD
(HT
-The square root of negative numbers
)HT
(SUBTITLE
-The
(F
-sqrt x
)F
- for
(F
- x lt 0
)F
)SUBTITLE
)HEAD
```

Figure 31. Placing Markup in an Element

7.6 The tree structure

When the elements in a document class have been established, the relationships between them should be determined. Some elements contain other elements. For memos, the memo element contains all others; the body element contains paragraphs and quotations. Paragraphs are **nested** inside body, which is nested inside memo.

This nesting of elements can be graphically expressed by a tree. The tree structure of the memo is shown in Figure 32. SGML is good at describing tree like objects.

A tree structure does, however, not describe all the relations that exist between elements. An element could be purposely excluded from another (although the tree would permit it to be there), or some elements may be included in parts of the structure (where it would not be permitted according to the tree). For example, a footnote can be allowed to appear in any element. These **inclusions** or **exclusions** can only be found by reviewing the contents of each element in detail.

A tree structure is also unable to indicate the required order or frequency of the elements. This information is described by the structure diagrams discussed in the next chapter.

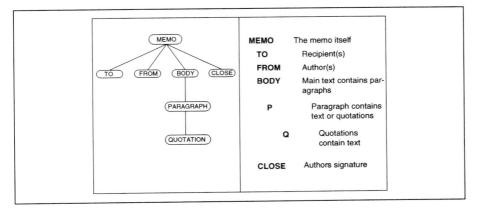

Figure 32. Memo Tree Structure

7.7 Exercise

Find a tree structure for a **LETTER** (see Figure 33.)

```
<!DOCTYPE LETTER SYSTEM "letter.dtd">
<LETTER>
<TO>
<NAME>Henry Ford</NAME>
<ADDRESS>Motor way, Detroit, U.S.A</ADDRESS>
<FROM>
<NAME>Eric van Herwijnen</NAME>
<ADDRESS>Geneva, Switzerland</ADDRESS>
<SUBJECT>thief-proof cars</SUBJECT>
<SALUT>Dear Henry,</SALUT>
<BODY>
<P>Wouldn't it be nice if you could design me a thief-proof car?</P>
</BODY>
<CLOSE>Sincerely yours,</CLOSE>
</LETTER>
```

Figure 33. A Letter (SGML)

7.8 Bibliography for Chapter 7

[1]   J.Graf
      Attributes and Elements. Tastes Great — Less Filling?, <TAG>,
      vol 1, no.6, Pages 11–14
      april 1988

8. Structure diagrams

To bridge the gap between the results of the document analysis and writing the formal DTD the use of **structure diagrams** can be helpful. Structure diagrams are a way of enriching the tree structure that is easy to translate into markup declarations for the DTD. Structure diagrams resemble "flow" diagrams, although the notation presented here may be different from the one that you are used to. The flow goes from left to right. To each node in the tree corresponds a structure diagram.

To obtain the complete set of structure diagrams for a document class, traverse the tree in the order defined by Figure 36. At each node, look at the elements below it and make its diagram using the seven types of structure diagrams described in the next section.

8.1 Seven types of structure diagrams

There are seven basic types of structure diagrams, which are shown in Figure 34. Each diagram corresponds to a fundamental structure for a node in the tree:

1. An element in a box means that this element appears once.

2. Two boxes one after the other ("in series") means that the element in the first box precedes the one in the second box. Both occur once.

3. Two boxes on top of the other ("in parallel") means that either one element or the other appears in that place, but not both.

4. Two boxes in series on top of the same two inverted ("in series and in parallel") means that both elements must appear in arbitrary order.

5. A box with an arrow pointing from right to left ("feedback") means that the element must appear at least once, but may appear an unlimited number of times.

6. A box with an arrow pointing from its left to its right ("bypass") means that the element is optional.

7. A box with two arrows ("feedback and bypass") means that the element may appear an indefinite number of times.

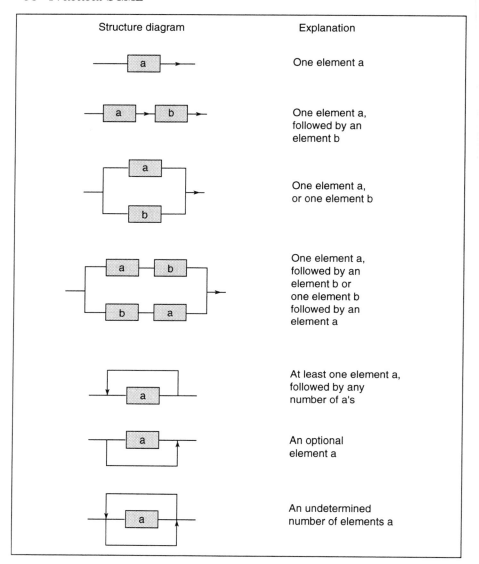

Figure 34. Seven Types of Structure Diagrams

If you are at a node which has no sub-nodes below it, you are at a terminal element. The structure diagram of a terminal element is a diagram of type 1 with a triangle in the bottom right hand corner.

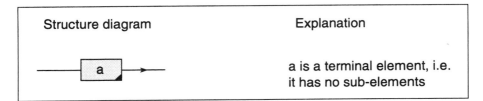

Figure 35. Structure Diagram for a Terminal Element

Even if an element is terminal, it is worth drawing a separate structure diagram since it has its own markup declaration.

8.2 Example of structure diagrams

In the case of the memo, the order for traversing the tree (also called "top-down") is shown in Figure 36.

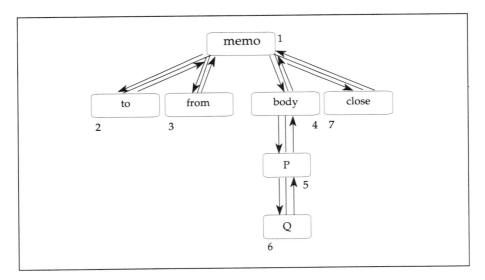

Figure 36. Traversing the Memo "top-down"

This is a systematic way of numbering all nodes in the tree and their sub-nodes. You start at the top and move down, moving from left to right, visiting all the nodes in the hierarchy; i.e. from the MEMO node move down to the TO node, move back up to the MEMO node, move down to the FROM node, etc.

When a node is first seen, it gets a number. Thus the MEMO node gets number 1, the TO node gets number 2, the FROM node gets number 3.

This method guarantees that all nodes will be visited, and hence, that no markup declarations will be forgotten.

For the memo tree, the first node is the MEMO element itself. It has sub-nodes 2 TO, 3 FROM, 4 BODY, and 7 CLOSE. To determine the structure diagram for the MEMO element, you need to supply information that cannot be read from the tree. How many times may the subelements appear and in what order?

You could, for example, decide that the TO and FROM elements may appear in arbitrary order. In this case, they would be put into structure diagram number four (Figure 37).

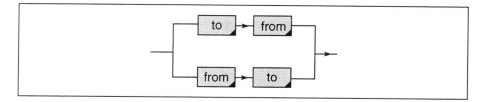

Figure 37. Structure Diagram for the Memo Element (First Part)

If the BODY element appears only once in a memo, this subdiagram would be of type number one. You could decide that the BODY element should follow the TO/FROM element block (Figure 38).

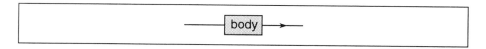

Figure 38. Structure Diagram for the MEMO Element (Second Part)

If you decide that the CLOSE element is optional, the third part of the memo structure diagram would be a subdiagram of type number six. You could decide that it should follow the BODY element (Figure 46).

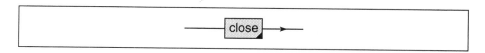

Figure 39. Structure Diagram for the MEMO Element (Third Part)

The complete structure diagram for the MEMO document is the sequence of the three subdiagrams (Figure 40).

The second node visited corresponds to the TO element. This element is a terminal element, so it has structure diagram number one, with a triangle in the bottom right-hand corner (Figure 41). In this case, the type of character data that the TO element contains is called parsed character data (see also section 10.1).

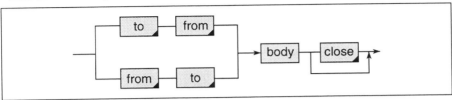

Figure 40. Structure Diagram for the MEMO Element (Complete) — Node 1

Parsed character data are indicated by the keyword **#PCDATA**. The symbol # preceeding PCDATA is a `reserved name indicator` (**RNI**). Its purpose is to prevent a confusion with an element that has name PCDATA.

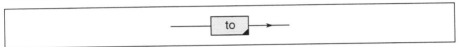

Figure 41. Structure Diagram for the TO Element — Node 2

The third node corresponds to the FROM element. This also is a terminal element, and it has structure diagram number one, with a triangle in the bottom right-hand corner (Figure 42). Like the TO element, the FROM element contains #PCDATA.

Figure 42. Structure Diagram for the FROM Element — Node 3

The fourth node corresponds to the BODY element. It has one subnode number 5, the element P. If BODY contains an unlimited amount of paragraphs, it has a structure diagram of type number seven (Figure 43).

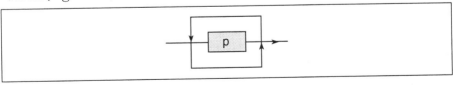

Figure 43. Structure Diagram for the BODY Element — Node 4

The fifth node corresponds to the P element. It has one subnode number 6, the element Q (quotations). It would be possible, but unusual, to decide that paragraphs are uniquely composed of quotations.

Paragraphs usually contain ordinary text (i.e. parsed character) data, with perhaps a quotation or two in the middle.

Elements that have subelements as well as #PCDATA are said to have **mixed content**. A flexible situation, that applies well to mixed content elements is obtained via subdiagrams number three and number seven (Figure 44).

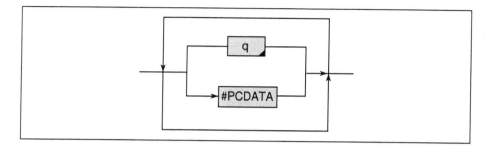

Figure 44. Structure Diagram for the P (Paragraph) Element — Node 5

The sixth node corresponds to the Q element. It is a terminal element with structure diagram number one and #PCDATA content (Figure 45).

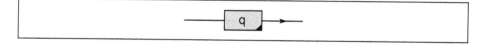

Figure 45. Structure Diagram for the Q (Quotation) Element — Node 6

The seventh and last node corresponds to the CLOSE element. It is a terminal element with diagram number one and #PCDATA content (Figure 46).

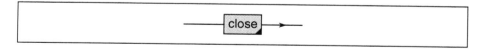

Figure 46. Structure Diagram for the Close Element — Node 7

8.3 Exercise

Draw the structure diagrams for the document class letters from the previous exercise. Use the tree structure in Figure 47.

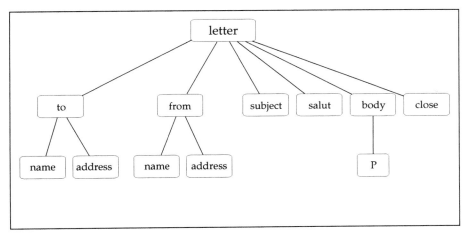

Figure 47. Letter Tree Structure

9. Markup declarations

In this chapter you will learn how to define markup declarations and how to construct them using structure diagrams.

Look at the DTD in Figure 48.

```
<!-- DTD for simple office memoranda                          -->
<!ENTITY % doctype "MEMO"  -- document type generic identifier -->
<!--          ELEMENTS   MIN  CONTENT              (EXCEPTIONS) -->
<!ELEMENT  %doctype;    - -  ((TO & FROM), BODY, CLOSE?)      >
<!ELEMENT  TO           - O  (#PCDATA)                        >
<!ELEMENT  FROM         - O  (#PCDATA)                        >
<!ELEMENT  BODY         - O  (P)*                             >
<!ELEMENT  P            - O  (#PCDATA | Q )*                  >
<!ELEMENT  PREF         - O  EMPTY                            >
<!ELEMENT  Q            - -  (#PCDATA)                        >
<!ELEMENT  CLOSE        - O  (#PCDATA)                        >
<!--          ELEMENTS   NAME  VALUE                  DEFAULT  -->
<!ATTLIST  %doctype;    STATUS  (CONFIDEN|PUBLIC) PUBLIC      >
<!ATTLIST  P            id      ID              #IMPLIED      >
<!ATTLIST  PREF         refid   IDREF           #IMPLIED      >
```

Figure 48. Memo DTD

This DTD displays the characteristics of most DTDs:

- all lines in a DTD start with "`<!`"; they are **markup declarations**;

- the three most commonly occurring ones are: **element**, **attribute**, and **entity**;

- elements, attributes and entities have **names**;

- the expressions within parentheses are **groups**;

- elements are followed by **occurrence indicators** (*,?) and linked together inside groups by **connectors** (&, |).

The expressions containing a percent ("%") are only there to show how parameter entities work. In a simple DTD such as this, you would normally not use a parameter entity in this way.

This DTD defines the markup language `<MEMO>`, `<TO>`, `<FROM>`, `<BODY>`, `<P>`, `<Q>`, `<PREF>`, and `<CLOSE>`. The markup declarations control the way the markup should be interpreted, i.e., `<MEMO>` is the outermost element, containing all the others in a certain order and with a certain frequency, etc.

More formally, the structure of a markup declaration is as follows. They contain a **keyword** (e.g. **ELEMENT, ATTLIST**, or **ENTITY)** depending on what type of declaration you are dealing with. The content follows the keyword. Table 9, which contains an example of an ELEMENT declaration, shows the four parts of a markup declaration.

Table 9. The parts of a markup declaration

Example: <!ELEMENT MEMO - - ((TO & FROM), BODY, CLOSE?) >			
Order	**Part**	**Description**	**Abstract Name**
1	<!	markup declaration open delimiter	MDO
2	ELEMENT	declaration type keyword	
3	MEMO - - ((TO & etc.	content of declaration	CONTENT MODEL or DECLARED CONTENT
4	>	markup declaration close delimiter	MDC

There may be several keywords in a markup declaration. These keywords are often **reserved names** (e.g., ELEMENT) which have a particular meaning to the SGML parser. There is *no* blank between the markup declaration open delimiter ("<!") and the first keyword (ELEMENT). In general, you should be aware that blanks are not always ignored; sometimes their presence or absence is considered significant markup.

The building blocks of a markup declaration are **groups, connectors, occurrence indicators**, and **names**. These concepts are defined in the following sections.

9.1 Names

The parts of an SGML **name** are shown in Table 10.

Table 10. The parts of an SGML name

Examples: To, confiden			
Order	**Part**	**Description**	**Abstract Name**
1	a-z, A-Z	name start character	LC LETTER UC LETTER LCNMSTRT UCNMSTRT
2-8	a-z, A-Z, 0-9, . , -	name character	as above + DIGIT

A name has no more than eight characters, starts with a **namestart** character (i.e., "a-Z") followed by **name** characters (i.e. "a-Z," "0-9,"".,""-"). Valid names are MEMO, TO, FROM, CH-1211.

9.2 Name tokens

Name tokens are similar to names, except they need not start with a namestart character.

A summary of possible tokens is given in Table 11.

Table 11. Tokens

Tokens	**Description**	**Abstract Name**
Name token	as a name, but no name start character required	NMTOKEN
Number	a name token consisting of digits only	NUMBER
Number token	must start with a digit, with up to 7 characters following it	NUTOKEN

A **name token** has no more than eight characters, and consists of **name** characters (i.e., "a-Z," "0-9," ".," "-"). Valid name tokens are -1211, .SGML, 1-KEY, and 2KEY.

9.3 Numbers

A **number** is a name token consisting only of digits (0-9). Valid numbers are 1234, 01, 12345678. Numbers are character strings, and so the number 01 is not the same as 1.

9.4 Number tokens

A **number token** is a name token that must start with a digit, but may have up to 7 name characters following it. Valid number tokens are 1abc, 1-4.5.

9.5 Groups

There are three[6] types of groups which you can come across in markup declarations:

1. **model** groups: a list of elements;

2. **name** groups: a list of names;

3. **name** token groups: a list of name tokens.

The structure of a group is shown in Table 12.

Table 12. The parts of a group

Example: (CONFIDEN | PUBLIC)			
Order	**Part**	**Description**	**Abstract Name**
1	(	group open delimiter	GRPO
2	CONFI-DEN	PUBLIC	group content	
3	)	group close delimiter	GRPC

A group's content consists of **tokens** (e.g., CONFIDEN, PUBLIC). Model groups may be nested (i.e., parentheses may appear within parentheses if they contain lists of elements). The objects inside them are related by **connectors** (commas, ampersands, and vertical bars).

---

[6] Strictly speaking there are five types, if we count the data tag and data tag template groups. Data tag minimization is not discussed in this book, since it is a less important SGML feature.

9.6 Model groups, occurrence indicators, and connectors

Model groups are used inside element declarations to define the possible contents (i.e. sub-elements or parsed character data) of an element. Table 13 shows the parts of a model group.

Table 13. The parts of a model group

Example: (TO ", *or* & *or* | " FROM)"? *or* + *or* *"			
Order	**Part**	**Description**	**Abstract Name**
1	(	group open delimiter	GRPO
2	TO & FROM	content token list	
3	,	sequence connector	SEQ
	&	and connector	AND
	|	or conncector	OR
4	)	group close delimiter	GRPC
5	?	optional occurrence indicator	OPT
	+	required and repeatable	PLUS
	*	optional and repeatable	REP

9.7 Connectors

Connectors indicate the relationship between elements. Several types of connectors exist, but only one type may appear per model group (look at the memo DTD in Figure 49 while you are reading this).

```
<!-- DTD for simple office memoranda                           -->
<!ENTITY % doctype "MEMO"   -- document type generic identifier -->
<!--          ELEMENTS   MIN  CONTENT                (EXCEPTIONS) -->
<!ELEMENT  %doctype;    - -  ((TO & FROM), BODY, CLOSE?)          >
<!ELEMENT  TO           - O  (#PCDATA)                            >
<!ELEMENT  FROM         - O  (#PCDATA)                            >
<!ELEMENT  BODY         - O  (P)*                                 >
<!ELEMENT  P            - O  (#PCDATA|Q|PREF)*                    >
<!ELEMENT  PREF         - O  EMPTY                                >
<!ELEMENT  Q            - -  (#PCDATA)                            >
<!ELEMENT  CLOSE        - O  (#PCDATA)                            >
<!--          ELEMENTS   NAME    VALUE              DEFAULT  -->
<!ATTLIST  %doctype;    STATUS  (CONFIDEN|PUBLIC) PUBLIC          >
<!ATTLIST  P            id      ID                 #IMPLIED       >
<!ATTLIST  PREF         refid   IDREF              #IMPLIED       >
```

Figure 49. Memo DTD

There is a direct correspondence between structure diagrams (see section) and model groups containing connectors.

1. **Sequence connectors.** They are represented by commas (","). Elements or model groups appearing on either side of the sequence connector must figure in the *same order*. For example, inside the MEMO element, the BODY element must appear after the element represented by the model group (TO & FROM).
   The model group (a,b) corresponds to the structure diagram "in series."

2. **And connectors.** They are represented by ampersands ("&"). Elements or model groups appearing on both sides of the and connector may appear in any order, but they *must both* appear in the document. For example, inside the MEMO element, both the TO element and the FROM element must appear, albeit in any order.
   The model group (a&b) corresponds to the structure diagram "in series and parallel."

3. **Or connectors.** They are represented by vertical bars ("|"). Either the element or model group on the left-hand side of the or connector must occur or the element on the right-hand side, but not *both*. For example, inside the attribute list for the MEMO element, the attribute with name STATUS must have value CONFIDEN or PUBLIC.
   The model group (a|b) corresponds to the structure diagram "in parallel."

9.8 Occurrence indicators

The complete list of correspondences between the connectors in model groups and structure diagrams is shown in Figure 50.

Structure diagram	Content model

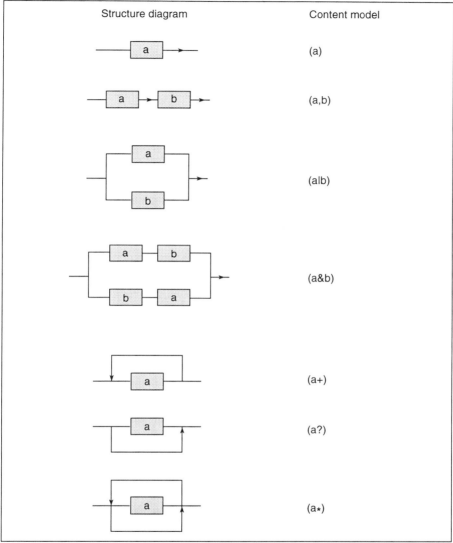

	(a)
	(a,b)
	(a|b)
	(a&b)
	(a+)
	(a?)
	(a∗)

Figure 50. Correspondence between Structure Diagrams and Model Groups

Occurrence indicators have a higher precedence than connectors. For example, if (#PCDATA|Q)∗ is the model group for the content of a paragraph, a paragraph may contain an arbitrary number of parsed character data strings mixed with an arbitrary number of quotations:

```
<P>First paragraph.<Q>First quotation.</Q> Rest of first
paragraph.</P>
```

```
<P><Q>Second quotation at the start of the second
paragraph.</Q> Rest of second paragraph.</P>
```

If the model group is (#PCDATA|Q*) a paragraph may contain an arbitrary number of parsed character data strings *or* an arbitrary number of quotations:

```
<P>Start of first paragraph in which no quotations are
allowed</P><P><Q>First quotation in second paragraph.</Q>
<Q>Second quotation</Q><Q>Third quotation</Q></P>
```

9.9 Model and name groups

A **name group** is a list of names.

For a name group, at least one valid name appears inside the group delimiters followed by an arbitrary number of other names with connectors between them. Only one type of connector should be used inside a name group: for example, (TO & FROM) or (CONFIDEN|PUBLIC) or (NAME,IZIP,LOC,COMPANY,DEPT,PHONE). They can be used in all types of markup declarations.

If the tokens of a name group are generic identifiers and there is only one type of connector (such as in (TO & FROM)) a name group is also a model group. It can then be used in entity and attribute declarations.

9.10 Name token groups

A name token group is a list of name tokens.

At least one valid name token appears inside the delimiters followed by an arbitrary number of others with connectors in between. Only one type of connector should be used inside a name token group. For example, (1KEY, 2KEY), (CH|-1211) and (8,--1234) are all valid name token groups. They can be used in all types of markup declarations. Names are also valid name tokens.

9.11 Exercises

1. Prove by writing down the structure diagrams and analyzing the possible states that (A|B?) is equivalent to (A|B)?.

2. Explain in words the meaning and draw the structure diagram of the model group (A*,(B|C)?).

3. Give the model group for 0 or many elements A, followed by 0 or 1 elements B, followed by one A.

10. Element declarations

Element declarations are constructed by introducing sequence connectors and occurrence indicators into model groups. The parts of element declarations are given in Table 14.

Table 14. The parts of a element declaration

Example: <!ELEMENT name omitted-tag-minimization contents >			
Order	**Part**	**Description**	**Abstract Name**
1	<!	markup declaration open delimiter	MDO
2	ELEMENT	declaration type keyword	
3	MEMO	the element's generic identifier	GI
4	- -	omitted tag minimization	
5	((TO & FROM),etc.)	contents of the characters that may appear between start-tag and end-tag	CONTENT MODEL or DECLARED CONTENT
6	>	markup declaration close delimiter	MDC

To each node of the tree, and to each structure diagram, corresponds an **element declaration** in the DTD (e.g. MEMO , TO or FROM). The DTD must contain a declaration for the document type name (MEMO).

The **omitted tag minimization** consists of two characters, one for the start-tag and one for the end-tag, a letter O if the tag may be omitted ("O") or a minus if it may not be omitted ("-"). The letter O may be uppercase or lowercase. The omitted tag minimization may be left out of an element declaration if the OMITTAG NO feature is selected in the SGML declaration (see section 16.1).

An element's content can be described via a **content model** or via **declared content**. Both content models and declared content are used to markup valid SGML characters. If you need to include non-SGML data such as a bitmap containing binary data, you should do so via an external entity declaration (data entities are discussed in section 12.3).

10.1 Content models

The content model of an element specifies the **model group** that defines the allowed content of the element.

During the discussion of structure diagrams, we encountered terminal elements that do not contain any subelements (e.g., TO and Q). The reserved name #PCDATA is used inside markup declarations to indicate zero or more parsed data characters for a content model without subelements.

These elements contain the textual data of the document. **#PCDATA** means **parsed character data**. It is called like this since the parser needs to determine if the data contains other markup such as entity references and start-tags.   The number sign ("#") is the **reserved name indicator (RNI)**. It distinguishes parsed character data from an element with the name PCDATA, which is a perfectly legal name that anyone is allowed to use. The model group

```
<!ELEMENT P        - O          (#PCDATA|Q)*           >
```

means that a P element can contain valid SGML data as well as Q elements. The data must be parsed to determine whether a given character is markup or character data.   #PCDATA has an implicit optional and repeatable occurrence indicator "*".

10.2 Included elements

It may happen that an element can occur in all the sub-elements of a given element. You could decide, for example, that a footnote (FN) element is allowed anywhere within the MEMO element. To include FN in all model groups would be cumbersome. The same effect may be achieved via an **inclusion** of elements which are not logically part of the document's hierarchical structure (cf. Table 14):

```
<!ELEMENT name minimization    (modelgroup)  +(inclusion)>
```

Here **PLUS** ("+") is the **inclusion delimiter**. For example:

```
<!ELEMENT MEMO - -     ((TO & FROM), BODY, CLOSE?) +(FN)>
```

means that the element FN may occur anywhere in MEMO (an unlimited number of times, including any of its sub-elements). Note:

1. The inclusion is a name group. Provided only one type of connector is used, a model group may be present following the inclusion delimiter (PLUS):

```
+(fig|xmp)         but NOT    +(fig|xmp,fn)
```

Inclusions should only be used for elements that are not part of the logical contents at the point where they occur in the document. Valid examples are keywords, index entries, table of contents entries, floating figures or tables, and so on. They should not be used for paragraphs or other basic document elements. To avoid unstructured documents, inclusions should only be used at the lowest possible level in the document's tree structure.

A **proper** sub-element is an sub-element which is permitted inside an element because of its content model. An element which appears as an inclusion is not a proper sub-element.

10.3 Excluded elements

It may happen also that an element should be excluded from showing up in all the sub-elements of a given element. An example is the footnote that should be prevented from occurring inside itself. This is achieved via an **exclusion**:

```
<!ELEMENT name minimization    (modelgroup)   -(exclusion)>
```

Here **MINUS** ("-") is the **exclusion delimiter**. For example:

```
<!ELEMENT FN     - -            (P+)                        -(FN)>
<!ELEMENT P      - O            (TEXT|FN)+                      >
<!ELEMENT TEXT O O            (#PCDATA)                       >
```

The content model for footnotes does not allow footnotes to occur at the top level of another footnote, but they could occur in a paragraph contained in a footnote. The exclusion group -(FN) prevents this from happening. The expression following the exclusion delimiter (MINUS) is a name group. The following restrictions apply to exclusions:

1. An element can only be excluded if it is optional, repeatable or if it occurs in an "or" group (e.g., (#PCDATA|FN)). You cannot exclude any required element. For instance, the following is an error:

```
<!ELEMENT FN     - -            (P+)                        -(P)>
```

2. You cannot change the required or optional status of an element by an exclusion group. For instance, the following is an error:

```
<!ELEMENT P      - O            (TEXT|FN)+         -(TEXT|FN)>
```

3. Inclusions and exclusions may occur in the same document element. If an element is excluded as well as included, the exclusion takes precedence.

Exclusions should be used to prevent recursion of an inclusion, or when a part of a DTD is an external, unmodifiable DTD. To prevent unstructured documents, exclusions should only be used at the lowest possible level in the document's tree structure.

10.4 ANY content

If an element's content model is **ANY**, this means that the element contains #PCDATA or any of the elements defined in the DTD, in any order. For example,

```
<!ELEMENT Memo        - - ANY                      >
<!ELEMENT P           - O (#PCDATA|Q|PREF)*         >
etc.
```

means that the PREF and Q elements can occur anywhere in the document, not only in the P element but also in the TO element. Do not leave elements with content model ANY in your DTD since this leads to unstructured documents. It should be used for debugging.

10.5 Declared content

Sometimes a text has elements that have to be treated in a special way by the parser. For example, if you are writing a book on SGML, you may have many examples with tags that you do not want to be processed. Depending on which type of data the element was declared to have, the parser takes different actions.

Some examples of these types of data are:

1. mathematical formulae, graphics;

2. formatted text;

3. text with markup.

In either case you want to prevent the parser from interpreting characters or accidental bit combinations as markup delimiters. This can be achieved by giving an element declared content.

There are three possible declared content types, each indicated by a reserved name. When used in an element declaration, they indicate the element's **declared content**.

CDATA   Character data. Elements that have this declared content data type may contain only SGML characters. All markup characters or delimiters are ignored, except for ETAGO ("</") delimiters or valid **null end tags** ("/", see section 16.1). This means that the element's end-tag

(or that of an element in which it is nested) is recognized, while an error occurs if the ETAGO is invalid. This is useful for data wherein SGML delimiters are used for another purpose. For example, in a textbook on quantum physics you could encounter the notation

```
<a> = <p c/|E|>
```

A parser would object to this if it were treated as #PCDATA. The above formula can be achieved with the following markup. Declaration:

```
<!ELEMENT Expvalue - - CDATA>
```

Use:

```
<Expvalue><a> =<p c/|E|></Expvalue>
```

Output:

```
<a> = <p c/|E|>
```

No reserved name indicator is needed in front of CDATA because a model group cannot have a content where character data is mixed with other elements since no markup is recognized inside it.

RCDATA   Replaceable character data. This declared content data type is similar to CDATA except that entity references and character references are recognized.

EMPTY   If the element does not have any content, it may have declared content EMPTY. For example, a **<DATE>** tag could tell the processing system that the date is required somewhere in the document:

```
<!ELEMENT DATE     - O EMPTY                    >
```

Another example is a table of contents, marked up by the empty **<TOC>** tag. This could tell the system to generate a table of contents. No other elements are allowed inside elements with EMPTY content. End-tags must be omitted for these elements because there is no content and the element does not need to be closed.

10.6 Other markup

Other markup that may be contained in an element are entity references, character references, markup declarations, and processing instructions. All these are ignored if the element has CDATA contents. If an element has RCDATA contents, markup declarations and processing instructions are ignored.

10.7 A mixture

An element is declared to have **mixed content** if its content model contains #PCDATA besides sub-elements; otherwise the element has **element content**. For example,

```
<!ELEMENT P        - O (#PCDATA|Q)*              >
```

is a mixed content element.   It is recommended that only the or connector ("|") is used in mixed content model groups, since the use of other connectors leads to problems.

10.8 Exercises

1. Why is the reserved name indicator (#) required in element declarations with PCDATA, but not with CDATA, RCDATA and EMPTY? Figure 51 shows the memo DTD after removing #P in element declarations:

```
<!DOCTYPE MEMO [
<!-- DTD for simple office memoranda                        -->
<!ELEMENT  MEMO        - -  ((TO & FROM), BODY, CLOSE?)       >
<!ELEMENT  (TO|FROM|CLOSE)    - O  (CDATA)                    >
<!ELEMENT  BODY        - O  (P)*                              >
<!ELEMENT  P           - O  (#PCDATA | Q )*                   >
<!ELEMENT  Q           - -  (#PCDATA)                         >
<!ATTLIST  MEMO         STATUS  (PUBLIC|CONFIDEN) PUBLIC      >]>
<MEMO>
<TO>Comrade Napoleon
<FROM>Snowball
<BODY>
<P>In Animal Farm, George Orwell says: <Q>...the pigs had to
expend enormous labour every day upon mysterious things called files,
reports, minutes and memoranda. These were large sheets of paper
which had to be closely covered with writing, and as soon as they
were so covered, they were burnt in the furnace...</Q>
Do you think SGML would have helped the pigs?
</BODY>
<CLOSE>Comrade Snowball</CLOSE>
</MEMO>
```

Figure 51. Removing the #P from #PCDATA

When this file is parsed, the error message shown in Figure 52 occurs. Interpret this message and explain the problem.

```
ASTATUS TOKEN PUBLIC
(MEMO
(TO
sgmls: SGML error at totmemo.sgm, line 19 at "n":
       No definition for CDATA implied start-tag;
       "CDATA O O ANY" assumed
(CDATA
-Comrade Napoleon  \n
(FROM
-Snowball
)FROM
(BODY
AID IMPLIED
(P
-In Animal Farm, George Orwell says:
(Q
-...the pigs had to\nexpend enormous labour every day upon mysterious
things called files,\nreports, minutes and memoranda. These were
large sheets of paper which \nhad to be closely covered with writing,
and as soon as they were so\ncovered, they were burnt in the furnace...
)Q
-\nDo you think SGML would have helped the pigs?
)P
)BODY
-\n
(CLOSE
-Comrade Snowball
)CLOSE
)CDATA
)TO
sgmls: SGML error at totmemo.sgm, line 30 at ">":
       MEMO element ended prematurely; required FROM omitted
)MEMO
```

Figure 52. The Output of the Parser after Removing the #P from #PCDATA

2. Write down the element declarations for the letter, using the tree you made in a previous exercise.

3. Correct the file in Figure 53, which contains characters that should not be interpreted as markup:

```
<!DOCTYPE wywa [
<!-- DTD for a while-you-were-away note                              -->
<!ENTITY % doctype "wywa" -- document type generic identifier  -->
<!--        ELEMENTS    MIN  CONTENT    (EXCEPTIONS)               -->
<!ELEMENT  wywa          - -  ((To & From & Of), Phone?, Notes?)    >
<!ELEMENT (To|From|Of|Phone|Notes) - O  (#PCDATA)                   >
]>
<wywa>
<To>The big pig</To>
<From>The small pig</From>
<Of called>The middle pif
<Phone>767 5087
<Notes>This is an example of markup in the text: supposing a<b.
</wywa>
```

Figure 53. Parsing Characters that are not Markup

The parser's reaction to this input is shown in Figure 54:

```
(WYWA
(TO
-The big pig
)TO
(FROM
-The small pig
)FROM
(OF
-The middle pig
)OF
(PHONE
-767 5087
)PHONE
(NOTES
sgmls: SGML error at /asis/eric/ebt_books/books/advanced/markup.sgm,
line 25 at record start: Undefined B. start-tag GI ignored; not used
in DTD
-This is an example of markup in the text: supposing a
)NOTES
)WYWA
```

Figure 54. Parsing Characters that are not Markup

11. Attribute declarations

It is not always obvious to make the choice between elements and attributes. For example, a letter may be a **business letter** and include a company logo, or a **private letter**, including a private address. You could add an element TYPE in the letter indicating which type is used:

```
<TYPE>private
<TYPE>business
```

but SGML cannot check if the data's content is "private" or "business." It is better to introduce an attribute TYPE on the LETTER element:

```
<LETTER TYPE="private">
<LETTER TYPE="business">
```

The parser checks the values of attributes. Attributes and their possible values are defined in the DTD by **attribute definition list** declarations. If there is no attribute definition list corresponding to an element, the element does not have any attributes. The parts of an attribute definition list declaration are shown in Table 15.

Table 15. The parts of an attribute declaration

Example: <!ATTLIST MEMO STATUS (PUBLIC I CONFIDEN) PUBLIC>			
Order	**Part**	**Description**	**Abstract Name**
1	<!	markup declaration open delimiter	MDO
2	ATTLIST	attribute definition list declaration keyword	
3	associated element	name of the element to which the list belongs	GI
4	attribute-name	name of the attribute	NAME
5	declared-value	declared value of the attribute, or keyword	NOTATION, NAME or a keyword

Example: <!ATTLIST MEMO STATUS (PUBLIC｜CONFIDEN) PUBLIC>			
Order	**Part**	**Description**	**Abstract Name**
6	default value	default value of the attribute, or keyword	
7	>	markup declaration close delimiter	MDC

Attribute names must satisfy the rules for SGML names. Like element names, attribute names are case insensitive. You can define as many attributes as you need. The length of any token in an attribute's declared value may not exceed 8. The possible declared value keywords are given in the table below.

Table 16. Possible declared value keywords for attributes

keyword	attribute value	value type	example
CDATA	character data	CDATA	<table arrange="1 2/3 4">
ENTITY	general entity name	SGML name	<artwork name="PIC">
ENTITIES	general entity name list	SGML names	<artwork name="PIC1 PIC2">
ID	id value	unique name	<BIB ID=Orwell>
IDREF	id reference value	name	<BIBREF REFID="Orwell">
IDREFS	id reference list	names	<BIBREF REFID="Orwell Huxley">
NAME	name	name	<Memo from="Fons">
NAMES	name list	names separated by spaces	<Memo from="Fons Hans">
NMTO-KEN	name token	name token	<Building no="R-021">
NMTO-KENS	name token list	name tokens	<Building no="R-021 R-023">

keyword	attribute value	value type	example
NOTA-TION	notation name		`<formula nota-tion="EQN">`
NUMBER	number	digit	`<c n="7">`
NUM-BERS	number list	digits	`<table no="5 0 8 7">`
NUTO-KEN	number to-ken	<9 chars	`<phone no="2157-1262">`
NUTO-KENS	number to-ken list	number to-kens with spaces	`<phone no="2157 - 262">`

In this table, it is a coincidence that under the examples for the declared values ID and NOTATION, the attribute names were also chosen to be ID and NOTATION. Notice the following constraints:

1. the length of any declared token may not exceed eight characters;

2. there may be one list per element, as many names as required;

3. ID and NOTATION may appear only once per element;

4. a token may not occur more than once per list, i.e.,

```
<!ATTLIST LIST TYPE (bullet,ordered) bullet
              CHAR (bullet, asterisk, number) number >
```

is illegal because two different attributes (**TYPE** and **CHAR**) can take the same value (**bullet**);

5. an ENTITY declared value means that this attribute must have as value the name of a data entity (see section 12.3), or the name of a SGML subdocument entity.

When using attributes, all spaces, record ends and separator characters are replaced by a single space. For example,

```
<PREF REFID="
xyz">
```

is equivalent to:

```
<PREF REFID=" xyz">
```

CDATA attribute values are an exception to this rule. In addition to the above replacements, all spaces between literal delimiters are retained. CDATA is the only declared value that may have an empty string as default:

```
<!ATTLIST MEMO STATUS CDATA "">
```

The default value of an attribute may be:

1. #FIXED followed by a token, meaning that if specified, the value must equal the fixed value;

2. a member of a token list given for the attribute;

3. one of the default value keywords in Table 17.

Table 17. Attribute defaults

Keyword	Description
#FIXED	keyword is followed by the attribute's value
#REQUIRED	attribute must always be given a value
#CURRENT	value is the most recently specified one
#CONREF	value is for cross references
#IMPLIED	value need not be given; the processing system chooses a default

To avoid confusion between these keywords and attribute values they are preceded by the reserved name indicator ("#").

#FIXED followed by a value means that the attribute always has this value. The user does not have to supply it. #CURRENT means that the user must supply a value on the first occurrence of a tag (as if #REQUIRED was used) with this attribute. The same value is used for any subsequent tag that uses this attribute. A value may be shared between many tags.

Your SGML guide advises...

As an example of using #CONREF, consider the following case. When you are working on a large document which you have split into several parts, it can happen that you want to refer to a textual element that belongs to a different part. To avoid unresolved references while processing the individual parts, the unique identifier attribute should be given the default value #CONREF:

```
<!ELEMENT Fig    - O EMPTY                        >
<!ELEMENT Figref - O (#PCDATA)                    >
<!ATTLIST Figref refid IDREF #CONREF              >
<!ATTLIST Fig    id    ID    #IMPLIED             >
```

If the attribute is given, the element's content can be empty:

```
<P>This is a figure: <Fig id="newdtd">.......</Fig>
<P>The memo DTD is shown in <Figref refid="newdtd">.
```

When there is no attribute, the figref element can have content:

```
<P>The memo DTD is shown in <Figref>Figure 12 on
page 46</Figref>.
```

11.1 Unique identifiers and cross-referencing

To distinguish one element from all the other elements, you should define a **unique identifier** attribute for it. This is done by declaring its value as ID:

```
<!ATTLIST P        ID ID #REQUIRED>
```

This declaration defines an attribute with name ID (a unique identifier) for the element P with declared value type ID. The default #REQUIRED means that the user must give a value for ID. The declared value ID means that its value is unique in this document.

```
<P ID="xyz">In Animal Farm,...
```

For consistency, you should give all unique identifier attributes in a DTD the same name, e.g., **ID**. Unique reference identifiers must have a declared default of either #REQUIRED or #IMPLIED. For #IMPLIED, if the value of **ID** is not provided, the element is not available for referencing. Only one attribute with declared value ID may be defined per element.

The purpose of unique identification is to be able to refer to it later (cross-referencing). This is done by giving to an attribute the declared value IDREF:

```
<!ATTLIST PREF  REFID IDREF #REQUIRED>
```

You can now link a paragraph reference to a paragraph by giving the **REFID** attribute the same value as the previously defined value of **ID**:

```
<PREF REFID="xyz">
```

Attributes of type ID and IDREF are useful for referring to figures, tables, chapters, sections, etc. The reference numbers themselves and the cross references to them are added by the processing application. The parser checks if for each IDREF a corresponding ID exists, or if an ID value is defined but never used. To add numbers, the processing system may need to run through the document a second pass.

11.2 Exercises

1. Write down the attribute declaration that gives a unique identifier to the affiliation element in the first page of the article, and the attribute declaration that gives a reference to a unique identifier to the author element.

2. Write down the attribute declaration that allows you to indicate whether a letter is a *personal* or a *business* letter.

12. Entity declarations

Entities are defined with an **entity declaration**. There are two types of entities: **general entities** and **parameter entities**.

A general entity's content can be one of the following four possibilities:

1. A parameter literal. This is the most common case. This situation described in Table 18 and below.

2. An external entity specification. This is to include external files in your document. It is described in section 12.3.

3. Data text. This facility is less used. For a discussion on data text see section 12.4.

4. Bracketed text. Section 12.5 describes bracketed text.

12.1 Parameter literals

The syntax of an entity declaration whose entity text is a **parameter literal**, is shown in Table 18.

Table 18. The parts of an entity declaration

Ex.: <!ENTITY CALS "Computer-aided Acquisition and Logistics Support">			
Order	**Part**	**Description**	**Abstract Name**
1	<!	markup declaration open delimiter	MDO
2	ENTITY	entity declaration keyword	
3	CALS	name of the entity	NAME
4	"	literal string delimiter to delimit the entity's content	LIT
	'	alternative literal string delimiter	LITA

Ex.: <!ENTITY CALS "Computer-aided Acquisition and Logistics Support">			
Order	**Part**	**Description**	**Abstract Name**
5	Computer-aided Acquisition and Logistics Support	content of the parameter literal	replaceable parameter data
6	"	literal string delimiter	LIT
	'	alternative literal string delimiter	LITA
7	>	markup declaration close delimiter	MDC

Entity names must follow the rules for SGML names (see section 9.1).

A parameter literal consists of character data inside which parameter entity references (see section 12.6) and character entity references are resolved.

If the content of the parameter literal includes double quotes, use the alternative literal string delimiter and vice versa.

12.2 Default Entity

The parser will report an error message when an undefined entity is found. If, however, a default entity has been declared, its content will be used in processing.

```
<!ENTITY #DEFAULT "Warning: This entity is not defined">
```

12.3 External Entities

External entities are **local** or **public**. A local entity is usually not known beyond the system where it is installed, whereas a public entity is registered in a standard way and available to everyone. The syntax of an external entity declaration is shown in Table 19.

Table 19. The parts of an external entity declaration

Example: <!ENTITY chapter external identifier>			
Order	**Part**	**Description**	**Abstract Name**
1	<!	markup declaration open delimiter	MDO
2	ENTITY	entity declaration keyword	
3	chapter	name of the entity	NAME
4	external identifier	system or public identifier	
5	>	markup declaration close delimiter	MDC

For local entities, a system identifier is required. The parts of a system identifier are shown in Table 20.

Table 20. The parts of a system identifier

Example: SYSTEM "c:\chapter.sgm"			
Order	**Part**	**Description**	**Abstract Name**
1	SYSTEM	system identifier keyword	
2	" or '	literal or alternative literal string delimiter	LIT or LITA
3	c:\chapter.sgm	a system identifier	system data
4	" or '	literal or alternative literal string delimiter	LIT or LITA

The keyword SYSTEM is followed by a literal string containing **system data**. System data are composed of valid SGML characters (see Table31).

See Figure 55 for an example of an external entity.

```
<!DOCTYPE book SYSTEM "/home/eric/book.dtd" [
<!ENTITY chap SYSTEM "/home/eric/chap.sgml"> ]>
<book>
<preface>
<p>This book explains SGML.</p>
</preface>
<body>
&chap;
</body>
</book>
```

Figure 55. Example of an External Entity

Your SGML guide advises...

The entity contains the SGML data for a chapter. Splitting a document into smaller parts makes them easier to manage. It also allows inclusion of parts that follow a different DTD, provided the SUBDOC feature is used [1] and [2]. In this case the SUBDOC keyword should follow the external identifier.

The parts of a public identifier are shown in Table 21.

Table 21. The parts of a public identifier

Ex.: PUBLIC "ISO 8879:1986//ENTITIES Publishing//EN" "c:\a.ent"			
Order	**Part**	**Description**	**Abstract Name**
1	PUBLIC	public identifier keyword	
2	" or '	literal or alternative literal string delimiter	LIT or LITA
3	ISO 8879...	a public text owner identifier	minimum data
4	" or '	literal or alternative literal string delimiter	LIT or LITA
5	" or '	literal or alternative literal string delimiter	LIT or LITA
6	c:\a.ent	a system identifier	system data
7	" or '	literal or alternative literal string delimiter	LIT or LITA

The keyword PUBLIC is followed by a **minimum literal** string. A minimum literal is delimited by the literal string delimiters and contains minimum data, that is, digits, upper- and lower-case letters, the characters '()+,-./:=?, record start, record end, and space.

A minimum literal is normalized by ignoring record starts, condensing record end and space characters into a single space, and by stripping off leading and trailing spaces. The minimum literal in a public identifier can be a public text owner identifier (see section 13.1). If two slashes ("//") separate the owner identifier from the text identifier, the public identifier is a formal public identifier.

Use of a public DTD or a reference to a public text in a DTD does not mean that these data are universally available. It is a standard way of referring to a standard object, giving all the information required for anyone wanting to obtain the public text. To use the public text, the data have to be made known to the system. A system identifier may follow the minimum literal in a public identifier.

To illustrate these points, consider the trivial document in Figure 56 that refers to the ISOnum public entity set.

```
<!DOCTYPE test [
<!ELEMENT test O O (#PCDATA) >
<!ENTITY % ISOnum PUBLIC
 "ISO 8879-1986//ENTITIES Numeric and Special Graphic//EN" >
%ISOnum;
]>
&half; is the first entity in the ISOnum set.
```

Figure 56. Referring to a Public Entity Set

Without telling the parser where it can find this entity set, it will not be able to resolve the reference to the entity `half`. Figure 57 shows what happens when the sgmls parser cannot find the public entity set.

```
sgmls: Error at /asis/eric/ebt_books/books/advanced/pubtext.sgm,
line 4 in declaration parameter 5:
     Could not find external parameter entity "ISOnum"
sgmls: SGML error at /asis/eric/ebt_books/books/advanced/pubtext.sgm,
line 5 at ";":
     No declaration for entity "%ISOnum"; reference ignored
sgmls: SGML error at /asis/eric/ebt_books/books/advanced/pubtext.sgm,
line 7 at ";":
     No declaration for entity "half"; reference ignored
(TEST
-is the first entity in the ISOnum set.
)TEST
```

Figure 57. Output of the Parser Trying to Find a Public Entity Set

To get the parser to find the entity set, it should be present somewhere on the system and the full pathname of the entity set (the system identifier) should be added to the declaration as shown in Figure 58. Some systems may have a way of identifying public entity sets without adding a system identifier, but SGML parsers are not required to do so.

```
<!DOCTYPE test [
<!ELEMENT test O O (#PCDATA) >
<!ENTITY % ISOnum PUBLIC
"ISO 8879-1986//ENTITIES Numeric and Special Graphic//EN" "c:\isonum">
%ISOnum;
]>
&half; is the first entity in the ISOnum set.
```

Figure 58. Referring to a Public Entity Set with a System Identifier

12.3.1 Data entities

This section requires an understanding of **NOTATION** (see section 17.1). If you want, you can skip this section and come back to it later.

The external entities I have discussed so far have been SGML text entities (with exception of SGML subdocument entities). Often, it is interesting to define external files that contain data of some kind or another (for example, PostScript, CGM or TₑX).

These entities are called **data entities**. A NOTATION that describes the datatype of the entity should be defined in the DTD. To indicate the datatype of an entity, a keyword denoting the datatype and the name of the NOTATION should be added after the file identifier of the external entity:

```
<!ENTITY Bike SYSTEM "/home/newbike.eps" CDATA PS>
```

Except for the keyword (e.g., CDATA) indicating the data type, the identification and declaration of data entities are the same as for subdocuments. If there is no keyword, the data type is SGML. The three other possible datatypes are:

1. **CDATA** (character data). The data consist of valid SGML characters, normally used for anything that a processing instruction can be used for. These data will not be scanned for markup by a parser and should be used for data that are specific to a processor (e.g., a mathematics processor such as TₑX). They may need to be changed when the document is interchanged: for example, in the case of a picture that uses a graphics notation that is not universally available.

2. **SDATA** (specific character data). The data consist of valid SGML characters. Data-generating instructions must be entered in SDATA entities. The only markup that is recognized is the terminating delimiter. SDATA entities would normally have to be changed for

different systems. The distinction between CDATA and SDATA is a subtle one. The only difference is whether the data is system dependent or not.

3. **NDATA** (non-SGML data). The data consist of other than valid SGML characters. It can be used for binary data such as bitmaps. NDATA is not necessarily processed by the parser.

It is not possible to define a notation for entities that contain SGML data.

Note that if an element has an attribute with declared value entity, this entity must be a data entity (see Figure 59).

```
<!DOCTYPE testnot [
<!ELEMENT testnot O O (ref)*>
<!ELEMENT ref      - O EMPTY >
<!ATTLIST ref target entity #IMPLIED >
<!NOTATION SGMLdoc public "-//ibm //NOTATION //EN" >
<!ENTITY doc1 SYSTEM "totmemo.sgm" >
<!ENTITY doc2 SYSTEM "totmemo.sgm" CDATA SGMLdoc>]>
<testnot>
<ref target=doc1>
<ref target=doc2>
```

Figure 59. Data entities

The parser complains against the first entity, because it is a general entity (see Figure 60).

```
(TESTNOT
sgmls: SGML error at testnot.sgm, line 10 at "1":
       TARGET = "doc1" entity not data entity; may affect processing
(REF
)REF
- \n
NSGMLDOC sgmldoc -//ibm\s//NOTATION\s//EN
Edoc2 CDATA SGMLDOC totmemo.sgm
ATARGET ENTITY doc2
(REF
)REF
-
)TESTNOT
```

Figure 60. Parsing data entities

A summary of the possible entity types is shown in Figure 61.

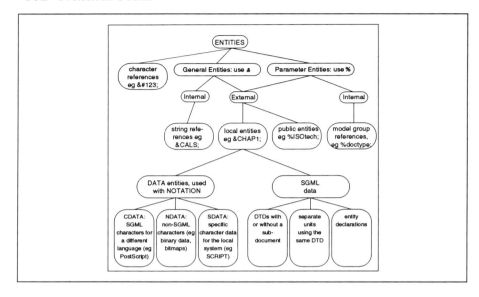

Figure 61. Possible Entity Types

12.4 Data text

There are three types of data text entity, each indicated by a keyword preceding the parameter literal in the general entity's declaration:

1. **CDATA.** The replacement text is character data.

2. **SDATA.** The replacement text is specific character data.

3. **PI.** The replacement text contains a processing instruction.

An example of an SDATA data text entity is the representation of special symbols in the specific form required by a text processor. The entity `Omega` could be replaced by the TEX command `\Omega`:

```
<!ENTITY Omega SDATA "\Omega">
```

Your SGML guide advises... Processing data text entities are a convenient and good way of defining processing instructions.

```
<!ENTITY cc PI ".cc 5">
```

Processing instructions defined in this way can easily be changed when the document is transported to a different system.

12.5 Bracketed text

This section is most meaningful in the context of marked sections and short references. You may skip it and come back to it later.

Bracketed text allows you to define entities whose replacement text is markup. There are four types of markup that each have a keyword that is placed before the parameter literal in the entity's definition:

1. **STARTTAG**. The text of the parameter literal is preceded by a start-tag open delimiter "<", and followed by a tag-close delimiter ">".

2. **ENDTAG**. The text of the parameter literal is preceded by an end-tag open delimiter "</", and followed by a tag-close delimiter ">".

3. **MS**. The text of the parameter literal is preceded by a marked section start delimiter "<![", followed by a marked section end delimiter "]]>".

4. **MD**. The text of the parameter literal is preceded by a markup declaration open delimiter "<!", and followed by a markup declaration close delimiter ">".

Examples can be found in the sections dealing with marked sections (18.3) and short references (19.2).

12.6 Parameter entities

Parameter entities can only be used inside markup declarations, and most of them are seen in DTDs. Their declaration and use is similar to that of general entities. The parameter entity reference open delimiter (**PERO**) is a percent '%' instead of an ampersand '&'.

The syntax of a parameter entity reference is shown in Table 22.

Table 22. The parts of a parameter entity reference

Example: %ISOtech;			
Order	**Part**	**Description**	**Abstract Name**
1	%	parameter entity reference open delimiter	PERO
2	ISOtech	parameter entity name	NAME
3	;	entity reference close delimiter	ERC

The PERO is followed by a blank, the parameter entity name and the entity text. There are four possible types of entities; in the commonest case the entity text consists of a parameter literal. Table 23 shows the syntax of such a parameter entity declaration.

Table 23. The parts of a parameter entity declaration

Example: <!ENTITY % doctype "MEMO" - - doctype name - ->			
Order	**Part**	**Description**	**Abstract Name**
1	<!	markup declaration open delimiter	MDO
2	ENTITY	parameter entity name	NAME
3	%	parameter entity reference open delimiter	PERO
4	doctype	name	NAME
5	" or '	literal or alternative literal delimiter	LIT or LITA
6	MEMO	parameter data	
7	" or '	literal or alternative literal delimiter	LIT or LITA
8	>	markup declaration close delimiter	MDC

Note the spaces around the %. The length of a parameter entity (seven characters) is one less than that of general entities. Parameter entities are useful for reusable structured objects in a DTD.

12.7 Bibliography for Chapter 12

[1]   M. Bryan
      An Author's Guide to SGML
      Addison-Wesley, Reading, 1988
[2]   C.F. Goldfarb
      The SGML Handbook
      Clarendon Press, Oxford, 1991

13. Putting the DTD together

This chapter describes how to assemble the DTD, how to include some standard entity sets, and how to refer to a DTD.

13.1 Public text owner identifiers

Publicly declared entity sets have public identifiers. Public entities are for sharing public text. Public text can be a set of entities or other markup declarations, even a complete DTD. It is defined as follows:

"Text that is known beyond the context of a single document or system environment and which can be accessed with a public identifier."

The public identifier must be given in the entity declaration. A separate standard (ISO 9070:1991[1]) controls the construction and registration of **public text owner identifiers**. The parts of a public text owner identifier are shown in Table 24.

Table 24. The parts of a public text owner identifier

Ex: +//ISO 9070 owner identifier//public text class public text description//language		
Order	**Part**	**Description**
1	+//	indicates an ISO 9070 registered owner identifier
2	ISO 9070 owner identifier	identifies the entity according to the rules of ISO 9070
3	//	ends the registered owner identifier, starts the text identifier
4	public-text-class	an SGML construct such as ENTITY, DTD, ELEMENTS, TEXT etc.
5	public-text-description	a description of the object: General Technical, Particle Entity Names
6	//	ends public identifier, starts language code
7	language	language code from ISO 639 (EN for English)

The rules of ISO 9070:1991 allow the registration of entity sets via ISBN numbers. For example, `ISBN 92-9083-041-7::CERN` is a valid ISO 9070 owner identifier. It also creates precise references to material in books. To refer to the PostScript Language Reference Manual, for example, use the owner identifier `ISBN 0--201--18127--4::Adobe`.

13.2 The DOCTYPE declaration

Every SGML document must contain a DTD or a reference to a DTD. The reference to the DTD is made by a markup declaration at the beginning of an SGML document called the DOCTYPE declaration. Figure 62 shows that the document type declaration starts with the DOCTYPE keyword.

```
<!DOCTYPE MEMO SYSTEM "memo.dtd">
```

Figure 62. The DOCTYPE Declaration

The parts of the DOCTYPE declaration are shown in Table 25.

Table 25. The parts of the DOCTYPE declaration

Ex.: <!DOCTYPE MEMO SYSTEM "/home/eric/memo.dtd">			
Order	**Part**	**Explanation**	**Abstract Name**
1	<!	markup delcaration open delimiter	MDO
2	DOC-TYPE	DOCTYPE keyword	
3	MEMO	document type name	NAME
4	SYSTEM	DTD is external, but on the system	
5	" or '	literal or alternative literal string delimiter	LIT or LITA
6	system or public identifier	the pathname or public name of the DTD	minimum data
7	" or '	literal or alternative literal string delimiter	LIT or LITA
8	>	markup declaration close delimiter	MDC

If a public identifier is given, it may be followed by a system identifier. To summarize:

- every document must refer to a DTD;

- every document must contain a DOCTYPE declaration;

- the DOCTYPE declaration does *not* belong to the DTD.

There is some confusion over the last point. Some commercially available products place the DOCTYPE declaration in the DTD.

13.3 The DOCTYPE Declaration Subset

When a DTD is stored outside the document, it is easier to maintain and can be shared among different documents. If, however, you have to send your document to a different system, you may want to add the DTD to a part of the document called the **document type declaration subset**. For an example of the doctype declaration subset, see Figure 63.

```
<DOCTYPE Memo SYSTEM "C:\MYDIR\MEMO.DTD"
[ --this is the declaration subset  --]>
```

Figure 63. The Position of the DOCTYPE Declaration Subset

The parts of the DOCTYPE declaration subset are shown in Table 26.

Table 26. The parts of the document type declaration subset

Example: [declaration subset]			
Order	**Part**	**Description**	**Abstract Name**
1	[	declaration subset open delimiter	DSO
2	declaration subset	private markup declarations or the DTD	
3	]	declaration subset close delimiter	DSC

Figure 64 shows a DTD in the document declaration subset.

```
<!DOCTYPE MEMO [
<!-- DTD for simple office memoranda                         -->
<!ELEMENT  MEMO    - -  ((TO & FROM), BODY, CLOSE?)           >
<!ELEMENT  (TO|FROM|CLOSE)  - O  (#PCDATA)                    >
<!ELEMENT  BODY        - O  (P)*                              >
<!ELEMENT  P           - O  (#PCDATA | Q )*                   >
<!ELEMENT  Q           - -  (#PCDATA)                         >
<!ATTLIST  MEMO        STATUS  (PUBLIC|CONFIDEN) PUBLIC   >]>
<MEMO>
<TO>Comrade Napoleon
<FROM>Snowball
<BODY>
<P>In Animal Farm, George Orwell says: <Q>...the pigs had to
expend enormous labour every day upon mysterious things called files,
reports, minutes and memoranda. These were large sheets of paper
which had to be closely covered with writing, and as soon as they
were so covered, they were burnt in the furnace...</Q>
Do you think SGML would have helped the pigs?</P>
<CLOSE>Comrade Snowball</CLOSE></MEMO>
```

Figure 64. The DTD in the Doctype Declaration Subset

The DOCTYPE declaration subset is the place for adding private markup declarations, either in the form of a complete DTD, or in addition to an external DTD. They may be used to:

- define general entities;

- include external SGML files (external entities);

- include graphical data (external entities with a special data type ;

- include objects that follow a special notation (see section 17.2, mathematics);

- achieve conditional processing of the data (marked sections, see section 18.1).

You can also add your own private element declarations, but without modifying the original DTD it will be difficult to include them in the model groups of elements, and you will not be able to use them. If a declaration re-defines an already existing object, it will be ignored.

13.4 Comments

Add comments to your DTD to explain why you did things in a certain way, and to keep track of who made modifications, why, and when.

Use a lot of comments, and make them obvious. Separate parts of the DTD by putting comments before them. Insert a comment for anything you might need to explain to someone, in particular why you did your document analysis in your way.

Make sure that the person using the DTD does not have to repeat your job. If you took a while to figure out why you did something, you can be sure it will be the same with anyone trying to understand your work. Make your DTD readable by adding meaningful comments!

The parts of comment declarations are shown in Table 27.

Table 27. The parts of an SGML comment

Example: <!- -This paragraph was added by the editor, EVH - ->			
Order	**Part**	**Description**	**Abstract Name**
1	- -	comment start delimiter	COM
2	The follow-ing ...	comment content	
3	- -	comment close delimiter	COM

Comments may appear anywhere inside a markup declaration and the document instance. Note the following points about comments:

• If a markup declaration starts with a comment, there is no blank between the markup declaration open delimiter (<!) and the comment open delimiter ("- -").

• For an example of comments in a DTD fragment, see Figure 65.

```
<!-- ========================================================= -->
<!--     THE DOCUMENT STRUCTURE                                -->
<!-- ========================================================= -->
<!--          ELEMENT     MIN   CONTENT        (EXCEPTIONS)    -->
<!ELEMENT (%doctype;)     - -   (front, body, appmat?, back?)
                                            +(%i.float;)       >
<!-- ========================================================= -->
<!--     FRONT MATTER ELEMENTS                                 -->
<!-- ========================================================= -->
<!-- the following 2 declarations are specific to Books        -->
<!ELEMENT front           O O   (titlegrp, authgrp, date?, pubfront?,
                                (%fmsec.d;)*, toc?)            >
<!ELEMENT (%fmsec.d;)     - O   %m.sec;                        >
<!-- +++++++++++++++++++++++++++++++++++++++++++++++++++++++++ -->
<!--     Title Group                                           -->
<!-- +++++++++++++++++++++++++++++++++++++++++++++++++++++++++ -->
<!ELEMENT titlegrp        O O   (msn?, sertitle?, no?, title,
                                            subtitle?)         >
<!ELEMENT (title|subtitle)
                          - O   %m.ph;                         >
<!-- +++++++++++++++++++++++++++++++++++++++++++++++++++++++++ -->
<!--     Author Group                                          -->
<!-- +++++++++++++++++++++++++++++++++++++++++++++++++++++++++ -->
<!ELEMENT authgrp         O O   (author|corpauth|aff)*         >
<!ELEMENT author          - O   %m.name;                       >
<!ELEMENT (fname|surname|role|degree|orgname|orgdiv)
                          - O   (#PCDATA)                      >
<!ELEMENT (aff|corpauth|school)
                          - O   %m.org;                        >
<!ELEMENT (%ade.ph;)      - O   (#PCDATA)                      >
<!-- +++++++++++++++++++++++++++++++++++++++++++++++++++++++++ -->
<!--     Publisher's Front Matter                              -->
<!-- +++++++++++++++++++++++++++++++++++++++++++++++++++++++++ -->
```

Figure 65. Comments in a DTD

Your SGML guide advises...

• An arbitrary number of comments may follow one another. Be sure the number of dashes is always a multiple of 4.

• Use comments to temporarily exclude markup and data from being processed:

```
<!--
<p>In Animal Farm...-->
```

Marked sections (see chapter 18) can sometimes be used as an alternative to comments.

14. Some advice on DTDs

14.1 Choosing a DTD

Some good DTDs exist in the public domain. They can provide a starting point for your own applications or as a source of inspiration.

1. The DTD in Annex E of ISO 8879:1986 [2]. This general purpose DTD is well documented in the ISO Technical Report ISO/TR 9573:1988 [3]. It is an example of general document elements for text processing applications.

2. The DTDs described in the ISO Technical Report ISO/TR 9573:1988. It contains DTDs for letters, memoranda, spreadsheets, mathematics, and examples on how to use non-Latin alphabets.

3. One of the DTDs given in the American Department of Defense Military specification MIL-M-28001. CALS [4] demands defence contractors to provide their documentation using these DTDs.

4. The American National Standard for Electronic Manuscript Preparation and Markup[5] (ANSI Z39.59–1988). This was formerly known as the AAP (Association of American Publishers) DTD, and is now in widespread use by the American publishing industry. It was prepared by the AAP for publishers, authors and editors. One of the goals of this DTD is to provide "some logical ways of representing special characters using only ASCII character sets." Therefore it contains an extensive set of entity definitions for special symbols.

Since this standard was designed before SGML had appeared, the AAP DTD suffered from various problems. The AAP DTD was extensively cleaned up and streamlined and became ISO12083:1993 [6]. ISO12083:1993 also contains facilities for the blind designed by the International Comittee for Accessible Document Design; it supports HyTime and it contains a new mathematics DTD (see chapter 24).

ISO12083:1993 has the support of some large publishers and professional organizations, such as the European Physical Society and the American Physical Society. This book was made with the ISO12083:1993 Book DTD.

5. The SNE/Cercle DTD. A proposal for the French publishers' world. This DTD is well documented and comes in machine readable form with the book by Dominique Vignaud [7].

6. The TEI DTD [8]. The Text Encoding Initiative's Guidelines for Electronic Text Encoding and Interchange are available from the TEI-L

fileserver described in chapter 6. It discusses problems of characters and character sets and provides non-technical guidance on choosing a character set and preparing documents for interchange.

14.2 Tips for writing DTDs

When putting elements, attributes, and entity definitions together in a DTD, it is helpful to stick to the following principles.

• *Place the common elements of different document classes together;* these can be shared between DTDs. Often two document classes have elements in common. For example, business letters and memos have different front matter (one has a postal address while the other does not), but their main body elements are the same (both have paragraphs). It is convenient to place the common elements in a separate DTD and to refer to it in the main DTD via an entity reference. You could go further and use a single DTD for both document classes if there are not too many differences. This can be done by making some elements optional.

• *Use existing DTDs wherever possible.* Some DTDs are now publicly available, which will probably become de facto standard DTDs. They are written by professionals and are tested and debugged. If they are part of a commercial product, they are sometimes accompanied by application procedures which save time and effort. It pays off to study existing DTDs after the document analysis to investigate whether one of them may be used, at least as a starting point. Although most existing public DTDs have some deficiency or other, using them makes documents and applications more portable.

• *It is often easier to modify an existing DTD than to create a new one from scratch.* Although you still need to do the document analysis, the major part of the structure has already been coded. In these cases, it is a good idea to remain "backwards compatible" with the modified DTD, in the sense that documents that are parsed correctly using the original DTD, are parsed successfully using the modified DTD.

• When writing a DTD from scratch, do it in the following order:

1. Decide on the *names* of the tags. Each logical element of a document class that has been identified in the process of document analysis should have a corresponding generic identifier.

2. Adapt the *flexibility* of the DTD to the target user community. Should it be a straight jacket or should it leave some freedom to the user? You could disallow examples inside figures, to make sure that examples are used only when they are meant as such. In an organization where it is possible to establish rules that are *law*, this approach is possible. In more flexible organizations the users do not appreciate the arguments

behind the rules. Provide adequate flexibility to give the users what they want (e.g., a monospaced font inside figures).

3.Bear the possible *applications* in mind when deciding on the flexibility of a DTD. Suppose that all articles written inside an organization are published in one magazine, which insists that tables are placed together with their contents at the end of an article. It would be easy to write a DTD that prohibits tables anywhere but at the end of an article. This works fine as long as one sticks to this single magazine (application). The day one wants to publish in another magazine, which demands tables inline with the rest of the text, a more flexible DTD is needed. It is not difficult to provide flexibility in a DTD, but creating text formatter macros that present the tables as they appear in the text and in another case keep them until the end of the article, means programming effort. What is gained in increased user happiness is lost by investing manpower in creating application procedures.

4.Decide on the *relationship* between the elements. Document analysis reveals the position of each element in the tree representation of the document class. Do not carry the deficiencies of an application procedure through to the DTD. For example, a formatter may not be able to mix text and graphics. Rather than forbid artwork by excluding it from the DTD, the SGML source file should be processed so that the artwork is removed and blank space is left before giving it to the text formatter.

5.Define the rules for tag markup *minimization*

6.Specify which *attributes* are allowed for each tag.

7.Define the *entity sets* that are defined for use with a given application. Several entity sets are publicly available such as those of Annex D of ISO 8879:1986.

8.Decide on any *short reference maps* that can make keying in markup easier. Use this facility with care, since it makes the DTD more complicated to write and a user is not aware of the adopted conventions undesired markup may result. Experience has shown that few users directly use short references. They could, however, be useful if a word processor is used as the SGML input system. In this case, the files are consistent and can be converted with short references to fully marked-up SGML files.

9.Define the *notation* that is allowed. Notation may be used for adding artwork (for example Encapsulated PostScript or CGM) or mathematics (T$_{E}$X, EQN, the troff-mathematics processor, or the Script Mathematical Formula Formatter, SMFF).

10.Remember that a DTD does not have to use *all* the constructs of the SGML language. Only use what you need!

11.*Code the DTD.*

12.*Test the DTD.* Use a validating parser that reports ambiguities in content models for thoroughly checking the DTD.

• Make sure every DTD is thoroughly explained, as well as the relationship between elements and their minimization. This is essential if no SGML input system is available and users must rely on documentation to create SGML files. It is also important for maintaining the system, since it is a definitive record of the interpretation of the DTD.

• Use the same DTD on different platform. If DTDs are used on different platforms to describe the same class of documents, they should be the same. Having different DTDs results in different SGML source files which may not be processable everywhere. In practice this means a severe constraint on a DTD, since some systems are hampered by problems such as size, memory, etc.

• Be careful with LINK, CONCUR, SUBDOC etc.: these features are not yet universally available.

Your SGML
guide warns...

14.3 Pitfalls

1. Be careful with **mixed content** elements. A mixed content element has a mixture of parsable character data (#PCDATA) and other elements:

```
<!ELEMENT P - O (#PCDATA|Q) >
```

Always use the "|" connector in such elements. See section 20.1 how to avoid ambiguities due to the interpretation of record end characters.

2. Agree on which processing instructions are supported by your system.   Processing instructions make a document less portable, but they can be used to patch up formatter deficiencies.   Keep the number of processing processing instructions to the absolute minimum. Encourage the use of processing entities.

3. Avoid elements that imply specific formatting. Tags such as *bold* mean very little to a non-formatting environment. Elements should be described rather by their logical function such as *highlighted phrase*, *quotation*, etc.

4. Allow users to put their own declarations in the document type declaration subset, but make it clear to them that they can create unportable documents.

5. Don't constrain the number of tags.

6. Be flexible. If you need a special font for your table which you can only obtain by placing an example inside a table, you will be upset if this is not allowed. An attribute containing formatting information (e.g., `<Table font=mono>`) is the least harmful solution in this case.

7. Avoid minimization and short references. One of the reasons for the complexity of SGML is the requirement that it should be easy to create SGML documents without an SGML input system. Some notorious errors resulting from the use of these techniques have been discussed in an article in the <TAG> magazine [9]. In the same issue some, in my opinion very sane, suggestions can be found for modifying the SGML standard (the article by J. Heath and L. Welsch). By simplifying the way you use SGML you gain in portability.

8. Be careful with parameter entities, since these can hide the structure. For example, look at Figure 66.

The problem with this document instance is that the content of the element **Xmp** is obscured by its definition in terms of parameter entities. It is not clear that **Xmp** contains itself. The assumption of the author was that **Xmp** has mixed content. Paragraphs, however, are not legal inside the **Xmp** element.

```
<!DOCTYPE parents [
<!ENTITY % ot.ph    "Xmp"                                           >
<!ENTITY % sent.ph "#PCDATA|%ot.ph;"                                >
<!ENTITY % bdel     "(%sent.ph;|P)"                                 >
<!ELEMENT  Parents    - -  (%bdel;)*                                >
<!ELEMENT  Xmp        - O  (%sent.ph;)*                             >
<!ELEMENT  P          - O  (%bdel;)*                              >]>
<parents>
<p>This example illustrates how nested parameter entities can be a
source of confusion. For example:</p>
<xmp>An example (this is surely PCDATA)
<p>The xmp element is defined as a sentence, which can be PCDATA or
other phrases. But we had forgotten that paragraphs are not
allowed !</p></xmp>
</parents>
```

Figure 66. Parameter Entity Definitions

The parser will therefore assume the **Xmp** element is closed when a paragraph start tag is found. When an **Xmp** end-tag is found later, an error will be reported, as shown in Figure 67. Of course, had the author used an SGML editor, this error would never have occurred.

```
(PARENTS
(P
-This example illustrates how nested parameter entities can be a
\nsource of confusion. For example:
)P
-\n
(XMP
-An example (this is surely PCDATA)
)XMP
(P
-The xmp element is defined as a sentence, which can be PCDATA or
\nother phrases. But we had forgotten that paragraphs are not
\nallowed !
)P
sgmls: SGML error at /asis/eric/ebt_books/books/advanced/parents.sgm,
      line 18 at ">":
       XMP end-tag ignored: doesn't end any open element
     (current is PARENTS)
)PARENTS
```

Figure 67. Problems with Parameter Entity Definitions

14.4 Exercises

1. Draw the tree structure and structure diagrams for "While-You-Were-Away" notes, an example of which is shown in Figure 68.

2. Write down the element, attribute, and entity declarations for the While-You-Were-Away notes; assemble the DTD.

```
WHILE-YOU-WERE-AWAY
===================

To:          Mr big pig                    ·

From:        Miss small pig      Seeme:      yes

Concerning:  The boss            Wantsyou:   yes
                                 Called:
                                 Phoned:     Götenburg 767 5087
                                 Replied:
                                 Came:
Notes:
Please call back about a pile of burnt memo's.
```

Figure 68. A While-You-Were-Away (WYWA) Note

3. Find the tree structure for the article in Figure 69.

4. Make the structure diagrams and write a DTD for the article.

CERN–TH.6545/92

ZZ' Mixing and Radiative Corrections at LEP I

A. Leike[1], S. Riemann[1] and T. Riemann[1,2]

[1]DESY – Institut für Hochenergiephysik, O-1615 Zeuthen, Germany

[2]Theory Division, CERN, CH-1211 Geneva, Switzerland

Abstract

We present a method for a common treatment of Z' exchange, QED corrections, and weak loops in e^+e^- annihilation. QED corrections are taken into account by convoluting a hard-scattering cross section containing γ, Z, and Z' exchange. Weak corrections and ZZ' mixing are treated simultaneously by a generalization of weak form factors. Using the properly extended Standard Model program for the Z line shape, $_{ZF}I^T T_{ER}$, we perform and compare two different analyses of the 1990 LEP I data in terms of theories based on the E_6-group and in terms of LR-symmetric models. From the LEP I data alone, the ZZ' mixing angle may be limited to $|\theta_M| \leq 0.01$ and the Z' mass to $M_2 > 118$–148 GeV, depending on the model (95% CL).

CERN–TH. 6545/92
June 1992

Figure 69. First Page of an Article

14.5 Bibliography for Chapter 14

[1] ISO
    ISO 9070:1991 SGML Support facilities — Registered procedures
    for public text owner identifiers
    Geneva, 1991

[2]   ISO
      ISO 8879:1986 Text and office systems — Standard Generalized
      Markup Language
      Geneva, 1986
[3]   ISO
      ISO/TR 9573:1988 Information processing - SGML support facil-
      ities - Techniques for using SGML
      Geneva, 1988
[4]   US Dept. of Defense
      Computer-aided Acquisition and Logistics Support
      Washington, 1988
[5]   American National Standardisation Institute
      American National Standard for Electronic Manuscript Prepara-
      tion and Markup ANSI/NISO Z39.59–1988
      1988
[6]   ISO
      ISO 12083:1993 Electronic Manuscript Preparation and Markup
      Geneva, 1993
[7]   Dominique Vignaud
      SGML: application à l'édition française
      Syndicat national de l'édition, Cercle de la librairie, Paris, 1989
[8]   Text Encoding Initiative
      TEI-DTD
      1993
[9]   W. Davis, D.C. Waldt
      Subtleties of SHORTREF and DATATAG, <TAG>, issue 9, Pages
      3–4
      april 1989

Part III. Customizing SGML

The aim of this part is to explain the SGML declaration, minimization, notation, short references, marked sections and ambiguities. It is intended for anyone who is interested in the more subtle features of SGML, or who needs to customize SGML because its default functionality is not adequate. At the end you should have learned:

- what the purpose of the SGML declaration is;
- what SGML features exist (minimization);
- what a notation is;
- how to use marked sections and short references;
- about ambiguities in DTDs and how to avoid them.

15. The SGML declaration

Each language has a **syntax**. Some aspects of the syntax of the English language, for example, are the fact that the characters with which we write are roman letters, that characters group together to form words, and that words are separated by blanks to form sentences. Sentences are started with a capital letter and terminated with a full stop.

The SGML language is defined indirectly, using what it calls **delimiter roles**, rather than specific characters when defining the syntax of the language. That is why it is an **abstract** syntax. The markup constructs of SGML are based on these delimiter roles which cause text to be interpreted as markup rather than as data.

Each of these delimiters is identified by a name in the abstract syntax and must be defined by a character string in the **concrete SGML syntax**. Some examples of roles are markup declaration open (MDO), markup declaration close (MDC), or start-tag open (STAGO) delimiter. The role of a delimiter is only recognized within a specific context, called **recognition mode**.

The role of the start-tag open delimiter (STAGO) is defined as the first character of a start-tag; this role is recognized in the content of elements, in marked sections (see chapter 18), and in a start-tag or an end-tag. Since this definition is abstract, there is no mention of a particular character.

Defining a concrete SGML syntax is assigning a character to a particular role, thus inventing a new concrete syntax but preserving the basic character of SGML. For example, the markup declaration open delimiter (MDO) could be defined as ("<!"), the markup declaration close delimiter (MDC) as (">") and the start-tag open delimiter (STAGO) as ("<"). In addition to defining delimiters, a concrete syntax can also describe:

- reserved names and keywords such as ELEMENT, ATTLIST, ENTITY, PCDATA etc.;

- characters that should not be used in documents (SHUNNED characters);

- characters used for FUNCTION characters (SPACE, RE, RS, etc.);

- naming rules (for example, which characters can be used in names);

- various quantities (for example, the maximum length of names).

SGML defines a concrete syntax which is called the reference concrete syntax (see section 15.5). The reference concrete syntax is used in the SGML declaration to define other syntaxes.

The characters used by the document are also defined in the SGML declaration, although these are not necessarily the same character definitions used to define the concrete syntax.

The SGML declaration, which precedes the DTD, is the first part of an SGML document. In its absence, the system will choose a default.

For an example of an SGML declaration, see Figure 70.

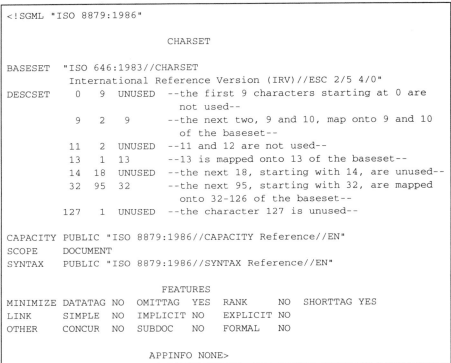

```
<!SGML "ISO 8879:1986"

                              CHARSET

BASESET    "ISO 646:1983//CHARSET
            International Reference Version (IRV)//ESC 2/5 4/0"
DESCSET     0    9  UNUSED   --the first 9 characters starting at 0 are
                              not used--
            9    2  9        --the next two, 9 and 10, map onto 9 and 10
                              of the baseset--
           11    2  UNUSED   --11 and 12 are not used--
           13    1  13       --13 is mapped onto 13 of the baseset--
           14   18  UNUSED   --the next 18, starting with 14, are unused--
           32   95  32       --the next 95, starting with 32, are mapped
                              onto 32-126 of the baseset--
          127    1  UNUSED   --the character 127 is unused--

CAPACITY PUBLIC "ISO 8879:1986//CAPACITY Reference//EN"
SCOPE    DOCUMENT
SYNTAX   PUBLIC "ISO 8879:1986//SYNTAX Reference//EN"

                              FEATURES
MINIMIZE DATATAG NO  OMITTAG  YES  RANK      NO   SHORTTAG YES
LINK     SIMPLE  NO  IMPLICIT NO   EXPLICIT  NO
OTHER    CONCUR  NO  SUBDOC   NO   FORMAL    NO

                         APPINFO NONE>
```

Figure 70. The SGML Declaration

The SGML declaration is intended to be read by humans as well as by machines. Its purpose is to determine whether an exchanged document can be processed without modification by the receiving system or whether some manual intervention is required.

The parts of the SGML declaration are shown in Table 28.

Table 28. Components of the SGML declaration

Keyword	Parameter	Explanation
CHARSET	document character set	start of description of document's character set
BASESET	public identifier	document's base character set

Keyword	Parameter	Explanation
DESCSET	0 9 UNUSED	document's character set, in terms of the base set
CAPACITY	public identifier	limits not to be exceeded by document
SCOPE	DOCUMENT	syntax applies to DTD as well as document
SYNTAX	public identifier	syntax used by document
FEATURES	start of features	describes features used (MINI-MIZE, LINK etc.)
APPINFO	NONE	application specific information

Note that BASESET and DESCSET are part of the CHARSET definition.

The SGML declaration must use the reference concrete syntax. The following sections contain an explanation of the objects defined in the SGML declaration.

15.1 The document character set

In the previous chapters I have occasionally alluded to the problems which may occur when transporting data between systems (see Chapter 4.8, Character Entities). Until you've faced a screen full of very odd-looking characters that comprised a document on another system, you probably had not given a great deal of thought to how a computer represents that document. So far, I have tacitly assumed that ASCII is the character set which we are working with. On IBM mainframes, however, the character set will be called EBCDIC[7].

Within ASCII and EBCDIC, there are many permutations, usually depending on the country where the data are created. It is an unpleasant fact of life that different conventions for representing characters are used on different computer systems.

The most obvious solution to this problem is simply to use the same representation for the same characters on all systems. In fact, there is an effort underway to propose just such a solution, namely ISO 10646, a standard for representing all characters and ideographs used throughout the world. Another standard called Unicode is designed to accomplish the same goal. Unicode will be a subset of ISO 10646, and both have been accorded much deserved attention. Unfortunately, these standards won't help us until computers, operating systems, and

---

[7] Extended Binary Coded Decimal Interchange Code

programs have been implemented to exploit this capability. Until then, we are faced with a world with many different versions of ASCII and EBCDIC, to accommodate all characters that are required, particularly by the publishing business.

To understand how SGML solves this problem, it is important to divorce the character (for example, an "A" is the first letter in the upper case Latin alphabet) and its meaning from its representation on particular system. Characters are identified with decimal number representations in their character set. This is called a "character number." These numbers are used in several places in the syntax definition. For example, the upper case "A" has position 65 in ASCII and 193 in EBCDIC.

To support the definition of a document character set, SGML must associate a character (which will have a number in a set) used in the document to that character's meaning. Unfortunately, it is verbose to define character meanings directly (although this can be done using text descriptions) so SGML allows them to be defined in terms of another known or standard character set. If you are writing your document on a system that uses the EBCDIC character set, you can associate your upper case "A" in position 193 in EBCDIC to an upper case "A" in ASCII in the SGML declaration, after the CHARSET parameter in the SGML declaration (see Figure 71).

```
                          CHARSET

BASESET  "ISO 646:1983//CHARSET
         International Reference Version (IRV)//ESC 2/5 4/0"
DESCSET ...

         193    1   65 -- Map 1 document character starting at 193
                          (EBCDIC A) to base set character 65
                          (ISO 646 A) --
         ...
```

Figure 71. Associating Document Characters to Baseset Characters

15.1.1 The BASESET

BASESET introduces the public identifier description of the character set being used as a reference or "base." The base set is typically a standard, registered, or at least well-known character set (see Figure 71, where the "base" character set is ISO 646:1983). The description must be a form that the expected recipients will understand, such as a public text owner identifier. It is convenient if the base set contains most, if not all, of the characters the document character set will use. It is also convenient if the base set closely resembles the document character set since this reduces the amount of specification that is required.

After the base set specification, DESCSET introduces the descriptions or mappings from the positions in the document character set to positions in the "base" set.

The facilities for specifying this mapping are quite flexible. You may use whatever base set(s) is understood by your system. If a character does not exist in the base set chosen, a literal may be used to describe the character meaning. The syntax also allows you to map multiple characters in the document character set to the base character set with a single declaration. In the above example, only one character was mapped, hence the "1" used in the example in Figure 71.

15.1.2 The DESCSET

Each mapping found in the DESCSET section consists of three entries:

1. The document character set character number being mapped. This is the character number of the character being defined in the document's character set.

2. The number of characters being defined. This parameter allows the SGML declaration writer to associate contiguous characters in the document character set and the base character set in one specification.

3. The base set character number which corresponds to the document character set number of the same entry. This field may also be the character string UNUSED which indicates that the document characters and character number(s) are not used in the document. This is known as a non-SGML character. This field may also be the literal which describes the character that exists in the document character set but does not exist in the base set.

Now when creating this mapping, you have to define the mapping for all the characters that exist in the document character set. Figure 72 contains an example that defines a subset of EBCDIC in terms of ISO 646:1983 (ASCII).

Your SGML
guide thinks...

There are several points to note here:

• Every EBCDIC character possible has been mapped. If there was no mapping, the keyword UNUSED was used to indicate this.

• Even control characters have been mapped (EBCDIC defines these differently than ISO 646:1983 does).

• Since "cent sign" is unknown in ISO 646:1983, it was defined using a text description. (See character number 74's mapping.)

• Commentary made the mappings much easier to understand and follow.

There will be instances when the characters used in a document are defined in multiple, different character sets. This is done by respecifying the BASESET parameter with the new base character set name and then continuing with the DESCSET mapping of document characters. This respecification of BASESET in terms of DESCSET may be done as many times as necessary.

```
BASESET
     "ISO 646:1983//CHARSET
     International Reference Version (IRV)//ESC 2/5 4/0"
     DESCSET
         0    5    UNUSED
         5    1    9              -- HT --
         6    7    UNUSED
        13    1    13             -- CR (RE) --
        14   23    UNUSED
        37    1    10             -- LF (RS) --
        38   26    UNUSED
        64    1    32             -- SPACE --
        65    9    UNUSED
        74    1                   "cent sign"
        75    1    46             -- period --
        76    1    60             -- less than sign --
        77    1    40             -- left paren --
        78    1    43             -- plus sign --
        79    1    124            -- vertical bar --
        80    1    38             -- ampersand --
        81   48    UNUSED
       129    9    97             -- a to i --
       138    7    UNUSED
       145    9    106            -- j to r --
       154    8    UNUSED
       162    8    115            -- s to z --
       170   23    UNUSED
       193    9    65             -- A to I --
       202    7    UNUSED
       209    9    74             -- J to R --
       218    8    UNUSED
       226    8    83             -- S to Z --
       234    6    UNUSED
       240   10    48             -- 0 to 9 --
       250    6    UNUSED
```

Figure 72. Mapping EBCDIC onto ISO 646:1983 (ASCII)

The most common case is that the document character set matches exactly a known, standard character set and the specification of the document character set becomes trivial; Figure 73 shows this in the case of ISO 646:1983.

```
                        CHARSET

BASESET
"ISO 646:1983//CHARSET
International Reference Version (IRV)//ESC 2/5 4/0"
DESCSET
     0 128   0
```

Figure 73. The ASCII Document Character Set

Even this simple specification is useful since it specifies something that would have to otherwise be assumed or discovered.

Once the document is presented to a parser, it will be in the document character set, and the document character set parameter is therefore ignored by the parser.

When presented with an erroneous character set definition (for example, one in which all the documents characters are described as non-SGML characters), the parser will present error messages, but nevertheless correctly continue to parse the document.

15.1.3 System character set

Within the SGML standard, there is the concept of the "system character set." This is the character set that is used to represent characters within a given SGML system. For the system to process a document, the document character set must be the same as the system character set. If they are different, one or the other must be changed. Either the document can be converted to the system character set for processing or the system can be configured to process the document character set.

The first alternative is a straightforward process of translating each character in the document to its equivalent in the system character set. There is a problem with performing this translation if there is no equivalent for a character in the document character set in the system character set. This is always a problem and is not a problem SGML has solved. One approach is to use character entity references, assuming that the appropriate entities are defined in the application being used; in any case, it is problematic.

This is a powerful argument for keeping the number of characters represented by numbers in the document character set small and insuring that they are a fairly common set of characters, using entity references for all other characters. (This requires that the DTD define a large standard set of entity definitions to work well. ISO/TR 9573:1988, part 13 defines a large number of such entities.)

The process of translating the document into the system character set must be followed by changing the document character set definition in the SGML declaration in the document, if it included an SGML declaration, since the document character set has been changed.

The idea of changing the system to process the document character set points out a limitation of the self-defining nature of an SGML declaration. The SGML declaration is part of an SGML document and is therefore written using the document character set. But the document character set is defined within the SGML declaration. This seems to make this portion of the declaration redundant since the document cannot be read unless the reader knows the character encoding used. This characteristic of SGML declarations is the reason there are two basic approaches to communicating the document character set definition:

• by an identifying name or number;

• by using a human-readable copy of the SGML declaration.

While on the face of it, this seems to be a severe limitation, the only alternative would be to define a character set standard for SGML declarations which would make them impossible to create, edit, or even read on some systems and would divorce them from the documents of which they are intended to be a part.

Given this a priori knowledge of the document character set, there is no reason that an SGML system could not process a complete document, even if it were encoded using a "foreign" character set, although handling the data after having done so is problematic.

15.2 Capacity

Capacities are a crude measure of the memory required to store the result of parsing an SGML DTD. The idea is to give a rough idea of the magnitude of a system's resources that will be required to process a given document. While this is a worthwhile objective in theory, in practice it is difficult to accomplish. Each SGML system uses different means to implement SGML processing. In practice, if a document exceeds one or more capacities, systems usually simply report the error and continue processing until complete or until system resources are actually exhausted.

Capacities are also used to set a baseline for conformance of SGML systems since they are used to specify a minimum that all conforming SGML systems must be able to parse. Any document that does not exceed the reference capacities (see Table 29) and conforms in all other respects must be processed by a conforming SGML system.

There are several classifications of capacities, each one designed to classify the memory requirements of a particular class of SGML object. For example, ENTCAP is a measure of the memory required to represent the fact that an entity was declared. A capacity set is calculated in units of **capacity points**. A point corresponds to a character of storage space (byte).

Table 29. The reference capacity set for a basic SGML system

Name	Maxi-mum value	Points per unit	Units for which points are counted
TOTALCAP	35000		Grand total of individual capacity points
ENTCAP	35000	8	Each entity defined
ENTCHCAP	35000	1	Each character of entity text
ELEMCAP	35000	8	Each element defined
GRPCAP	35000	8	Each content token at any level of a content model
EXGRPCAP	35000	8	Each exceptions group
EXNMCAP	35000	8	Each name in an exceptions group
ATTCAP	35000	8	Each attribute defined, plus 8 for each occurrence in an entity declaration of a notation name
ATTCHCAP	35000	1	Each character of an attribute value defined as a default value, or explicitly defined in a data attribute specification
AVGRPCAP	35000	8	Each token defined in an attribute value name group or name token group
NOTCAP	35000	8	Each data content notation defined
NOTCHCAP	35000	1	Each character in a notation identifier
IDCAP	35000	8	Each ID attribute specified in the instance
IDREFCAP	35000	8	Each IDREF attribute specified in the instance
MAPCAP	35000	8	Each short reference map declared, plus for each map 8 per short reference delimiter defined

In ENTCAP's case, this value is equal to the value of the NAMELEN quantity (which is defined in the syntax) that is the maximum length of an entity name. This value is then multiplied by the number of occurrences of the object being counted to calculate the total value for each category of capacity. In the case of ENTCAP, this is the number of entities declared. Continuing the ENTCAP example, assuming that 120 entities are defined in the DTD under consideration and that NAMELEN for the concrete syntax is 12, the value of ENTCAP for this document is 1440 (12 times 120). This total is then compared to the value indicated in the SGML declaration to assure that the value in the declaration has not been exceeded.

The reference capacity set defines 35000 characters as the upper limit of storage space for a DTD, which corresponds to 35K bytes. This limit is considered to be on the low side nowadays, and it is ignored by many implementations of SGML.

The capacity limit for each of the quantities in this table is 35000 characters, provided the sum of all limits does not exceed 35000 characters.

Figure 74 shows the capacities of the example memo.

```
TOTALCAP    220/35000
  ENTCAP      8/35000
ENTCHCAP      4/35000
  ELEMCAP    64/35000
   GRPCAP    96/35000
   ATTCAP    24/35000
 ATTCHCAP     8/35000
 AVGRPCAP    16/35000
```

Figure 74. Capacities Used by the Memo

Although the capacity set poses constraints on the size and complexity of the DTD and the document by limits on the number of attributes and other constructs, it is not affected by the amount of textual or other data inside a document (except IDCAP and IDREFCAP).

Many people (and certainly many implementors) consider capacities a nuisance that add little to the standard. They can generate error messages that can be confusing. Although they can usually be safely ignored (at least until system errors occur indicating that memory is exhausted), you can avoid questions from novice or cautious users if you update the SGML declaration for your application to indicate the appropriate maximums.

Figure 75 shows an example of changing the CAPACITY SET.

In this example, CAPACITY SGMLREF introduces this section of the SGML declaration and reminds the writer that categories that do not have a specification will take the value indicated in the reference capacity set. The specifications that follow then modify only those capacities specified.

In some cases, rather than specifying a list in the declaration itself, a formal public identifier is included which references a file containing the capacity specifications.

```
CAPACITY     SGMLREF
             TOTALCAP  80000
             ELEMCAP   65000
             GRPCAP    65000
             ATTCAP    65000
```

Figure 75. Changing the CAPACITY SET

15.3 Exercises

1. Calculate the While-You-Were-Away note's capacity in Figure 76.

```
<!DOCTYPE wywa [
<!-- DTD for a while-you-were-away note                       -->
<!ENTITY %  doctype "wywa"      --document type generic identifier-->
<!--         ELEMENTS   MIN   CONTENT (EXCEPTIONS)             -->
<!ELEMENT  wywa         - -   ((To & From & Of), Phone?, Notes?)    >
<!ELEMENT  To           - O   (#PCDATA)                        >
<!ELEMENT  From         - O   (#PCDATA)                        >
<!ELEMENT  Of           - O   (#PCDATA)                        >
<!ELEMENT  Phone        - O   (#PCDATA)                        >
<!ELEMENT  Notes        - O   (#PCDATA)                        >
<!--         ELEMENTS   NAME      VALUE           DEFAULT      -->
<!ATTLIST  From         seeme     (seeme)         #IMPLIED     >
<!ATTLIST  Of           called    (called)        #IMPLIED
                        phoned    (phoned)        #IMPLIED
                        came      (came)          #IMPLIED
                        replied   (replied)       #IMPLIED
                        wantsyou  (wantsyou)      #IMPLIED     >]>
<wywa>
<To>The big pig</To>
<From>The small pig</From>
<Of called>The middle pig
<Phone>767 5087
<Notes>Please call back about a pile of burnt memo's.
</wywa>
```

Figure 76. The WYWA Note (SGML)

2. Why is the value of GRPCAP 88, not 96?

15.4 Scope

The SCOPE parameter indicates what data are governed by the delimiters and other parts of the syntax which were defined there. The

SGML declaration allows the concrete syntax used in the DTD to be different from that in the document instance. This can be useful for public DTDs which use a syntax different from the syntax a particular group is used to using (for example, the public DTD may use the reference concrete syntax while the document uses a local variation). The scope is selected by giving one of the two following choices:

DOCU-MENT indicates that the DTD and the document instance (the document data and markup that follow the DTD) both use the declared syntax. Remember that the SGML declaration always uses the reference concrete syntax. Also remember that the entire SGML document must use the document character set defined above.

INSTANCE indicates that only the document instance is marked up using the syntax that is being defined. In this case, the DTD, like the SGML declaration, must use the reference concrete syntax.

Figure 77 shows the specification that indicates the scope of the defined syntax is the entire document, not just the document instance.

```
SCOPE      DOCUMENT
```

Figure 77. Defining the Scope of the Syntax

15.5 Syntax

The **concrete syntax** refers to the mappings of characters to delimiter roles, control characters that have special meaning, naming rules, reserved names, and quantities used in the markup of the document. In other words, the concrete syntax describes what characters are used as start-tag open and tag-close delimiters, entity reference open and close delimiters and other character sequences found in markup. All of these may be changed to obtain a syntax that looks quite different from anything one normally thinks of as SGML data. This is a powerful facility that can be useful if used wisely.

The start of the syntax definition is identified with the keyword SYNTAX. There are two alternatives for what follows. Either a public syntax may be referenced using a public identifier or a full syntax specification may follow. The reference to a public concrete syntax is used if there is already a defined syntax that describes the syntax to be used within the document. The most commonly used public syntax is the reference concrete syntax. The purpose of the keyword SWITCHES is to identify a pair of character numbers that have been switched. This allows reuse of public syntaxes if there are only trivial differences.

In the example in Figure 78, the syntax is declared to be the reference concrete syntax with the *line feed* and *carriage return* character meanings reversed (which may have some use on Unix-based systems, where the carriage return character is not typically used in data).

```
SYNTAX    PUBLIC "ISO 8879:1986//SYNTAX Reference//EN"
          SWITCHES 10 13
```

Figure 78. A Trivial Change to the Reference Concrete Syntax

If a public syntax is not referenced, a full syntax definition specification must follow. The parts of a syntax definition are illustrated in Table 30 and described in the next section.

15.5.1 The reference concrete syntax

The **reference concrete syntax** (see Figure 79) is SGML's proposal for a concrete syntax.

```
         SYNTAX
 SHUNCHAR CONTROLS 0  1  2  3  4  5  6  7  8  9 10 11 12 13 14 15 16 17
          18 19 20 21 22 23 24 25 26 27 28 29 30 31 127
BASESET  "ISO 646:1983//CHARSET
          International Reference Version (IRV)//ESC 2/5 4/0"
DESCSET  0 128 0
FUNCTION RE               13
         RS               10
         SPACE            32
         TAB      SEPCHAR  9
NAMING   LCNMSTRT ""
         UCNMSTRT ""
         LCNMCHAR "-."      -- Lower-case hyphen, period are --
         UCNMCHAR "-."      -- same as upper-case (45 46).   --
         NAMECASE GENERAL YES
                  ENTITY  NO
DELIM    GENERAL  SGMLREF
         SHORTREF SGMLREF
NAMES    SGMLREF
QUANTITY SGMLREF
```

Figure 79. The Reference Concrete Syntax

The reference concrete syntax can be modified and the result is a **variant** concrete syntax (an example of a variant concrete syntax is shown in Figure 78). The parts of the reference concrete syntax are shown in Table 30.

Table 30. Components of the reference concrete syntax

Keyword	Parameter	Explanation
SYNTAX		start of concrete syntax part in SGML declaration
SHUN-CHAR	CONTROLS 0 1 2...	control characters which are ignored by the parser
BASESET	public identifier	base character set of the concrete syntax
DESCSET	0 128 0	concrete syntax character set, in terms of the base set
FUNCTION	RE 13, RS 10, SPACE 32...	characters that perform a function (record end = 13)
NAMING	LCNMSTRT ""	lower case name start characters are a-z
DELIM	GENERAL SGMLREF	general delimiters are from reference concrete syntax
NAMES	SGMLREF	reserved names are from reference concrete syntax
QUANTITY	SGMLREF	quantity set values are from reference concrete syntax

Before explaining these parts in the following sections, a review of the way SGML classifies characters is required as shown in Table 31.

The SGML characters in a document are parsed to determine whether a character is data or whether it has a role such as markup.

FUNCTION characters are characters that have a special purpose to SGML, in addition to being recognized as markup. Markup characters can be data whenever they are not recognized as markup.

NONSGML characters are used for special data objects, such as scanned images, binary data, etc. NONSGML characters may represent different characters after file transfer, because the new document character set may use a different way of assigning characters.

Table 31. The way SGML classifies characters

Type	Description		Character
non SGML characters	All UNUSED or SHUNNED, except FUNCTION characters		in ISO 646: 0-8, 11-12, 14-31, 127
SGML charac-ters	FUNCTION	characters which have a purpose (e.g., separators)	RE, RS, SPACE, TAB, SEPCHAR
	name	characters that can be used in a name	a-Z, 0-9, . , -
	delimiters	characters that cause the text to be interpreted as markup instead of data	See Table 32
	data	all other characters	#PCDATA

15.5.2 Shunned character number identification

The shunned character number identification portion of the syntax definition specifies the characters that should not be used in any document character set using the syntax. This is done because the indicated characters may cause problems for processing systems using the data. This is not an absolute prohibition, however.

Shunned characters may be used to represent markup or minimum data characters (RS, RE, SPACE, lower case letter, upper case letter, digit, or special) but should not be used for other ordinary data characters. The reason for these exceptions is that markup characters will not be passed to the application by the parser and therefore will not cause problems. A keyword that may be specified here is CONTROLS. This keyword indicates that any character number that is used as a control character in the system character set is a shunned character as well.

Shunned characters should not be translated when translating from one character set to another. This could cause problems because within EBCDIC, the tab character is encoded differently than in ASCII and both are typically indicated as shunned characters. Care must therefore be exercised when specifying characters as shunned.

Figure 80 shows a typical specification for this section.

This example defines two graphic characters as shunned characters, 127 and 255. While these are graphics in some character sets, they may cause problems to some systems and were therefore identified as shunned. In most cases, this is excessive. If any character is not allowed in a character set, it may be defined as a non-SGML character in the document character set and therefore be prohibited from occurring in the document.

```
SHUNCHAR CONTROLS
          0  1  2  3  4  5  6  7  8  9 10 11 12 13 14 15
         16 17 18 19 20 21 22 23 24 25 26 27 28 29 30 31
         127 255
```

Figure 80. Shunned characters

15.5.3 The syntax character set

After the shunned character number identification, the next section defines the syntax reference character set. The purpose of this character set is to define the character set used when specifying character numbers.

The specification of the syntax reference character set is identical to the specification of the document character set which was discussed in a previous section. It uses the BASESET specification to identify a known character set. The DESCSET specification is then used to define the syntax reference character set in terms of the base character set.

15.5.4 Function character identification

The function character identification section identifies the character numbers in the syntax reference character set that represent several important function characters: RS, RE, and SPACE.

In addition to these function characters, other special function characters may be defined. To do so, you must define a name for the function and assign a function class and a character number. There are five function classes; here are their definitions:

FUNCHAR   Identifies characters that may have some significance to the system but that have no SGML function defined.

MSOCHAR   Identifies characters that inhibit the recognition of markup (markup scan out) in the data that follow. The MSICHAR function character is used to restore markup recognition.

MSICHAR   Identifies characters that restore markup (markup scan in) recognition when it was suppressed by the use of a character defined as a MSOCHAR character.

MSSCHAR   Identifies characters that inhibit the recognition of markup (markup scan suppress) for the character that immediately follows the function character in the same entity.

SEPCHAR Identifies characters that are allowed as separators (like RE, RS and SPACE) and will be replaced by SPACE in all contexts in which RE is replaced by SPACE. One commonly defined such function character is TAB.

Figure 81 shows an example of the identification of function characters:

```
FUNCTION  RE              13
          RS              21
          SPACE           64
          TAB     SEPCHAR 5
```

Figure 81. The Identification of Function Characters

In this example, character number 13 (carriage return) has been defined as RE (record end), character number 21 (line feed) has been defined as RS (record start), and character number 64 (space) has been defined as SPACE. In addition, character number 5 (tab) has been defined as the function TAB with the function class SEPCHAR. These function character definitions would appear in an EBCDIC character set definition.

15.5.5 Name rules

The definition of SGML names, numbers, and tokens has been given earlier (see section 9.1). Here we explain how the rules with which they are constructed, are defined in the concrete syntax.

The naming rules definitions allow you to specify characters (in addition to alphabetic characters and digits) to be used in names and as name start characters. The definitions also allow the specification of uppercasing rules for the added name characters. The categories that may be defined are:

LCNMSTRT Lowercase name start characters. These characters are considered lowercase and may be used as the first character in a name.

UCNMSTRT Uppercase name start characters. These characters are considered uppercase and may be used as the first character in a name. Characters may occur multiple times in this definition to allow different lowercase characters to map to the same uppercase character. For letters which do not distinguish between lower and uppercase, the same character is used in both LCNMSTRT and UCNMSTRT.

LCNM-CHAR   Lowercase name characters.   These characters are considered lowercase and may be used within a name.

UCNM-CHAR   Uppercase name characters.   These characters are considered uppercase and may be used in names.

NAMECASE   Determines the extent of uppercase substitution during markup processing. It allows you to determine whether case may be used to differentiate entity names, element names, attribute names, etc.   There are two different specifications possible for NAMECASE:

GENERAL   Determines whether all names, name tokens, number tokens, and delimiter strings (besides entity names and references) will be folded to uppercase.

ENTITY   Determines whether all entity names and entity references will be folded to uppercase.

You must specify either a "**YES**" or a "**NO**" for both.

Figure 82 shows an example of a typical naming rules section.

```
NAMING   LCNMSTRT  ""
         UCNMSTRT  ""
         LCNMCHAR  "&#46;&#45;" -- ".-" --
         UCNMCHAR  "&#46;&#45;" -- ".-" --
         NAMECASE GENERAL   YES
                  ENTITY    NO
```

Figure 82. A Naming Rules Section in the Syntax Definition

In the example of Figure 82, no name start characters have been added to the defined minimum set (upper and lowercase letters). That is why the LCNMSTRT and UCNMSTRT have null character strings as arguments. The name characters (which at a minimum contain the name start characters and the digits, 0 through 9) have two additional characters added, the period and the hyphen.

Case is not an issue for these characters so they are specified using the same character numbers in both LCNMCHAR and UCNMCHAR.

The NAMECASE specification indicates that all names except entity names (in declarations and references) will be folded to uppercase, which is the case in the reference concrete syntax, the default in this book.

Notice that the LCNMSTRT and the others take a character string called a parameter literal, not character numbers. This allows these characters to be specified directly, which is much easier than using the character number. This could, however, give unexpected results if the document and syntax character set are not the same.

A method for avoiding this problem is to use numeric character references in the literal strings to specify the character used in the syntax reference character set. This is shown in the example of 82. Notice that if this method is used, the syntax definition specification may be translated to a different character encoding without affecting the assignment of characters to roles in the syntax.

15.5.6 Delimiters

The delimiter set definitions assign delimiter roles to specific characters or character strings. There are two classes of delimiters defined:

1. general delimiters defining the characters used to represent the delimiter roles in the document;

2. short reference delimiters defining the character strings that are available for use in short reference maps for mapping these strings to entity references.

The delimiter characters in the reference concrete syntax were selected after considering the following questions:

1. Which systems are used to create SGML documents?

2. Which delimiter symbols would be easily distinguishable from data by both humans and computers?

3. Is there a suitable character for each role?

The classification of the characters according to their roles is shown in Table 32. The first column contains the typical presentation, or glyph; the second column contains the delimiter role; the third column shows the character number in the syntax reference character set (ISO 646:1983) of the reference concrete syntax.

Table 32. Delimiters defined by the reference concrete syntax

Glyph	Delimiter role	ISO 646 #	Abstract Name
&	and connector	38	AND
– –	comment start or end	45 45	COM
&#	character reference open	38 35	CRO
]	declaration subset close	93	DSC
[	declaration subset open	91	DSO
]	data tag group close	93	DTGC
[	data tag group open	91	DTGO
&	entity reference open	38	ERO
</	end-tag open	60 47	ETAGO
)	group close	41	GRPC
(	group open	40	GRPO
"	literal start or end	34	LIT
'	literal start or end (alternative)	39	LITA
>	markup declaration close	62	MDC
<!	markup declaration open	60 33	MDO
-	minus; exclusion	45	MINUS
]]	marked section close	93 93	MSC
/	null end-tag	47	NET
?	optional occurrence indicator	63	OPT
|	or connector	124	OR
%	parameter entity reference open	37	PERO
>	processing instruction close	62	PIC
<?	processing instruction open	60 63	PIC
+	required and repeatable; inclusion	43	PLUS
;	reference close	59	REFC
*	optional and repeatable	42	REP
#	reserved name indicator	35	RNI

Glyph	Delimiter role	ISO 646 #	Abstract Name
,	sequence connector	44	SEQ
<	start-tag open	60	STAGO
>	tag close	62	TAGC
=	value indicator	61	VI

The reference concrete syntax defines 31 delimiters (excluding the short reference characters). Whenever you want to use these characters in the text as data, you should use entity references. For example, if you need to use a less-than sign ("<") and be sure its delimiter role will not be applied, you should use (for example) the entity reference ("<").

The keyword **GENERAL** introduces the section where general delimiters may be defined. All SGML delimiters may be changed. If a delimiter is not changed in the SGML declaration, it is assigned to the delimiter defined in the SGML reference concrete syntax. The GENERAL keyword must be followed by the keyword **SGMLREF**.

Rules for defining delimiters

When changing delimiter definitions remember the following:

1. A delimiter must differ from any other delimiter that may be recognized in the same mode. This prevents the declaration from defining an ambiguous condition.

2. The use of a name start character or a number in a delimiter string is discouraged. This prevents you from using "<e" as the end tag open delimiter since this would make it impossible to have any elements whose name begins with an "e."

3. Delimiter strings must be less than NAMELEN characters in length.

Any delimiter can be changed in the reference concrete syntax after the DELIM keyword by giving the abstract name of the delimiter followed by, for example, a numeric character reference as shown in Figure 83.

This example redefines several of the delimiter roles to use a GML-like set of delimiters. Notice that the **ETAGO** is not ":e" as would be expected for GML starter set compatibility. This could be specified as ":e" but this would be contrary to the recommendation that name start characters should not be defined as part of delimiter strings.

```
DELIM GENERAL SGMLREF
              ETAGO      "&#58;&#47;"   -- ":/" --
              PIO        "&#RS;&#46;"   -- "&#RS;." --
              REFC       "&#46;"        -- "." --
              STAGO      "&#58;"        -- ":" --
              TAGC       "&#46;"        -- "." --
```

Figure 83. Redefinition of Delimiter Characters in the Syntax

15.5.7 *Reserved names and keywords*

Markup declarations use reserved words such as DOCTYPE, ELE-MENT, ATTLIST, etc. Each of these has a role that is identified by its name in the reference concrete syntax.

This portion of the syntax declaration allows you to substitute a name for many of the reserved names used in the reference concrete syntax. None of the reserved names used in the SGML declaration may be replaced since the SGML declaration is always written in the reference concrete syntax. All names defined here must follow all the rules for names (for example, they must be composed of name characters) in the declared concrete syntax.

Although SGML technically allows you to make these changes, I have personally never had the need to do so. But if you want to do a national language customization or have another reason for changing the reserved names, Table 33 shows the reserved names and keywords used by SGML. The ones marked by an asterisk (*) may be changed by defining a variant concrete syntax.

Table 33. Reserved names and keywords in SGML

A-E	E-M	M-R	R-Z
AND	ETAGO	MSICHAR	RNI
ANY (*)	EXCLUDE	MSOCHAR	RS (*)
APPINFO	EXGRPCAP	MSOCHAR	SCOPE
ASN1	EXNMCAP	MSSCHAR	SDATA (*)
ATTCAP	EXPLICIT	NAME (*)	SDIF
ATTCHCAP	FEATURES	NAMECASE	SEPCHAR
ATTCNT	FIXED (*)	NAMELEN	SEQ
ATTLIST (*)	FORMAL	NAMES (*)	SEQUENCE
ATTSPLEN	FUNCHAR	NAMING	SGML
AVGRCAP	FUNCTION	NDATA (*)	SGMLREF

A-E	E-M	M-R	R-Z
BASESET	GENERAL	NET	SHORTREF (*)
BSEQLEN	GRPC	NMTOKEN (*)	SHORTTAG
CAPACITY	GRPCAP	NMTOKENS (*)	SHUNCHAR
CDATA (*)	GRPCNT	NO	SIMPLE (*)
CHANGES	GRPGTCNT	NONE	SPACE (*)
CHARSET	GRPLVL	NONSGML	SRCNT
COM	GRPO	NORMSEP	SRLEN
CONCUR	ID (*)	NOTATION (*)	STAGO
CONREF (*)	IDCAP	NUMBER (*)	STARTTAG (*)
CONTROLS	IDLINK (*)	NUMBERS (*)	SUBDOC (*)
CRO	IDREF (*)	NOTCAP	SWITCHES
CURRENT (*)	IDREFCAP	NOTCHCAP	SYNTAX
DATATAG	IDREFS (*)	NUTOKEN (*)	SYSTEM (*)
DEFAULT (*)	IGNORE (*)	NUTOKENS (*)	TAGC
DELIM	IMPLICIT	O (*)	TAGLEN
DELIMLEN	IMPLIED (*)	OMITTAG	TAGLVL
DESCSET	INCLUDE (*)	OPT	TEMP (*)
DOCTYPE (*)	INITIAL (*)	OR	TEXT
DOCUMENT	INSTANCE	OTHER	TOTALCAP
DSC	LCNMCHAR	PACK	UCNMCHAR
DSO	LCNMSTRT	PCDATA (*)	UCNMSTRT
DTAGLEN	LINK (*)	PERO	UNPACK
DTD	LINKTYPE (*)	PI (*)	UNUSED
DTEMPLEN	LIT	PIC	USELINK (*)
DTGC	LITA	PILEN	USEMAP (*)
DTGO	LITLEN	PIO	VALIDATE
ELEMCAP	LKNMCAP	PLUS	VI
ELEMENT (*)	LKSETCAP	POSTLINK (*)	YES

A-E	E-M	M-R	R-Z
ELEMENTS	LPD	PUBLIC (*)	
EMPTY (*)	MAPCAP	QUANTITY	
ENDTAG (*)	MD (*)	RANK	
ENTCAP	MDC	RCDATA (*)	
ENTCHCAP	MINIMIZE	RE (*)	
ENTITIES (*)	MINUS	REFC	
ENTITY (*)	MODEL	REP	
ENTLVL	MS (*)	REQUIRED (*)	
ERO	MSC	RESTORE (*)	

The reference concrete syntax reserved name is used for any name not replaced by this definition. Figure 84 contains an example of a specification.

```
NAMES     SGMLREF
          O         "OMIT"
```

Figure 84. Changing an SGML Keyword

In the example, the reserved name "**O**" is replaced by the name "OMIT". The keyword SGMLREF is required and is a reminder that unspecified reserved names default to their values in the reference concrete syntax.

15.5.8 The quantity set

Quantities are a set of limits on markup constructs. These are important for implementations — for example — of a parser. The limit of 40 on the ATTCNT quantity, which is the number of attribute names and name tokens in an attribute definition list, has a direct consequence for the size of the buffer in which the parser will store these names. The reference concrete syntax defines the quantities shown in Table 34.

Table 34. The reference quantity set

Name	Value	Description
ATTCNT	40	Number of attribute names and name to-kens in an *attribute definition list*
ATTSPLEN	960	Normalized length of a start-tag's *attribute specifications*
BSEQLEN	960	Length of a blank sequence in a short reference string
DTAGLEN	16	Length of a datatag
DTEMPLEN	16	Length of a datatag template or pattern template (undelimited)
ENTLVL	16	Nesting level of entities
GRPCNT	32	Number of tokens in a group
GRPGTCNT	96	Grand total of content tokens at all levels of a content model
GRPLVL	16	Nesting level of model groups (including the first level)
LITLEN	240	Length of a *parameter literal* or *attribute value literal*
NAMELEN	8	Length of a *name, name token, number*, etc.
NORMSEP	2	Used instead of separators when calculating normalized lengths
PILEN	240	Length of a *processing instruction*
TAGLEN	960	Length of a *start-tag*
TAGLVL	24	Nesting level of open elements

Figure 85 contains an example of a quantity set specification:

```
QUANTITY SGMLREF
         ATTCNT    64
         GRPGTCNT 128
         NAMELEN   32
```

Figure 85. A Quantity Set Specification in the Syntax

In the example, the maximum number of attributes that may be defined in an ATTLIST declaration has been set to 64. The maximum number of content tokens that may occur at all levels of a content model (this includes element names and delimiters) has been set to 128. Finally, the maximum length of names has been raised to 32 characters. Here again, the keyword SGMLREF is required and is a reminder that unspecified quantities default to their value in the reference concrete syntax.

15.5.9 Exercise

Modify the SGML declaration to include a variant syntax that redefines the NAMELEN quantity.

15.5.10 Basic SGML documents

If a conforming SGML document uses the reference concrete syntax throughout, the reference capacity set, and only the SHORTTAG and OMITTAG features, it is a **basic** SGML document. These basic documents are the easiest to exchange between different systems.

15.5.11 Core concrete syntax

The core concrete syntax is the reference concrete syntax with NONE as value for SHORTREF (i.e. no short references are possible).

15.5.12 Changing the reference concrete syntax

By changing the reference concrete syntax, you can increase the length of the names of elements, change the syntax character set (see section 15.5), change the short reference delimiters (see section 19.1), and so on.

Or you may need to change the syntax character set: for example, if your computer uses a non-ASCII character set or if you want to use a national extension to ASCII.

Your SGML
guide advises...

Changing the reference concrete syntax is not a problem, as long as you stay within the system where your documents were generated. If you want to export such documents, you need an SGML system that can analyze the SGML declaration containing your syntax. This is not required of a conforming SGML system.

Since every conforming SGML syntax **must** support the reference concrete syntax or core concrete syntax, it is best to stick to this if you want to ensure the widest possible interchange of your documents. If you absolutely need to define a variant syntax, you should design it so that you can easily convert your documents to the reference concrete syntax should this be required.

15.6 Application specific information

The text following the APPINFO keyword in the SGML declaration contains any application specific information that is applicable to the document. NONE means there is none.

15.7 The system declaration

The system declaration is included in the documentation for a conforming SGML system. It specifies the features, concrete syntaxes, character set, and data content notations (see section 17.1) that are supported by the system. It is structured in the same way as the SGML declaration, except that the parameters refer to the capability of the system rather than to individual documents.

It should be provided as part of the documentation describing the SGML product that you have chosen to install on your system.

Figure 86 shows an example of a system declaration. Such a declaration is shipped with IBM's SGML Translator DCF Edition product[2].

The differences with respect to the SGML declaration are:

1. CHANGES to describe changes to specified concrete syntaxes. Sub parameters are SWITCHES, DELIMLEN, SEQUENCE, SRCNTand SRLEN.

2. VALIDATE to specify if the system has a validating SGML parser and which optional validation services are provided. Sub parameters are:

a. GENERAL: markup errors are found and reported

b. MODEL: ambiguous content models are reported

c. EXCLUDE: exclusions that could change a token's required or optional status are reported

d. CAPACITY: exceeding a capacity limit will be reported

e. NONSGML: the occurrence of at least one non-SGML character will be reported

f. SGML: an error in the SGML declaration will be reported

```
                  CHARSET
BASESET   "-//IBM/PGM 5684-025//CHARSET Codepage 00037/1 // "
          -- This is found in file "EHMCP037 CHARSET *" --
DESCSET   0    256  0
                  CHARSET
BASESET   "-//IBM/PGM 5684-025//CHARSET Codepage 00395/1 // "
          -- This is found in file "EHMCP395 CHARSET *" --
DESCSET   0    256  0
CAPACITY  PUBLIC     "ISO 8879:1986//CAPACITY Reference//EN"


                  FEATURES
 MINIMIZE DATATAG    NO    OMITTAG   YES   RANK NO    SHORTTAG   YES
 LINK     SIMPLE     NO    IMPLICIT  NO    EXPLICIT   NO
 OTHER    CONCUR     NO    SUBDOC    NO    FORMAL     YES


 SCOPE    DOCUMENT

 VALIDATE GENERAL    YES
          MODEL      NO
          EXCLUDE    YES
          CAPACITY   YES
          NONSGML    YES
          SGML       NO
          FORMAL     YES


 SDIF     PACK       NO
          UNPACK     NO>
```

Figure 86. An SGML System Declaration

g. FORMAL: errors in formal public identifiers will be reported

SDIF: to specify whether the system can exchange SDIF documents

Some points to watch for are :

• Which character sets are used as base and described character sets (if you are using different systems).

• Which features are used by the system. Only SHORTTAG and OMITTAG are needed for *basic* SGML documents.

• Maximum capacity set (see section 15.2) used by the system. The capacity set defines limits on the number of quantities that may appear in a DTD and a document instance. These limits are defined to enable systems with limited memory to process conforming DTDs and documents. Nowadays computers have more memory, and this aspect is less important. Having a system that is unable to use anything but the reference capacity set may cause unwanted constraints.

15.8 Bibliography for Chapter 15

The material from this chapter has been adapted from the excellent tutorial in [1]. I am grateful to Wayne Wohler and SGML Associates for being able to use this material.

[1] Wayne Wohler
     The DTD may not be enough: SGML declarations, <TAG>, vol 5, no. 10 and vol 6, no. 1 and 2
     1992–1993
[2] IBM Corporation
     IBM SGML Translator DCF Edition
     Boulder, 1989

16. SGML features

To customize SGML, a number of "optional" features are defined. Whenever an optional feature is discussed in this book, I point this out. Not all features are available in all implementations.

The SGML features that can be defined in the SGML declaration are shown in Figure 87.

```
                        FEATURES
MINIMIZE DATATAG NO  OMITTAG  YES  RANK     NO  SHORTTAG YES
LINK     SIMPLE  NO  IMPLICIT NO   EXPLICIT NO
OTHER    CONCUR  NO  SUBDOC   NO   FORMAL   NO
```

Figure 87. Features Defined in the SGML Declaration

The following optional SGML features exist:

1. Markup minimization features.

2. LINK type features. These are not discussed in this book.

3. CONCUR, SUBDOC and FORMAL. I do not discuss CONCUR and SUBDOC in this book.

16.1 Minimization

An important part of an element declaration is the tag minimization and omission. This, however, is not the only type of minimization that can be applied. Markup minimization may be achieved in five different ways: by OMITTAG (see section 16.1), SHORTTAG (see section 16.1), DATATAG (see section 16.1), RANK (see section 16.1), and SHORTREF (see section 19.2).

The minimization features, with the exception of shortref, are optional SGML features. To use them the word YES must follow the name of the feature in the SGML declaration, and they must be supported by the parser.

The DTD is not affected by minimization. Omitted (minimized) markup should be added if a document is sent to a system that does not support a minimization feature.

16.1.1 OMITTAG

OMITTAG allows you to leave out tags: for example,

```
<TO>Comrade Napoleon
```

is the same as the un-minimized case:

```
<TO>Comrade Napoleon</TO>
```

The OMITTAG feature changes the meaning of the SHORTTAG assumptions.

Minimization was introduced into SGML when there were no WYSI-WYG editors available, and it was thought that this feature would make it easier to create SGML documents. With a WYSIWYG editor, all arguments for minimization fall away. In addition, you will see that minimization can cause some nasty surprises. My recommendation is not to use minimization, but if you absolutely want to, this section tells you how you do it.

The following three conditions must be satisfied if you want to omit tags:

1. OMITTAG YES must be given in the SGML declaration. Without this feature, no tags may be omitted.

2. Minimized tag information must be given in the element's markup declaration. For example, in

```
<--         Elements Min Content --               >
<!ELEMENT MEMO      - - ((TO & FROM), BODY, CLOSE?) >
<!ELEMENT TO        - O (#PCDATA)                  >
<!ELEMENT FROM      - O (#PCDATA)                  >
```

the two columns under MIN indicate whether the start- and end-tag may be minimized. Both parameters must be given; the minus ("-") indicates that a tag may not be omitted while the capital letter O means that the tag may be omitted.

If the element has content EMPTY, the end-tag must be omitted.

Only if OMITTAG NO is specified in the SGML declaration may the omitted tag minimization be left out of the element declaration: for example,

```
<!ELEMENT MEMO ((TO & FROM), BODY, CLOSE?)>
```

The complete memo, whose DTD does not have omitted tag minimization, is shown in Figure 88.

```
<!SGML "ISO 8879:1986"
                          CHARSET
BASESET   "ISO 646:1983//CHARSET
          International Reference Version (IRV)//ESC 2/5 4/0"
DESCSET 0  9 UNUSED --the first 9 characters starting at 0 are not used--
        9  2  9       --the next two, 9 and 10, map onto 9 and 10 of the
                        baseset--
       11  2 UNUSED  --11 and 12 are not used--
       13  1 13      --13 is mapped onto 13 of the baseset--
       14 18 UNUSED  --the next 18, starting with 14, are unused--
       32 95 32      --the next 95, starting with 32, are mapped
                       onto 32-126 of the baseset--
      127  1  UNUSED --the character 127 is unused--
 CAPACITY PUBLIC "ISO 8879:1986//CAPACITY Reference//EN"
SCOPE       DOCUMENT
SYNTAX    PUBLIC "ISO 8879:1986//SYNTAX Reference//EN"
                        FEATURES
MINIMIZE DATATAG NO  OMITTAG  NO  RANK     NO  SHORTTAG YES
LINK       SIMPLE  NO  IMPLICIT NO   EXPLICIT NO
OTHER      CONCUR  NO  SUBDOC   NO   FORMAL   NO
                       APPINFO NONE>
<!DOCTYPE MEMO [
<!ENTITY % doctype "MEMO"  -- document type generic identifier -->
<!--         ELEMENTS    MIN  CONTENT                  (EXCEPTIONS) -->
<!ELEMENT  %doctype;    ((TO & FROM), BODY, CLOSE?)              >
<!ELEMENT  TO           (#PCDATA)                                >
<!ELEMENT  FROM         (#PCDATA)                                >
<!ELEMENT  BODY         (P)*                                     >
<!ELEMENT  P            (#PCDATA | Q )*                          >
<!ELEMENT  Q            (#PCDATA)                                >
<!ELEMENT  CLOSE        (#PCDATA)                                >
<!ATTLIST  %doctype;    STATUS  (CONFIDEN|PUBLIC) PUBLIC    >]>
<MEMO>
<TO>Comrade Napoleon</TO>
<FROM>Snowball</FROM>
<BODY>
<P>In Animal Farm, George Orwell says: <Q>...the pigs had to
expend enormous labour every day upon mysterious things called files,
reports, minutes and memoranda. These were large sheets of paper which
had to be closely covered with writing, and as soon as they were so
covered, they were burnt in the furnace...</Q>
Do you think SGML would have helped the pigs? </P>
</BODY>
<CLOSE>Comrade Snowball</CLOSE>
</MEMO>
```

Figure 88. Memo without Omitted Tag Minimization

16.1.2 Start-tag omission

In the following example,

```
<TO>Comrade Napoleon
<FROM>Snowball
<P>In Animal...
```

the **<BODY>** start-tag can be omitted since no other element can occur in the position immediately following the **<FROM>** end-tag.

Start-tag omission is permitted if the following two conditions are satisfied:

1. The omitted tag is required at that place in the instance. In the above example, the **<BODY>** start-tag may be omitted since no other element can occur in the position immediately following the **</FROM>** end-tag.

Omitting the **<TO>** start-tag would create an ambiguity since either the **<TO>** or the **<FROM>** start-tags are allowed at that point in the document instance. That is illustrated by Figure 89.

```
ASTATUS TOKEN PUBLIC
(MEMO
sgmls: SGML error at /asis/eric/ebt_books/books/advanced/minex1.sgm,
       line 18 at "n":
       Data not allowed at this point in MEMO element
sgmls: SGML error at /asis/eric/ebt_books/books/advanced/minex1.sgm,
       line 18 at ">":
       TO end-tag ignored: doesn't end any open element (current is
       MEMO)
sgmls: SGML error at /asis/eric/ebt_books/books/advanced/minex1.sgm,
       line 19 at ">":
       FROM element not allowed at this point in MEMO element
sgmls: SGML error at /asis/eric/ebt_books/books/advanced/minex1.sgm,
       line 20 at ">":
       P element not allowed at this point in MEMO element
sgmls: SGML error at /asis/eric/ebt_books/books/advanced/minex1.sgm,
       line 20 at record end:
       MEMO element ended prematurely; required subelement omitted
-\nSnowballIn Animal Farm, ...
)MEMO
```

Figure 89. Ambiguity Created by Start-tag Omission

2. Any other elements that could occur at that place are optional.

There are three exceptions to this rule:

1. The element has a required attribute (see section), or declared content (see section 10.5) CDATA, RCDATA, or EMPTY. If, in the example above, **TO** and **FROM** had CDATA content, the start-tag of both elements would have been required since the parser has to know when to stop checking for markup.

2. The content of the element is EMPTY. The start-tag can never be omitted since otherwise the element is never recognized.

3. If the element's content starts with a short reference (see section 19.2) delimiter whose mapping is changed by the elements short reference map, the start-tag can not be omitted.

16.1.3 *End-tag omission*

An example of end-tag omission of `</CLOSE>` is:

```
<CLOSE>Comrade Snowball</MEMO>
```

The conditions for end-tag omission are:

1. The element is followed by the end tag of an open element (`</MEMO>` in the example above).

2. The element is followed by an element or SGML character not allowed in its context: for example,

```
text....<CLOSE>
```

Again, the parser implies the closing of the open element.

16.1.4 *SHORTTAG*

SHORTTAGs are tags from which all or part of the usual markup is omitted.

Tags may only be minimized if SHORTTAG YES is specified on the SGML declaration.

Short start-tags have three possible forms:

1. **Empty start-tag**. The generic identifier (GI) is left out of the tag (<> in stead of <q>). In the case of an empty start-tag, the GI is assumed to be one of the following three possibilities:

1.The GI of the most recently started open element (if OMITTAG YES is in force). For example,

```
<P>text <> more text
```

is equivalent to

```
<P>text <P> more text
```

2.The GI of the most recently ended element (if OMITTAG NO is in force). For example,

```
<P>text <Q>quotation text <>...
```

is equivalent to:

```
<P>text <Q>quotation text </Q>...
```

3. The GI of the document element if no other element is opened or closed. For example,

```
<><TO>Comrade Napoleon...
```

is equivalent to:

```
<MEMO><TO>Comrade Napoleon...
```

2. **Unclosed start-tag**. The STAGC (">") delimiter may be omitted from a tag that is immediately followed by another tag. For example,

```
<BODY<P>
```

is equivalent to:

```
<BODY><P>
```

As you can see, applying unclosed start-tag minimization results in obscure markup.

3. **NET-enabling start-tag**. The STAGC delimiter is replaced by the **null end-tag** (NET) delimiter ("/"). In this case, the end-tag is replaced by the NET . For example,

```
<Q/...the pigs...the furnace/
```

A null end-tag is only interpreted as an end-tag for the element in which it was used instead of the STAGC delimiter (i.e. as a NET-enabling start-tag).

Short end-tags also have three possible forms:

1. **Empty end-tag.** The GI is left out of the tag: `</>`. In the case of an empty end-tag, the GI is assumed to be the one of the most recently started open element: for example, in

```
<BODY><P>In Animal ...</>
```

the empty end-tag would belong to the P element.

2. **Unclosed end-tag**. The ETAGC (">") delimiter may be omitted from an end-tag that is immediately followed by another start- or end-tag. For example,

```
</P</BODY>
```

is equivalent to:

```
</P></BODY>
```

(i.e. the unclosed end-tag is equivalent to the paragraph end-tag).

3. **Null end-tag**. If an element's start-tag is delimited by the NET enabling character, the element may be closed by a NET:

```
<P/In Animal.../
```

16.1.5 Minimization of attribute values

Minimization of attribute values is possible if SHORTTAG YES is specified on the SGML declaration. There are two ways to minimize giving an attribute a value:

1. If the attribute value is a token consisting of name characters, the literal delimiters may be omitted:

```
<phone type="stk">
```

is equivalent to

```
<phone type=stk>
```

2. If the declared values are a group of names rather than a keyword, the attribute name and value indicator may be omitted:

```
<phone type="stk">
```

is equivalent to

```
<phone stk>
```

This is why different attributes (for the same element) cannot use the same declared value.

Other ways of minimizing attribute values, independent of SHORT-TAG YES are possible when the defaults #FIXED or #CURRENT are used for the default of an attribute. #FIXED followed by a value means that the attribute always has this value. The user does not have to supply it. #CURRENT means that the user must supply a value on the first occurrence of a tag (as if #REQUIRED was used) with this attribute. The same value is used for any subsequent tag that uses this attribute. A value may be shared between many tags.

16.1.6 DATATAG

If the DATATAG feature is used markup can be added automatically
when certain characters occur with regularity in an element. For
example, a comma (",") could be interpreted as the end-tag of an
element. To achieve this, the following content model should be
defined:

```
<!ELEMENT keywlist - - ([key1,"," ],key2)>
<!ELEMENT key1     O O (#PCDATA)          >
<!ELEMENT key2     O O (#PCDATA)          >
```

where the left square bracket ("[") is the **data tag open** delimiter
(**DTGO**) and the right square bracket ("]") is the **data tag close**
delimiter (**DTGC**). This technique allows you to define a template within
thedata tag open and the data tag close delimiters. Using this model,
the following keyword list can be marked up:

```
<keywlist>First keyword,second keyword
```

The comma implies the end-tag of the element **key1**; it is not part
of the data. The next contextually required element is **key2**. The
interested reader can find a complete discussion of the DATATAG
feature in Annex C section 1.4 of the SGML standard.

16.1.7 RANK

By using **RANK**, nested elements can be entered with abbreviated
generic identifiers (using the rank **stem**) instead of with the complete
generic identifier. The interested reader can find a complete discussion
of the RANK feature in Annex C section 1.5 of the SGML standard.

16.2 Exercise

Discuss all cases of minimization you can recognize in the second
While-You-Were-Away note in the figure below. Which ones are wrong?

```
<!-- DTD for a while-you-were-away note              -->
<!ENTITY % doctype "wywa" --document type generic identifier-->
<!--        ELEMENTS   MIN  CONTENT (EXCEPTIONS)        -->
<!ELEMENT   wywa       - -  ((To & From & Of), Phone?, Notes?)>
<!ELEMENT   To         - O  (#PCDATA)                    >
<!ELEMENT   From       - O  (#PCDATA)                    >
<!ELEMENT   Of         - O  (#PCDATA)                    >
<!ELEMENT   Phone      - O  (#PCDATA)                    >
<!ELEMENT   Notes      - O  (#PCDATA)                    >
<!--        ELEMENTS   NAME     VALUE          DEFAULT-->
<!ATTLIST   From       seeme    (yes|no)       #REQUIRED>
<!ATTLIST   Of         called   (called)       #IMPLIED
                       phoned   (phoned)       #IMPLIED
                       came     (came)         #IMPLIED
                       replied  (replied)      #IMPLIED
                       wantsyou (wantsyou)     #IMPLIED >
]>
<wywa>
The big pig</To>
The small pig
<Of called>The middle pig
<Phone>767 5087
<Notes>Please call back about a pile of burnt memo's.
</wywa>
```

Figure 90. Tag Minimization Examples

16.3 FORMAL

If FORMAL YES is specified in the SGML declaration, this means that all public identifiers must be formal public text identifiers (see section 12.3). This feature is useful for linkage to external objects by hypertext systems. The FORMAL feature is a requirement for HyTime (see section 24.5).

17. Notation

17.1 Data content notation

There are several examples of types of data which require special processing:

- mathematical formulas and graphics;
- formatted text;
- binary data, bitmaps;
- music, digitized audio, or video.

These data all have their own data content notation. The disctinction between them can be made with a **NOTATION** declaration in the DTD that indicates how the data should be processed. The parts of a NOTATION declaration are shown in Table 35.

Table 35. The parts of a notation declaration

Example: <!NOTATION TeX SYSTEM "file-identifier">			
Order	**Part**	**Description**	**Abstract Name**
1	<!	markup declaration open delimiter	MDO
2	NOTATION	keyword identifying a notation declaration	
3	TeX	name of the notation	NAME
4	SYSTEM "file-identifier"	file with information about the notation	
5	&gt;	markup declaration close delimiter	MDC

The example in this table declares the notation "TeX" with an empty external identifier. The keyword SYSTEM must be given, even if there is no file identifier following it. The purpose is to indicate a file (e.g. a READ-ME or HELP file) on the system containing further information about the NOTATION and how to process it.

NOTATIONs can be defined for elements whose content is CDATA or RCDATA, but also for data entities (see section 12.3).

To add a NOTATION to an element, you have to define an attribute with declared value (see section) NOTATION for this element:

```
<!NOTATION TeX SYSTEM "" >
<!NOTATION Eqn SYSTEM "" >
<!ELEMENT Formula - O CDATA>
<!ATTLIST Formula notation NOTATION (TeX|Eqn) #CURRENT>
```

A NOTATION attribute may appear only once per attribute list. It cannot be applied to an empty element, nor can it contain SGML data. In the example above, the NOTATION attribute's name is "notation," but it may be anything.

17.2 Using NOTATION to describe mathematics

As an example of a NOTATION consider mathematics, for example, the formula in Figure 91.

$$\Gamma\left(J/\psi \to \eta_c\gamma\right) = \frac{\alpha Q_c^2}{24}\left|A\left(J/\psi \to \eta_c\gamma\right)\right|^2 \frac{m_\psi^3}{m_{\eta_c}^2}\left(1 - \frac{m_{\eta_c}^2}{m_\psi^2}\right)^3$$

Figure 91. A mathematical formula

In the DTD, we have the following declarations:

```
<!NOTATION TeX SYSTEM ""                                     >
<!NOTATION Eqn SYSTEM ""                                     >
<!ELEMENT Formula - O CDATA                                  >
<!ATTLIST Formula notation NOTATION (Tex|Eqn) #CURRENT>
```

Various languages exist for typesetting mathematical formulas; two examples are TₑX and EQN. By defining notations for these languages, a mathematical formula which is written in either of them can be included in an SGML document.

In EQN, you can obtain the formula with the following commands:

```
<Formula notation=Eqn>
Gamma(J/psi rarrow eta sub c gamma) = < alpha Q sup 2 sub c > over 24
left vbar A ( J/psi rarrow eta sub c gamma ) right vbar sup 2 < m sup
3 sub psi > over < m sup 2 sub < eta sub c > > left ( 1 - < m sup 2
sub < eta sub c > > over < m sup 2 sub psi > right ) sup 3
```

If not EQN, but T_EX is available, TEX commands are used:

```
<Formula notation=TeX> $${ \Gamma(J/\psi \rightarrow \eta_c \gamma)}
= {{ \alpha Q_c^2 } \over 24}  \left| A ( J/\psi \rightarrow \eta_c
\gamma) \right|^2 {{ m_\psi^3 } \over { m_{ \eta_c}^2}} \left ( 1 -
{{ m_{ \eta_c }^ 2 } \over {m_\psi ^ 2 }} \right )^3$$
```

Chapter 22 discusses using SGML for mathematics.

17.3 Using NOTATION to describe graphics

As another example of using NOTATION consider graphics. Figure 92 shows a picture of a bike.

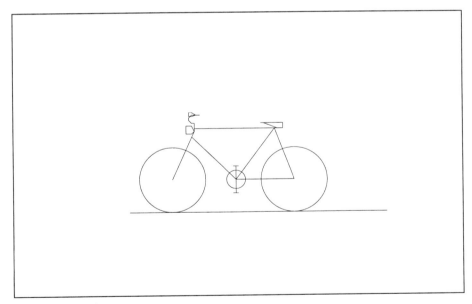

Figure 92. A Picture of a Bike

This picture may have been created with a number of graphics or drawing programs, and it may be stored in a number of different graphics formats or languages, such as PostScript, CGM, GKS, or Phigs.

The data corresponding to the figure can be included in an SGML document by defining a NOTATION in the DTD:

```
<!NOTATION PS SYSTEM "" --PostScript Notation-->
<!NOTATION CGM SYSTEM "" --Computer Graphics Metafile Notation-->
<!ELEMENT Picture - O CDATA>
<!ATTLIST Picture notation NOTATION (PS|CGM) #IMPLIED>
```

If the data for the picture is available in PostScript, it could then be included in an SGML document as shown in Figure 93.

```
<Picture notation='PS'>
%!
%%BoundingBox: 0 0 537 537
%begin(plot)
gsave /d {rlineto} def /m {moveto} def /lw {setlinewidth}
def /s {stroke} def /c {setrgbcolor} def /f {eofill} def
/cl {closepath} def /df {/Times-Roman findfont} def /sf
{scalefont setfont} def
.25 .25 scale 100 100 translate
0.000 0.000 0.000 c [] 0 setdash 1 lw 128
504 m 1997 0 d s 461 762 m 172 386 d
0 64 d s 633 1170 m 644 0 d 0 0 d s 1170
1212 m 107 -42 d 43 0 d 0 42 d
-172 0 d s 633 1212 m -22 0 d -21 22 d 0
21 d 21 22 d 0 0 d 43 0 d 0 0 d 22 0 d
0 0 d s 955 762 m 0 -108 d 21 0 d -43 0 d
0 0 d s 955 762 m 0 107 d 21 0 d
-43 0 d s 955 762 m -344 343 d s 955 762 m
451 0 d -151 408 d cl s 590 1298 m
0 -32 d 21 0 d 33 11 d -33 21 d -21 0 d cl
s 568 1191 m 0 -64 d 43 0 d 22 21 d
-22 43 d cl s 955 762 73 0 360 arc s 461 762
257 0 360 arc s 1406 762 257 0 360
arc s
showpage grestore
%end(plot)
</Picture>
```

Figure 93. PostScript for the Bike Picture

17.4 Exercise

Create a notation for PostScript and include the bike figure. Do not include the PostScript code in the SGML file, but define an external entity for it.

17.5 Data attributes

In the same way that elements may have attributes, a notation may also have an attribute. These are **data attributes**. They allow you to give additional information about an entity that uses the notation. For example, in the case of a graphics object it might be useful to mark its size.

Data attributes are declared in a way which is similar to those on elements, as shown in Table[36].

Table 36. The parts of a data attribute declaration

Example: <!ATTLIST #NOTATION CGM width CDATA #IMPLIED>			
Order	**Part**	**Description**	**Abstract Name**
1		markup declaration open delimiter	MDO
2	ATTLIST	attribute definition list declaration keyword	
3	associated notation name	#NOTATION notation-name (here: CGM)	
4	attribute-name	name of the attribute (e.g. width)	NAME
5	declared-value	declared value of the attribute, or keyword	
6	default value e.g. public	default value of the attribute, or keyword	
7	>	markup declaration close delimiter	MDC

The values of data attributes can be specified on the entity declaration of the entity that uses the notation. This is done in a declaration subset (i.e. within the DSO (declaration subset open, "[") and DSC (declaration subset close, "]") delimiters following the name of the notation:

```
<!ATTLIST #NOTATION ps width CDATA #IMPLIED>
<!ENTITY BIKE SYSTEM "/home/newbike.ps" CDATA ps
 [ width="3i" ]>
```

18. Marked sections

Marked sections are used to show which parts of a document should not be processed or should only be processed under certain conditions. For example, parts that are destined for different groups of readers may be kept together in a single document and the parser can be instructed to process the document for one or the other group.

Another example of text that should be processed conditionally is a part of a document that contains tags as text, such as the examples in this book. It may be used to tell the parser to ignore the markup.

The way marked sections are indicated in a document is shown in Table 37.

Table 37. The parts of a marked section

Example: <![status keyword [text with or without markup]]>			
Order	**Part**	**Description**	**Abstract Name**
1	<![	marked section start delimiter	MDO, DSO
2	e.g. IGNORE, INCLUDE	status keyword	
3	[	declaration subset open delimiter	DSO
4	text with or without markup	data	
5	]]	marked section close delimiter	MSC
6	>	markup declaration close delimiter	MDC

There are no blanks between the MDO and DSO delimiters at the start of the marked section, nor between the MSC and MDC delimiters at the end. The possible values of the "status keyword" and their meaning is as follows:

1. **IGNORE.** This section is omitted from processing. It will not be passed to the application by the parser. The only characters that are recognized are those of nested marked sections and the marked section

close delimiter ("]] ") to enable the parser to find the end of the section. The contents of nested marked sections are ignored.

2. **INCLUDE.** This section is not omitted from processing. A nested marked section is recognized and treated according to its keyword. An IGNORE section in an INCLUDE section is ignored, but an INCLUDE section in an IGNORE section is not included.

3. **TEMP.** This section is a temporary part of the document that could be removed later. It is treated by the parser like an INCLUDE section.

4. **CDATA.** This section contains character data. The data contain valid SGML characters but it is destined for a different processor (such as PostScript). Any markup in this section is ignored. This means that nested marked sections are not allowed because the first marked section close delimiter ("]] ") met by the parser ends the marked section.

5. **RCDATA.** This section contains replaceable character data. The data are treated like CDATA, except that entity references are replaced.

Multiple keywords may be given in a marked section declaration. The order of precedence of the marked section keywords is: IGNORE, CDATA, RCDATA, INCLUDE.

18.1 Marking sections as IGNORE and INCLUDE

Consider a multilingual document with parts in English, French, and Dutch. A flag can be set at the beginning of the document so that only one language is INCLUDEd from processing while the others are IGNOREd. Figure 94 shows the SGML of such a document.

Three parameter entities are declared in this example: ENGLISH, FRENCH, and DUTCH; the entity ENGLISH is given the value INCLUDE while the other two have the value IGNORE. Since these are parameter entities (see section 12.6), they are only for use inside markup declarations.

Whenever these entity names are used, they are replaced by either INCLUDE or IGNORE at the start of the marked section. The example in Figure 94 generates an English version of the document; other languages are obtained by changing the corresponding entity to INCLUDE. The advantage of this method is that there is one set of tags that is used for all three versions of the document. This guarantees that the structure of the same for all languages.

Your SGML
guide thinks...

```
<!DOCTYPE ERICBOOK  [
<!ELEMENT Ericbook - - (title, preface) >
<!ELEMENT title    - O (#PCDATA) >
<!ELEMENT preface  - O (ptitle, p*)>
<!ELEMENT ptitle   O O (#PCDATA) >
<!ELEMENT p        - O (#PCDATA|q)* >
<!ELEMENT q        - - (#PCDATA) >
<!ATTLIST title stitle CDATA #IMPLIED>
<!ENTITY % ENGLISH "INCLUDE">
<!ENTITY % FRENCH  "IGNORE">
<!ENTITY % DUTCH   "IGNORE"> ]>
<Ericbook>
<![ %ENGLISH [ <Title stitle="Practical SGML">Practical
SGML ]]>
<![ %DUTCH [ <Title stitle="SGML in de praktijk!">SGML in
de praktijk]]>
<![ %FRENCH [ <Title stitle="SGML en pratique!">SGML en
pratique]]>
<![ %ENGLISH [ <Preface>Preface ]]>
<![ %DUTCH [ <Preface>Voorwoord ]]>
<![ %FRENCH [ <Preface>Introduction ]]>
<P>
<![ %ENGLISH [ During the past 30-40 years we have witnessed
an enormous growth in the different areas of computer
applications. Initially, computers were mainly used
by scientists to perform numerically intensive calculations
(<q>number crunching</q>). These days, computers have found
their way into our homes and offices. It is by no means
exceptional in a modern company to find non-scientific staff,
for example administrators, to be equipped with powerful
networked personal computers instead of with typewriters.]]>
<![ %DUTCH [ Gedurende de afgelopen 30-40 jaar hebben we
een enorme uitbreiding van de diverse toepassings gebieden
van computers meegemaakt. In het
```

Figure 94. Using Marked Sections in a Multilingual Document

Another example of the use of IGNORE and INCLUDE marked sections is for version control. See Figure 95 for an example.

```
<!ENTITY % confiden "INCLUDE">
<!ENTITY % public   "IGNORE" >
...
<![ %confiden; [We are happy to announce that this year
the managers will receive a 30% pay-rise. ]]>
<![ %public; [Unfortunately the depressed economic
situation forces us to limit this year's pay rise to 2% ]]>
```

Figure 95. Version Control with Marked Sections

This example shows how you can obtain different documents for two groups of readers by defining parameter entities for confidential and public versions.

18.2 Marking sections as CDATA or RCDATA

The parser will not analyze any of the data in a CDATA section. The meaning of CDATA is the same as for data entities and elements: data with valid SGML characters, but intended for a different processor. This is often useful if some data include markup, and is not to be interpreted as such (e.g., mathematics).

For example:

```
<![ CDATA [
<-- The following paragraph was added by the copy-editor
EVH -->
<P>Quod licet Jovi ...
 ]]>
```

The content of the example is treated as character data and so the comment and the tag inside it are not recognized.

By marking a section as RCDATA entity references are ignored, but nothing else. Tags are not recognized:

```
<![ RCDATA [
<-- Le paragraph suivant &eacute;tait ajout&eacute; par
l&eacute;diteur,EVH -->
Pendant les derni&egrave;res ...
 ]]>
```

18.3 General advice on using marked sections

18.3.1 *Bracketed text and marked sections*

If a marked section occurs often it is convenient to define it as an entity:

```
<!ENTITY formula MS "RCDATA [ <a> = <p c/|E|>]">
```

where the MS keyword shows that the entity contains a marked section, that is, it is preceded by a marked section start ("`<![`") and followed by a marked section end ("`]]>`") delimiter. This is **bracketed text** . Other brackets can be MD for text within markup declaration open ("`<!`") and close ("`>`") delimiters, STARTTAG for text within start-tag open ("`<`") and close ("`>`") delimiters and ENDTAG for text within end-tag ("`</`") open and close ("`>`") delimiters.

For more examples of bracketed text, see chapter 19 on short references.

18.3.2 *Processing instructions and marked sections*

It is good practice to place processing instructions (see section 4.10) within a marked section:

```
<![ IGNORE [<?.cc 5>]]>
```

If a document has to be processed by several systems it is convenient to define a parameter entity for the marked section keyword and to define entities with the same name for similar functions. This is shown in Figure 96.

```
<!ENTITY % TeX "IGNORE">
<!ENTITY % Script "INCLUDE">
<![ %TeX; [
<!ENTITY newpage "<?\newpage>"> ]]>
<<![ %Script; [
<!ENTITY newpage "<?.pa>"> ]]>
]>
&newpage;
```

Figure 96. Marked Sections for Processing Instructions

By changing the value of the parameter entities one can prepare the file for a different processor, while keeping the SGML file unaltered.

18.3.3 *Marked section tips*

Although marked sections are handy, they can often be avoided. To prevent tags from being processed, the "<" entity reference can be used in the text instead of the markup open delimiter ("<") and the ">" instead of the markup close delimiter (">"). For example,

```
&lt;!-- The next paragraph was added by the copy-editor EVH--&gt;
&lt;P&gt;Quod licet Jovi ...
```

It is better to define an entity SGML for the STAGO delimiter ("<") and an entity **ESGML** for the TAGC delimiter (">"), since lt and gt are names that have a priori nothing to do with SGML markup.

It is desirable to avoid marked sections because it makes the data difficult to validate. All valid combinations of marked section keywords must be tried. The interactions in markup can cause problems since marked sections simply include or exclude sequences of characters which may be data or markup and need not follow the tree described by the DTD.

Remember that after processing the document has no trace of which sections were marked. To obtain this information you should always go back to the original SGML source.

19. Short references

One of the objectives of SGML is to make it possible to use familiar typewriter and word-processing conventions for adding markup to a document. This is particularly useful if there is no SGML editor available for creating SGML documents. **Short references** are short entity references where the entities contain element tags. The entities are created specifically to support the short references. Using them, it is possible to interpret text without markup as if tags were present.

Minimization through short references is unlike any of the other ways of minimizing. It is not a feature, but rather a variation of the SGML syntax.

19.1 Use of short references

Short references are strings of characters with a special purpose: they can be replaced by tags.

For example, the double quotes (") can be mapped into the quotation start-tag:

```
George Orwell says: "...
the pigs had to expend
```

is the same as:

```
George Orwell says: <Q>...
the pigs had to expend
```

This mapping is achieved by a **short reference map** in the DTD that tells the parser which **short reference delimiter** to replace with markup. The short reference string is mapped into an entity reference that expands into a tag via bracketed text (see section 12.5).

Inside the quotation, the map can be changed to the end-tag.

Table 38 contains the short reference delimiter characters defined by the reference concrete syntax.

Table 38.   Short reference delimiters defined by the reference concrete syntax

Delimiter	Meaning	Usage example	Delimiter	Meaning	Usage example
&#TAB;	horizontal tab	tables	+	plus sign	
&#RE;	record end	end-tag	,	comma	markup
&#RS;	record start	start-tag	-	hyphen	
&#RS;B	leading blanks	start-tag	- -	two hyphens	
&#RS;&#RE;	empty record	paragraph	:	colon	
&#RS;B&#RE;	blank record	paragraph	;	semi colon	
B&#RE;	trailing blanks	end-tags	=	equals sign	
&#SPACE;	space		@	commercial at	
BB	two or more blanks		[	left square bracket	
"	quotation mark	quotations	]	right square bracket	
#	number sign		^	circumflex accent	
%	percent sign		_	underscore	
'	apostrophe	quotations	{	left curly bracket	
(	left parentheses	markup	}	right curly bracket	

Delimiter	Meaning	Usage example	De-lim-iter	Meaning	Usage exam-ple
)	right paren-theses	markup	˜	tilde	
*	asterisk				

The short reference delimiters defined by the reference concrete syntax correspond to most of the nonalphabetic characters that are not used for markup, such as record start (RS), record end (RE), blank (B) and quotes ("). Some examples of typewriter conventions that they can recognize are indicated in the third column of the table. Only one delimiter is allowed per mapping. Additional delimiters may be defined by introducing a variant syntax.

The general entity can be defined as a tag or an arbitrary character string that may contain tags. The parser substitutes the short reference with markup. A general entity is needed for this since the short reference can be substituted with a named entity reference if the document is exported to a system that is unable to recognize short references.

Short reference delimiters are recognized in the content of an element and in any marked section that may occur in it (except if the content of or marked section is CDATA or RCDATA). Not all ISO 646:1983 characters are included as short reference delimiters since some characters already have different roles in certain contexts. Other characters can be defined as short reference delimiters by modifying the reference concrete syntax.

The possibility of automatically adding markup to a document makes creating SGML documents easier. Warning: some "parsers" are unable to recognize short reference delimiters.

Your SGML guide warns...

19.2 Definition of short references

For each short reference, three markup declarations are required in the DTD:

1. A **short reference mapping** declaration defines a name for a mapping and maps a short reference character string into an entity reference.

2. A **general entity** declaration contains the character string into which the short reference is mapped.

3. A **short reference use** declaration names the element(s) inside which a map should be used.

Short reference mapping declarations are constructed as shown in Table 39.

Table 39. The parts of a short reference mapping declaration

Example: <!SHORTREF MAP-TO &#RS;B&#RE; MAP1>			
Order	**Symbol**	**Name**	**Abstract Name**
1	<!	markup declaration open delimiter	MDO
2	SHORTREF	SGML keyword	
3	MAP-TO	a unique map-name	
4	&#RS;B&#RE;	short reference delimiter	SHORTREF
5	MAP1	general entity	ENTITY
6	>	markup declaration close delimiter	MDC

The general entity contains the action of the map. The table below shows how to construct short reference usemap declarations:

Table 40. The parts of a usemap declaration

Example: <!USEMAP MAP-TO TO>			
Order	**Part**	**Name**	**Abstract Name**
1	<!	markup declaration open delimiter	MDO
2	USEMAP	SGML keyword	
3	MAP-TO	name of a map	
4	TO	element or model where the map is in force	
5	>	markup declaration close delimiter	MDC

If a map is already in force for a given element and a second map is defined, it will be ignored. Declaring a usemap will destroy any that may already exist.

A usemap declaration may be given inside the document instance rather than in the DTD. The element parameter is then omitted from the declaration, and the map applies to the following data within the element in which the usemap declaration appears. This is useful for constructing maps. The map with name #EMPTY disables all maps currently in force.

19.3 Example of the use of short references

To appreciate what can be done with short references, consider the memo example that has been quoted ad nauseam in this book.

Almost all the markup in this example can be automatically added by defining short references.

The memo can be presented to a parser as shown below.

```
<!DOCTYPE  MEMO [
<!ELEMENT  MEMO          - -  ((TO & FROM), BODY, CLOSE?)            >
<!ELEMENT  (TO|FROM|CLOSE)  - O (#PCDATA)                           >
<!ELEMENT  BODY          - O (P)*                                   >
<!ELEMENT  P             - O (#PCDATA|Q)*                           >
<!ELEMENT  Q             - - (#PCDATA)                              >
<!ATTLIST  MEMO       STATUS  (CONFIDEN|PUBLIC)      PUBLIC         >
<!ENTITY   MAP1          STARTTAG "TO"                              >
<!ENTITY   MAP2          "</TO><!USEMAP MAP-FROM>"                  >
<!ENTITY   MAP3          STARTTAG  "FROM"                           >
<!ENTITY   MAP4          "</FROM><BODY><!USEMAP MAP-INBO>"          >
<!ENTITY   MAP5          STARTTAG "P"                               >
<!ENTITY   MAP6          ENDTAG "P"                                 >
<!ENTITY   MAP7          STARTTAG "Q"                               >
<!ENTITY   MAP8          ENDTAG "Q"                                 >
<!ENTITY   MAP9          "</BODY><CLOSE>"                           >
<!ENTITY   MAP10         "</CLSOE></MEMO>"                          >
<!SHORTREF MAP-TO        "&#RS;&#RE;"           MAP1                >
<!SHORTREF MAP-INTO      "&#RE;"                MAP2                >
<!SHORTREF MAP-FROM      "&#RS;&#RE;"           MAP3                >
<!SHORTREF MAP-INFR      "&#RE;"                MAP4                >
<!SHORTREF MAP-INBO      "&#RS;&#RE;"           MAP5
                         "&#RS;B"               MAP9                >
<!SHORTREF MAP-INPA      "&#RS;&#RE;"           MAP6
                         '"'                    MAP7                >
<!SHORTREF MAP-INQU      '"'                    MAP8                >
<!SHORTREF MAP-INCL      "&#RE;"                MAP10               >
<!USEMAP   MAP-TO        MEMO                                       >
<!USEMAP   MAP-INTO      TO                                         >
<!USEMAP   MAP-INFR      FROM                                       >
```

```
<!USEMAP    MAP-INPA    P                                           >
<!USEMAP    MAP-INQU    Q                                           >
<!USEMAP    MAP-INCL    CLOSE                                     >]>
<Memo>
```

Comrade Napoleon

Snowball

In Animal Farm, George Orwell says: "...the pigs had to expend enormous
labour every day upon mysterious things called files, reports, minutes
and memoranda. These were large sheets of paper which had to be closely
covered with writing, and as soon as they were so covered, they were
burnt in the furnace..."

Do you think SGML would have helped the pigs?

Comrade Snowball

The DOCTYPE declaration is required because the system needs to know where to find the DTD. The first tag, <MEMO> is also required because short references are inside elements, and since this is the first element it has to be opened before any other short reference maps can be activated. This tag, however, could be omitted if the minimized tag omission for the MEMO element would allow us to do so.

If the following typewriter conventions are used, you can define short references for all the other elements:

1. The TO element is opened by a blank line. It is the first element of the memorandum.

2. It is closed by the first record end found inside it.

3. The FROM element is opened by a blank line. It is the second element of the memorandum.

4. It is closed by the first record end found inside it. This opens the BODY element.

5. Inside BODY, paragraphs are opened by the first record start. It is closed by the first record start followed by one or more blanks, which immediately opens the CLOSE element.

6. Inside paragraphs, quotations are opened by quotes ("). Paragraphs are closed by blank lines.

7. Inside quotations, quotations are closed by quotes.

8. The CLOSE element is closed by blanks followed by a record end. This immediately closes the MEMO element as well.

To obtain the correct interpretation of these conventions, eight maps are needed with ten corresponding entities:

1. The first, inside the MEMO element, maps a blank line onto the TO start-tag.

2. The second map, inside the TO element, maps a record end onto the TO end-tag followed by a declaration to use the third map. The map has to be changed because after the TO end-tag, the first map will be in force again.

3. The third map, after the TO element, maps an empty line onto the FROM start-tag.

4. The fourth map, inside the FROM element, maps a record end onto the FROM end-tag, starts the BODY element and uses the fifth map (for the same reason as above).

5. The fifth map, inside the BODY element, maps a record start onto the P start-tag. It also maps a record start followed by one or more blanks onto the BODY end-tag immediately followed by the CLOSE start-tag. Although the two delimiters in this map start with the same character there is no confusion since SGML uses the best match it finds (a record start followed by a blank matches CLOSE better than P).

6. The sixth map, inside a paragraph, maps quotes onto the Q start-tag and a blank line onto a paragraph end-tag.

7. The seventh map, inside a quotation, maps quotes onto a Q end-tag.

8. The eighth map, inside CLOSE element, maps blanks onto the CLOSE end-tag, followed by the MEMO end-tag.

19.4 Limitations of short references

The previous example shows that it is not easy to achieve simple results with short references. Properly trained people can use short references to enter specific sets of data very efficiently. Use short references with care, because:

• they can only be used under controlled circumstances and are not suitable for arbitrary documents;

• the delimiter set in the reference concrete syntax is limited;

• more complex mapping situations soon cause a combinatorial explosion of maps;

• they obscure markup;

• the action of short reference delimiters is system dependent. In UNIX, for example, there is no record end character. A document that is correctly parsed on UNIX may need extra blank lines to achieve the same result on DOS.

Consider, for example, the case where " is mapped into
<Q>everywhere.   This could have the undesired effect of having
markup appear in illegal places.   Or consider mapping blanks into
paragraphs. This could have the result of starting paragraphs where
none are required (in lists for example). To avoid this problem, use as
<!> separator instead of blank lines.

If you want to add other delimiters to your syntax, avoid the following
characters: &#, &&, [, ;</, <(, >, <!,], /, <?.

19.5 Exercise

Modify the DTD from above to allow you also to omit the <MEMO>
opening tag. Hint: the omission of the <MEMO> tag can be achieved
by start-tag minimization.

20. Record boundaries and ambiguities

This chapter deals with the treatment of record start and record end characters and ambiguities. Both of these can be the cause of surprises.

20.1 Treatment of record boundaries

On some operating systems, files (and therefore documents) are defined as a collection of records. Each record starts with a **record start character** or line feed (RS) (e.g., ASCII 0A) and ends with a **record end character** (RE) or carriage return (e.g., ASCII 0D); no document, however, or part of a document, is deemed to start with an RS or end with an RE unless it really does. On an IBM mainframe for example, records are not indicated by the data but by the organization of the data on the storage device. There is no record start or end character stored on the device. This is not a problem for SGML. There is no record end character in UNIX.

Record boundaries are treated differently depending on whether they occur in between markup or as part of parsed character data.

20.1.1 Record boundaries in markup

In markup, both RS and RE are treated as spaces. They serve to separate the components of a markup declaration. For example,

```
<!DOCTYPE Memo SYSTEM "MEMO.DTD" [
]>
```

is the same thing as:

```
<!DOCTYPE Memo SYSTEM "MEMO.DTD" [ ]>
```

If an RE appears inside a processing instruction, such as

```
<?.cc
5>
```

the treatment depends on the processing system. Processing instruction entities are not treated as data. Specific character data entities, non-SGML data entities, or SGML sub-documents are all treated as data, and record boundaries are handled in the way described in the next section.

20.1.2 Record boundaries in contents

1. An RS is ignored, except if a short reference maps an RS into an entity:

```
<!ENTITY MAP-P STARTTAG "P">
<!SHORTREF MAP-P "&#RS;" MAP1>
```

maps each record start onto the entity **MAP1**. This means that blank lines will only be ignored if there is no short reference map active.

2. A RE (after replacement of references and markup, i.e., in #PC-DATA) is treated as part of the data, unless its presence is due to markup:

a. The first RE in an element is ignored if no RS, data, or proper sub-element precede it (i.e. any intervening markup declaration, processing instruction, or included sub-element; an included element is not a proper sub-element). For example,

```
<P>
Text
```

is equivalent to:

```
<P>Text
```

b. The last RE in an element is ignored if no data or proper sub-element follow it. For example,

```
Text
</p>
```

is equivalent to:

```
Text</p>
```

c. An RE that does not follow an RS is ignored if no data or proper sub-element intervene (note &#TAB; is data). For example:

```
&#RS;&#TAB;&#RE      = &#TAB;&#RE;
&#RS;text&#RE;       = text&#RE;
text1&#RE;&#RS;<!--comment-->&#RE;&#RS;text2 = text1&#RE;text2
```

3. The decision that RE is data (i.e. belongs to #PCDATA) is made during recognition of markup, before the decision to omit it. For elements like:

```
<!ELEMENT P         -  O   (#PCDATA|Q)*                          >
<!ELEMENT Q         -  -   (#PCDATA)                             >
```

this is correct:

```
&#RS;<P>                                                    &#RE;
&#RS;In Animal Farm,              ...                       &#RE;
&#RS;<Q>the pigs                  ...                       &#RE;
&#RS;                             ...                  fire &#RE;
&#RS;Do you                       ...                       &#RE;
&#RS;
```

the events that occur may be described as follows.

a. `&#RS;` found in content. Ignored.

b. `<P>` start-tag found. Element `P`, which has mixed content, opened. Look for #PCDATA or `Q`.

c. `&#RE;` found in content. `Q` start-tag may be omitted. Could be `<Q>` or #PCDATA. Short reference delimiter with map to `Q` is double quotes, so it is #PCDATA. It is the first, so omit it.

d. `&#RE;` found in content, so omit it.

e. `<Q>` start-tag found, open `Q` element which has #PCDATA content.

f. `&#RE;` found in mixed content is data.

g. `&#RS;` found in content so omit it.

h. `</P>` end-tag found. Element closed.

Finally you should note that a record end (RE) following an inclusion is ignored, while one following a proper sub-element is treated as data.

20.2 Ambiguity type 1

When writing a DTD, it is possible to create an **ambiguous content model**. The definition of an ambiguous content model is:

A content model for which an element or character string occurring in the document instance can satisfy more than one primitive token without look-ahead.

Gulp. This means that when a parser encounters some markup, it cannot determine which token it applies to. It might be able to if it continues further down in the document, but this is not allowed.

Ambiguous content models are prohibited in SGML, but parsers do not need to report the error, until a document tries to use it. It is possible, for example, to have an ambiguous content model in the DTD and the parser will not complain about it unless a document is created which brings this ambiguity to light. For an example, look at Figure 97.

```
<!DOCTYPE test [
<!ELEMENT test O O (Keywlist)>
<!ELEMENT Keywlist - - (Keyword?, Keyword) >
<!ELEMENT Keyword  - O (#PCDATA) >
]>
<Keywlist>
<Keyword>key
</Keywlist>
```

Figure 97. Ambiguity Type 1

When parsing this file, you obtain the following output:

```
sgmls: SGML error at /asis/eric/ebt_books/books/advanced/ambig1.sgm,
       line 3 in declaration parameter 4: Content model is ambiguous
(TEST
(KEYWLIST
(KEYWORD
-key
)KEYWORD
sgmls: SGML error at ambig.sgm, line 8 at ">":
       KEYWLIST element ended prematurely; required KEYWORD omitted
)KEYWLIST
)TEST
```

Figure 98. Parsing an Ambiguity Type 1

What is the problem? The parser notes the ambiguity, although it does continue correctly.

In the case of a single keyword, the parser correctly recognizes its start-tag, but it does not know whether this satisfies the first primitive token of the content model **(Keyword?,Keyword)** or the second.

If the parser were allowed to look at the tag following the element, it would find a **</Keywlist>** start-tag, and it would know that keyword satisfies the second primitive token. That is what is meant by **look-ahead**. Since this is not allowed, the parser has two possibilities. Therefore, there is an ambiguity.

The reason why look-ahead is not allowed by SGML is that it could happen that the parser needs to look very far ahead before finding another tag that would result in a large overhead in storage and processing time.

20.3 Content models with OR and * connectors

Suppose you are trying to describe data — for example — a "service," which can be of a certain "type" followed by a "name", or of a certain "type" followed by a "phone" number. Figure 99 contains the markup declarations corresponding to this situation, that induces ambiguity type 2.

```
<!DOCTYPE service [
<!ELEMENT Service - - ((Type, Name)|(Type, Phone))>
<!ELEMENT Type     - O (#PCDATA) >
<!ELEMENT Name     - O (#PCDATA) >
<!ELEMENT Phone    - O (#PCDATA) > ]>
<service>
<type>Help-desk
<phone>4952
</service>
```

Figure 99. Ambiguity Type 2

The parser displays the output shown in Figure 100.

```
sgmls: SGML error at /asis/eric/ebt_books/books/advanced/ambig2.sgm,
       line 2 in declaration parameter 4: Content model is ambiguous
(SERVICE
(TYPE
-Help-desk
)TYPE
sgmls: SGML error at /asis/eric/ebt_books/books/advanced/ambig2.sgm,
       line 9 at ">":
       NAME start-tag implied by PHONE start-tag; not minimizable
(NAME
sgmls: SGML error at /asis/eric/ebt_books/books/advanced/ambig2.sgm,
       line 9 at ">":
       Start-tag omitted from NAME with empty content
)NAME
sgmls: SGML error at /asis/eric/ebt_books/books/advanced/ambig2.sgm,
       line 9 at ">":
       Out-of-context PHONE start-tag ended SERVICE document element
       (and parse)
)SERVICE
```

Figure 100. Parsing an Ambiguity Type 2

Again, the parser is confused as to which group the **type** element belongs. The solution is to use different elements to contain the two groups containing `type`, or to take the `type` element outside the two model groups.

20.4 Mixed content models

A mixed content model is a content model that has element content as well as #PCDATA content. For example,

```
<!ELEMENT P - O (#PCDATA|Q)* >
```

Your SGML guide advises...

SGML recommends that #PCDATA be used only when data characters are permitted *anywhere* in the content of the element. That means that:

1. Either #PCDATA is the only token in the model,

2. Or, the "|" is the only connector used in the model.

This recommendation will prevent any ambiguities from occurring due to mixed content elements. See what happens if you use a different connector in the next example, which displays ambiguity type 3.

```
<!DOCTYPE Service [
<!ELEMENT Service - - (Type, #PCDATA) >
<!ELEMENT Type - O (#PCDATA)>
]>
<Service>

<Type>Help desk
</Service>
```

Figure 101. Ambiguity Type 3

The parser's reaction is shown in Figure 102.

```
(SERVICE
sgmls: SGML error at /asis/eric/ebt_books/books/advanced/ambig3.sgm,
       line 5 at record end:
       TYPE start-tag implied by data; not minimizable
(TYPE
)TYPE
sgmls: SGML error at /asis/eric/ebt_books/books/advanced/ambig3.sgm,
       line 7 at ">":
       Out-of-context TYPE start-tag ended SERVICE document element
       (and parse)
)SERVICE
```

Figure 102. Parsing an Ambiguity Type 3

The problem is caused by the second record end being interpreted as data in a mixed content element. This then triggers that start-tag of the contextually required element, which causes a problem when the parser finds the real start-tag. This problem should not really be called an ambiguity: it is a problem with the treatment of record boundaries as data.

For further discussions of ambiguities, see [1],[2] and [3].

20.5 Bibliography for Chapter 20

[1]   L.A. Price
      The Problem with Ambiguous Content Models, SGML Users'
      Group Bulletin 3/1, Pages 25–26
      1988
[2]   A. Brueggemann-Klein, D. Wood
      Deterministic Regular Languages, Bericht 38
      Universität Freiburg, 1991
[3]   J. McFadden, S. Wilmott
      Ambiguity in the Instance: An Analysis, <TAG>, issue 9, Pages
      3–5
      april 1989

Part IV. Special applications

The aim of this part is to present some special SGML applications:

1. How to use SGML for EDI messages;

2. A discussion on the usefulness of SGML for describing mathematics;

3. Using SGML for describing graphics.

Finally I show how SGML integrates with the various ISO text processing standards.

21. SGML and EDI

Electronic Data Interchange (EDI) originated in the late seventies from a desire to improve commercial and other communications between organizations. It was first known as Trade Data Interchange (TDI). At first sight EDI, which is applicable to the world of trade, seems to be of interest to a different group of professionals than SGML. Some of the problems that EDI and SGML try to solve, however, are similar. They both standardize the exchange of documents by defining a structure that is independent of a particular application.

The relevant ISO committees responsible for SGML and EDI, ISO/IEC JTC1/SC18/WG8 and ISO/TC154 have issued a statement on the compatibility and complementarity of the two standards [1].

Like with mathematics and graphics, an SGML document can include an EDI document by defining a NOTATION. In this chapter, I describe how the logical and layout structures of EDI documents can be described with SGML, and how EDI can benefit from this.

21.1 What is EDI?

EDI is the electronic exchange of messages between business partners in a form that permits both parties to process the content of these messages in whatever way is required.

Nowadays computers are widely used in many organizations to manage business information. Purchasing, inventory, stores and accounting are controlled electronically, thereby replacing the traditional paper shuffling associated with these activities. The communication between companies, however, is still largely done by exchanging orders, delivery forms, and invoices on paper. In Switzerland alone, 250 million of these documents are sent per year[2].

The next step is to find computerized business partners and to link to their systems via EDI (see Figure 103). Purchase orders, invoices, order changes, product information, and delivery schedules can then be communicated from computer to computer. Automatically feeding the content of these messages into existing MIS applications results in quicker and more reliable processing. Organizations using EDI have a competitive advantage.

Agreements have to be made about the way the information is presented in a message, both on the syntactical (i.e., symbol **x** separates data field **y**) as well as on the semantical level (this data field contains the delivery date). Since most organizations have more than one trading partner, a standard format for EDI messages is in everybody's interest.

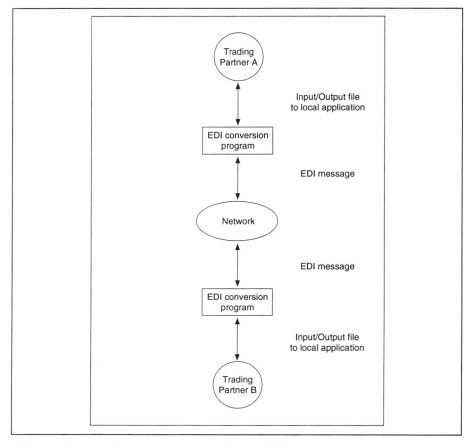

Figure 103. A Schematic Overview of EDI

EDI should not be confused with electronic mail. Electronic mail is the computerized exchange of nonstructured information between users of the same computer or between users of different computers linked by a network. The message contents is enveloped in a layer containing the electronic mail address of the recipient, the sender, the subject of the message, as described in the standard for electronic mail, X.400. You can put an EDI message inside an electronic mail.

21.2 EDIFACT

The United Nations Economic Commission for Europe **(UN/ECE)**, which works on trade facilitation, developed a set of syntax rules for the preparation of messages to be interchanged between partners in the fields of administration, commerce and transport. These rules are known as **EDIFACT**, described byISO 9735:1988 [3].

Each unit that is exchanged in an EDIFACT connection is called an **interchange**. Several interchanges may take place during a connection. Each interchange consists of one or more **messages**.

EDIFACT messages consist of the characters shown in Table 41. The codes corresponding to these characters are defined in ISO 646:1983, or in any other set agreed on by the communicating partners.

Table 41. The "level A" EDIFACT character set

Character	Sym-bol	Reserved for use as
Letters, upper case	A-Z	
Numerals	0-9	
Space character		
Full stop	.	
Comma	,	
Hyphen/minus sign	-	
Opening parenthesis	(	
Closing parenthesis	)	
Oblique stroke (slash)	/	
Equals sign	=	
Apostrophe	'	segment terminator
Plus sign	+	segment tag and data separator
Colon	:	component data element separator
Question mark	?	release character
Exclamation mark	!	
Quotation mark	"	
Percent sign	%	
Ampersand	&	

Character	Sym-bol	Reserved for use as
Asterisk	*	
Semi-colon	;	
Less-than sign	<	
Greater-than sign	>	

Figure 104 shows the tree representation of the messages in an interchange.

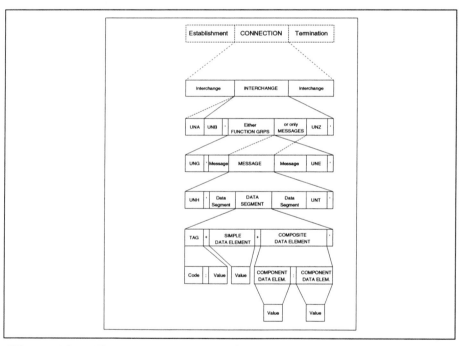

Figure 104. The Tree Structure of EDI Interchanges

The definitions of the elements in Figure 104 are given in the table below. A message with the EDIFACT syntax is an ordered sequence of segments. Each type of business transaction, be it an invoice, purchase order, or a request for quote, has its own sequence. The applications are often simplified with respect to the full EDIFACT message structure.

Table 42. The elements of an EDIFACT interchange

Element	Description	
Connec-tion	A connection is preceded by an establishment and ended by a termination. They may be based on the Open Systems Interconnection model ISO 7498	
Inter-change	contains:	
	1	an optional string UNA (service string advice)
	2	a mandatory string UNB (interchange header)
	3	either Functional groups or Messages
Functional Group	contains:	
	1	an optional string UNG (functional group header)
	2	one or more messages of the same type
	3	an optional string UNE (functional group trailer)
Message	contains:	
	1	an optional string UNH (message header)
	2	a **heading** section containing one or more data segments with information relating to the entire message
	3	a **detail** section containing one or more data segments overriding similar information in the heading section
	4	a **summary** section with totals, e.g. invoice total
	5	a mandatory string UNT (message trailer)
Segment	contains:	
	1	a mandatory segment **tag** e.g. CUX
	2	simple data elements
	3	composite data elements
Segment tag	contains:	
	1	a mandatory segment **code** e.g. 6345
	2	repeating and nesting value(s)

Element	Description
Simple data element	contains:
	a single data element value
Composite data element	contains:
	component data elements
Component data element	contains:
	a single data element value

An example of an EDIFACT message is shown below. It is a standard commercial invoice (see the next section for a full description). Each segment starts at the beginning of a new line for readability. In reality this is not necessarily the case.

```
UNA:+.?: : '
UNB+UNOA:1+5012345678901:14+123456:91+871215:123619+REF01+PASSW+INVOIC
+00001: '

UNH+INV001+INVOIC:3: '
BIN+01/051/H/503879+871215+IN: '
NAD+SU+501458000065:91+IMPERIAL CHEMICAL INDUSTRIES PLC:PO BOX 14:
    THE HEATH:RUNCORN, CHESHIRE, WA7 4QG:UK: '
RFF+238458241:VA: '
CTA+CW+1991:CG: '
CTA+IC++0928514444:TE: '
CTA+IC++629655:TL: '
CTA+IC++ICI MONDIV RUNCORN:TG: '
NAD+BY++ICI FRANCE ET SOPRA:1 AVENUE NEWTON:94142 CLAMART:FRANCE: '
RFF+637977:CR: '
CUX+FRF:IN: '
PAT+02++880110:003+06:2:1:90: '
TRD+10: '
NAD+ST+++OISSEL: '
TOD+01+EXW:01++++UNCLEARED DUTIES AND TAXES UNPAID: '
GPD+160+SK: '
MEA+PL+N+3200:K: '
MEA+CH+ZAS+80:K: '

UNS+D: '
LIT+++160:12:PCK+12.34::1:K+3200+39488: '
IMD++THIXOMEN: '
FTX+PKG++160X20KG PAPER SACKS PACKED 20 PER PALLET: '

UNS+S: '
TIA+39488: '
```

```
VAL+IN+5678.90+GBS: '
FTX+CUS++CERTIFIE CONFORME A L?: 'ORIGINAL:
    -NOUS CERTIFIONS QUE LES MARCHANDISES FAISANT L?: 'OBJET:
    DE CETTE FOURNITURE SONT DE FABRICATION GRANDE BRETAGNE:
    (PAR NOUS MEME) ET QUE LA VALEUR SOUS MENTIONEE EST JUSTE:
    ET CONFORME A NOS ECRITURES.: '
FTX+STN++GOODS ARE OF UNITED KINGDOM ORIGIN:GOODS ARE IN FREE
    CIRCULATION WITHIN EEC: '
UNT+31+INV001: '

UNT+1+REF01
```

Segments can be mandatory (e.g., **UNH** in the invoice above), they can depend on certain conditions imposed by the communicating partners (conditional or optional in SGML, e.g. **RFF**) and they can be repetitive (e.g. **CTA**). The description of EDIFACT messages corresponding to each different type of transaction must include a description of the segments. It is usually given in a **branching diagram**.

Figure 105 shows the summary part of the branching diagram corresponding to the invoice.

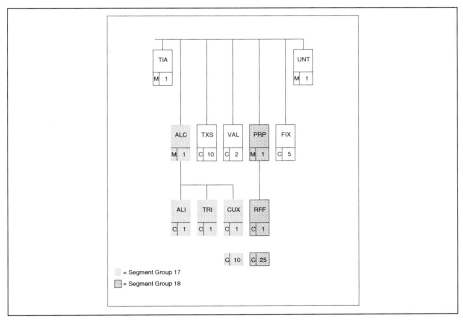

Figure 105. The Summary Part of the Branching Diagram for an EDIFACT Invoice

Each segment appears in the branching diagram as a box: within it are its name, the number of times it may be repeated, an **M** if the segment is mandatory, and a **C** if it is optional.

Segments consist of a sequence of compound (e.g., GWT1991:CG) or simple data elements (e.g., IC). Data elements either have values defined by a code pointing to the Trade Data Elements Directory, ISO 7372 [4], or have a format stating the number and type of characters. How this works in detail will be explained in the next section. Purchase order and quality data EDIFACT implementations exist in draft form and others are planned.

21.3 The standard commercial invoice

This message was set up by the UN/ECE as one of an integrated set following the EDIFACT syntax [5]. Since EDIFACT messages have a hierarchical structure, SGML can be used to describe them. The invoice message has a header section, a detail section, and a summary section. I restrict myself to the summary section because it is the smallest. The interested reader should find sufficient information here to be able work out the application in full details.

The definition of each segment is given in ISO 7372. I present the definitions of two segments (UNS and VAL) to illustrate the general principles in Table 43.

Table 43. The definition of two invoice segments

Name	Function			
UNS	To separate header, detail and summary section of a message			
	UNCE #	**Name**	**M/C**	**Value**
	0081	Section Identifier	M	D or S
VAL	To specify valutation of goods and services for customs or insurance			
	UNCE #	**Name**	**M/C**	**Value**
	5849	Valutation function code	M	CU, IN or TR
	5848	amount	M	1-15 numeric characters
	6345	currency code	C	e.g. USD, GBP, NLG

Each segment is a sequence of mandatory or optional data elements, which are defined by a reference number. Each reference number corresponds to an entry in UN/ECE Trade Data Element Directory, where the values that these fields can take are given. The value of a data element is one out of a finite set (e.g., 5849, the valutation function code can have values CU, IN, or TR), or given as a format (e.g., 5848, the amount is 1-15 numeric characters).

21.3.1 A DTD for the standard electronic message commercial invoice

The hierarchical structure of EDIFACT messages suggests they can be described with SGML. In this section I show how all EDIFACT information is adequately transmitted by using an SGML syntax and by interpreting the SGML elements according to the EDIFACT semantics.

Writing a DTD for EDIFACT applications is not difficult. A DTD for the summary section of the commercial invoice is shown in the figure below. Notice the following about this DTD:

1. To use it, it has to be modified in several places. It is only intended to display principles.

2. A list of dots (...) means that the list of declared values of an attribute was too long to fit in the figure.

3. Attributes have been used for all elements with a finite set of values. In the EDIFACT syntax, a segment or data element is identified by the order in which it appears in the message. By using attributes the order is lost, but a segment or data element is identified by the name of the attribute.

4. Enforcing finite repetition is done by defining entities. This is only practical for repetition figures below 100. I recommend using a * and checking that the limit is not exceeded in the translation program. Another possibility is to dynamically create a DTD corresponding to each number of repetitions.

5. Different types of business transactions have many segments in common. Consequently the corresponding elements should be placed together in a common DTD which is imbedded by the different DTDs for invoice, purchase order, and so on.

6. The data type (such as floating point numbers) of an element cannot be described by a DTD. An SGML input system will therefore not be able to check it.

The DTD for the summary section of a commercial invoice is shown in the example below.

```
<!-- DTD for summary section of commercial invoice            -->
<!ENTITY % FTX5   "((FTX, (FTX, (FTX, (FTX, FTX?)?)?)?)?)"     >
<!ENTITY % TXT5   "((TXT, (TXT, (TXT, (TXT, TXT?)?)?)?)?)"     >
<!ENTITY % SEG1710 "(SEG17?, SEG17?, SEG17?, SEG17?, SEG17?, SEG17?,
                     SEG17?, SEG17?, SEG17?, SEG17?)"          >
<!ENTITY % TXS10   "(TXS?, TXS?, TXS?, TXS?, TXS?, TXS?, TXS?, TXS?, TXS?,
                     TXS?)"                                    >
<!ENTITY % VAL2    "(VAL, VAL)"                                >
<!ENTITY % SEG1825 "(SEG18?, SEG18?, SEG18?, SEG18?, SEG18?, SEG18?,
SEG18?, SEG18?, SEG18?, SEG18?, SEG18?, SEG18?, SEG18?, SEG18?,
SEG18?, SEG18?, SEG18?, SEG18?, SEG18?, SEG18?, SEG18?, SEG18?,
                     SEG18?)"                                  >
<!ELEMENT INVSUM  - -  (TIA,(%SEG1710;),(%TXS10;),(%VAL2;),(%SEG1825;),
                        (%FTX5;),UNT)                          >
<!ELEMENT TIA     - O  (IAMOUNT, ITOTAL?, ASDISCT?, ASTAX?, IAAMOUNT?,
                        TATOTAL?, PPTOTAL?) -- total amount--  >
<!ELEMENT IAMOUNT - O  (#PCDATA)          --total invoice amount--  >
<!ELEMENT ITOTAL  - O  (#PCDATA)          --invoice article items total-->
<!ELEMENT ASDISCT - O  (#PCDATA)          --amount subject to payment
                        discount--                            >
<!ELEMENT ASTAX   - O  (#PCDATA)          --amount subject to tax--  >
<!ELEMENT IAAMOUNT - O  (#PCDATA)         --invoice additional amount-- >
<!ELEMENT TATOTAL - O  (#PCDATA)          --tax amount total--  >
<!ELEMENT PPTOTAL - O  (#PCDATA)          --prepayment totals--  >
<!ELEMENT SEG17   - O  (ALC, ALI?, TRI?, CUX?) --total allowances,
                                            charges  -->
<!ELEMENT ALC     - O  (AOCN?, SSERVID?, RATE?, ACAMOUNT?, ACPERCNT?,
                        AOCQ?, %TXT5?) --allowances and charges-->
<!ELEMENT AOCN    - O  (#PCDATA)          --allowance of charge number-->
<!ELEMENT SSERVID - O  EMPTY       --special services identification-->
<!ELEMENT RATE    - O  (RATEPU, UPRICE?)  --rate--            >
<!ELEMENT ACAMOUNT - O  (#PCDATA)         --allowance or charge amount-->
<!ELEMENT ACPERCNT - O  (AOCPRCNT, ACPB?)  --allowance or charge
                                            percentage--  >
<!ELEMENT AOCPRCNT - O  (#PCDATA)     --allowance or charge percent--  >
<!ELEMENT ACPB    - O  (#PCDATA)      --allowance or charge pct basis--  >
<!ELEMENT AOCQ    - O  (#PCDATA)      --allowance or charge quantity--  >
<!ELEMENT ALI     - O  EMPTY         --additional line information--  >
<!ELEMENT TRI     - O  (TAXCAT?, TAXRATE?, TAXAMNT?) --tax related
                        information--                         >
<!ELEMENT TAXCAT  - O  (#PCDATA)          --tax category--  >
<!ELEMENT TAXRATE - O  (#PCDATA)          --tax rate--  >
<!ELEMENT TAXAMNT - O  (#PCDATA)          --tax amount--  >
<!ELEMENT CUX     - O  (REFCUR, TARCUR?, EXRATE?, DRATE?) --currencies-->
<!ELEMENT REFCUR  - O  (EMPTY)            --reference currency--  >
<!ELEMENT TARCUR  - O  (EMPTY)            --target currency--  >
<!ELEMENT EXRATE  - O  (#PCDATA)          --rate of exchange--  >
<!ELEMENT DRATE   - O  (DATE?,TIME?)      --date and time of rate--  >
<!ELEMENT DATE    - O  (#PCDATA)          --date--  >
<!ELEMENT TIME    - O  (#PCDATA)          --time--  >
<!ELEMENT TXS     - O  (TAXCAT?, TAXRATE?, ASTAX?, TAXAMNT?, ASTTBTD?)
                        --tax subtotals--
<!ELEMENT ASTAX   - O  (#PCDATA)          --amount subject to tax--  >
<!ELEMENT ASTTBTD - O  (#PCDATA)          --amount subject to tax before
                        terms discount--                     >
<!ELEMENT VAL     - O  (STVALUE)          --valuation--  >
<!ELEMENT SEG18   - O  (PRP, RFF)         --amounts already payed and
```

```
                            related references--                      >
<!ELEMENT PRP      - O  (PAMOUNT,ASTT?)     --pre payment--           >
<!ELEMENT ASTT     - O  (#PCDATA)           --amount subject to tax-- >
<!ELEMENT RFF      - O  (REFERENC, DRATE?) -- references --           >
<!ELEMENT REFERENC - O  (REFNO?, SREFNO?)  --references--             >
<!ELEMENT REFNO    - O  (#PCDATA)           --reference number--      >
<!ELEMENT SREFNO   - O  (#PCDATA)           --secondary reference number-->
<!ELEMENT FTX      - O  (%TXT5;)            --free text--             >
<!ELEMENT TXT      - O  (#PCDATA)    --up to 70 alphanumeric characters-->
<!ELEMENT UNT      - O  (NOSITM, MESREFNO) --message trailer--        >
<!ELEMENT NOSITM   - O  (#PCDATA)      --number of segments in  message-- >
<!ELEMENT MESREFNO - O  (#PCDATA)           --message reference number-- >
<!ATTLIST ALC          AOCIND  (A,D,C,E,N)
                               #REQUIRED --allow. or ch. indicator--
                       SETTLMT (1,6,5,4,ZZ,8,2,7,3)
                               #IMPLIED  --settlement--               >
<!ATTLIST SSERVID      SSCODE  (AC,AM,AJ,AA,AN,A0010,A0020,A0030,B0010,...)
                               #REQUIRED --special services code--
                       AGCODE  (AX,AA,ST,AI,BI,CM,CI,NE,NR,OP,SI,TD,TI,UN)
                               #REQUIRED --agency code--
                       CLISTID (21,92,91,18,07,01,09,10,17,11,51)
                               #IMPLIED  --code list identifier--     >
<!ATTLIST (RATE,AOCQ) MUSPEC  (BAG,BL,BLI,BLK,BRD,BOT,BOX,CAN,CAR,CTN)
                               #IMPLIED  --measure unit specifier--   >
<!ATTLIST ALI          COOC    (AF,AR,BG,CH,CS,DA,NL,EN,EO,FI,FR,DE,GR,...)
                               #IMPLIED  --country code--
                       POCODE  (0,1)
                               #IMPLIED  --preference origin code--   >
<!ATTLIST TAXCAT       TAXTYPC (VAT)
                               #IMPLIED  --tax type code--            >
<!ATTLIST (TRI,TXS)    TAXCATC (X,E,F,G,H,J,K,I,A,O,S,T,V,Z)
                               #IMPLIED  --tax category code--        >
<!ATTLIST              CUCODED (AFA,DZD,AWG,ARP,AUD,BSD,BHD,THB,PAB,BBD,...)
                               #IMPLIED  --currency code--
                   CUFUNQU (CV,01,03,02,IN,OC,PY,LQ,PC,QC,RL,06,SL,SC,07,04)
                               #IMPLIED  --curr. function qualifier-- >
<!ATTLIST TARCUR       CUCODED (AFA,DZD,AWG,ARP,AUD,BSD,BHD,THB,PAB,BBD,...)
                               #IMPLIED  --currency code--
                   CUFUNQU (CV,01,03,02,IN,OC,PY,LQ,PC,QC,RL,06,SL,SC,07,04)
                               #IMPLIED  --curr. function qualifier-- >
<!ATTLIST CUX          CURCODE (AMS,FRA,IMF,LNF,LNS,NYC,PHI,ZUR)
                               #IMPLIED  --currency market exchange-- >
<!ATTLIST STVALUE      CUCODED (AFA,DZD,AWG,ARP,AUD,BSD,BHD,THB,PAB,BBD,...)
                               #IMPLIED  --currency code--            >
<!ATTLIST VAL          VAFCODE (CU,IN,TR)
                               #REQUIRED --valuation function code--  >
<!ATTLIST DRATE    DTQUAL  (70,35,11,46,57,44,95,62,53,1,61,108,21,20,...)
                               #REQUIRED --date,time qualifier--
                       TIZONE  (053,EST,GMT,054)
                               #IMPLIED  --time zone specifier--      >
<!ATTLIST REFERENC     REFNOQ  (VU,VV,WR,WM)
                               #IMPLIED  --reference numb. qualifier-- >
<!ATTLIST FTX      TRCODE  (ALL,CHS,CUS,DEL,DUT,GEN,HAZ,INS,INV,LIN,ZZZ...)
                               #IMPLIED  --text reference code--
                       TFCODE  (2,3,1)
                               #IMPLIED  --text function code--       >
```

The invoice in SGML form, marked up using this DTD is shown below. Needless to say, humans would never be expected to type data in this form.

```
<UNA CDESEP=":" DESEP="+" DECNOT="." RELIND="?" RESERV=" " SEGTERM="'">
<UNB SYNTAXID="UNOA" VERSION="1">
<SENDER IDQUAL="14">5012345678901</SENDER>
<RECEIVER IDQUAL="191">871215</RECEIVER>
<PREPAR DATE="871215" TIME="123619">
<REFNO>REF01</REFNO>
<PWD>PASSW</PWD>
<APPLIC>INVOIC</APPLIC>
<PRIORITY>00001</PRIORITY></UNB>

<UNH MREF="INV001" MTYPE="INVOIC" MVERSION="3">
<BIN NO="01/051/H/503879" DATE="871215" TYPE="IN">
<SEG1>
<NAD PACODE="SU" IDCODE="501458000065" CLISTID="91">
<ADDRESS><ALINE>IMPERIAL CHEMICAL INDUSTRIES PLC</ALINE>
<ALINE>PO BOX 14, THE HEATH</ALINE>
<ALINE>RUNCORN, CHESHIRE, WA7 4QG</ALINE>
<ALINE>UK</ALINE><ADDRESS></NAD>
<RFF><REFERENC REFNOQ="VA"><REFNO>23845821</REFERENC></RFF>
<CTA FUNCODE="CW"><DEPT CODE="1991" NAME="CG"></DEPT></CTA>
<CTA FUNCODE="IC"><COMCON NO="0928514444" QUALIF="TE"></COMCON></CTA>
<CTA FUNCODE="IC"><COMCON NO="629655" QUALIF="TL"></COMCON></CTA>
<CTA FUNCODE="IC"><COMCON NO="ICI MONDIV RUNCORN" QUALIF="TG"></COMCON>
</CTA></SEG1>
<SEG1>
<NAD PACODE="BY">
<ADDRESS><ALINE>FRANCE ET SOPRA</ALINE>
<ALINE>1 AVENUE NEWTON</ALINE>
<ALINE>94142 CLAMART</ALINE>
<ALINE>FRANCE</ALINE></ADDRESS></NAD>
<RFF><REFERENC REFNOQ="CR"><REFNO>637977</REFERENC></RFF></SEG1>
<CUX><REFCUR CUCODED="FRF" CURFUNQ="IN">
<PAT TERMTYPE="02">
<TERMS DATE="880110" QUALIF="003">
<INFO TREFCODE="06" TRELCODE="2" PERIOD="1"NO="90"></PAT>
<SEG2>
<TRD><<MODE CODE="10"></TRD>
<NAD PACODE="ST"><PLACE>
<PLINE>OISSEL</PLINE></PLACE></NAD></SEG2>
<TOD CODE="01">
<TERMS CODE="EXW" CODEID="01">
<TLIST><TLINE>UNCLEARED DUTIES AND TAXES UNPAID</TLINE></TLIST></TOD>
<SEG4>
<GPD NO="160" TYPE="SK">
<MEA MEAID="PL" DIMID="N"><VALUE UNIT="K">3200</VALUE></MEA>
<MEA MEAID="CH" DIMID="ZAS"><VALUE UNIT="K">80</VALUE></MEA></GPD>
```

```
</SEG4>
<UNS IDESC="D">

<SEG5>
<LIT>
<QUANTITY NO="160" QUALIF="12" UNIT="PCK">
<PRICE AMOUNT="12.34" BASIS="1" UNIT="K">
<UNITS>39488</UNITS></LIT></SEG5>
<IMD><DESCRIPT><DLINE>THIXOMEN</DLINE></DESCRIPT></IMD>
<FTX TRCODE="PKG">
<TXT>160X20KG PAPER SACKS PACKED 20 PER PALLET</TXT>
<UNS IDESC="S">

<TIA><IAMOUNT>39488</IAMOUNT></TIA>
<VAL VAFCODE="IN"><STVALUE CURCODE="GB">5678.90</STVALUE></VAL>
<FTX TRCODE="CUS"><TXT>CERTIFIE CONFORME A L'ORIGINAL</TXT>
<TXT>-NOUS CERTIFIONS QUE LES MARCHANDISES FAISANT L'OBJET</TXT>
<TXT>DE CETTE FOURNITURE SONT DE FABRICATION GRANDE BRETAGNE</TXT>
<TXT>(PAR NOUS MEME) ET QUE LA VALEUR SOUS MENTIONEE EST JUSTE</TXT>
<TXT>ET CONFORME A NOS ECRITURES.</TXT></FTX>
<FTX TRCODE="STN"><TXT>GOODS ARE OF UNITED KINGDOM ORIGIN</TXT>
<TXT>GOODS ARE IN FREE CIRCULATION WITHIN EEC</TXT></FTX>
<UNT><NOSIM>31</NOSIM><MESREFNO>INV001</MESREFNO></UNT>
```

This shows that EDIFACT messages can be marked up using SGML while preserving all their information, although data types are not explicitly indicated.

21.3.2 Why use SGML with EDIFACT?

I have shown that the SGML syntax can be used instead of the EDIFACT syntax. The essential information can be extracted by applying the EDIFACT semantics to the elements and attributes. SGML could be applied with EDI in two ways:

1. As an internal standard. Translation to and from EDIFACT is used for communication with the outside world.

2. As a replacement of the EDIFACT syntax.

3. Keeping the EDIFACT syntax, but using SGML as a way to impose semantics on the EDIFACT messages.

The first alternative is not so interesting since you have to always translate the SGML syntax to and from EDIFACT. This is not a big problem in itself, but SGML becomes an extra layer in the system without bringing any clear advantages. It would be useful if EDIFACT messages were created interactively, since you could then use an

SGML editor to make them without errors. They are, however, usually made by programs.

The second proposition is more interesting for the following reasons:

• The SGML parser will make sure that segments appear in the correct order, that no mandatory elements are omitted, that repeatable elements are repeated the correct number of times, and so on. EDIFACT messages can be parsed whenever they are modified or whenever they are received.

• Once an EDIFACT message exists in SGML form, it is easier to process: it can be translated into EDIFACT form, it can be translated into word-processor commands for printing, it can be added to a database, or it can be translated to an internally used form. Translating EDIFACT messages is not easy, but good software is available for translating SGML

• Messages in SGML form are easier to change: changing the DTD only requires the approval of the parties involved in the exchange.

• Transmitting an EDIFACT message that uses the SGML syntax will guarantee that there will be no character conversion problems when a message is sent from a 7–bit ASCII system to an 8–bit EBCDIC system for example. The EDIFACT characters in Table 43, however, usually translate without problems between EBCDIC and ASCII systems.

The third alternative requires software that does not exist. Its great advantage is that the EDIFACT syntax may be maintained, and that SGML DTDs can be made for each type of existing message, thus enabling standard messages to be checked by an SGML like system. We may well see several such applications of SGML into various unlikely areas in the coming years.

SGML, however, cannot completely replace EDIFACT, since there is no facility to check whether a data element has a certain length or whether its value consists of numbers, letters, or alphanumeric characters. An SGML attribute, for example, may have a required datatype of NUMBER that requires its value to be numerical but says nothing about its length. Some additional checking will always have to be done; in a future version of the SGML standard the support for datatypes should be considered.

An example of an organization who are using SGML to describe forms (grant applications) that are exchanged electronically is the UK Science and Engineering Research Council (SERC)[6].

21.4 Bibliography for Chapter 21

[1]   T.F. Frost
      EDI in Text and Office Systems — User Requirements (WG8 N830)
      Geneva, 1989

[2] R. Schwab
     L'EDI: un facteur de réussite, Panorama IBM
     Switzerland, 1989
[3] ISO
     EDIFACT- Application level Syntax Rules (ISO 9735)
     Geneva, 1988
[4] ISO
     Trade and Data Interchange — Tradce Data Elements Directory
     (ISO 7372)
     Geneva, 1988
[5] United Nations Economic and Social Council
     EDIFACT rapporteurs, Proposal for UN/ECE Standard Electronic
     Message Commercial Invoice Version No.3
     Geneva, 1987
[6] B. Robinson, G. Wu and K. Jeffery
     Using SGML for the exchange of the RG2 grant application form
     Oxford, 1989

22. SGML and mathematics

22.1 Why describe mathematics with SGML?

As you have seen in the previous chapters, generalized markup is based on two postulates:

1. Markup should describe a document's structure and other attributes rather than specify processing to be performed on it, as descriptive markup need be done only once and will suffice for all future processing.

2. Markup should be rigorous so that the techniques available for processing rigorously defined objects like programs and databases can be used for processing documents as well.

There is no reason why this should not be valid for mathematical formulas. If an unambiguous structure is required, restrictions should be imposed on the kind of mathematical formulas that can be described. The field of mathematics is so vast that it may be impossible to design a single DTD that covers every kind of mathematical formulas. In sciences that use mathematics as a tool — for example, physics — the mathematics used in many physics papers can be described as "advanced calculus." This definition can be made more precise by referring to some standard textbooks containing these types of formulas: for example, from the "Handbook of Mathematical Functions"[2] and the "Tables of Integrals, Series and Products"[3].

If a rigorous encoding of mathematical formulas (the second postulate above) is the objective, a DTD is required that will provide the descriptive markup to:

1. convert the formulas between different word processors;

2. store the formulas in and extract them from a database;

3. allow programs to input or output formulas in descriptive markup.

An example of the first application would be the conversion of mathematical formulas coded in LaTeX to, say, MS Word via SGML. Having an unambiguous description of a formula could also facilitate its translation into Braille, provided the description captures all the visual information in the formula.

An example of the second application would be encoding and storing the complete contents of the above-mentioned "Handbook of Mathematical Functions" and "Table of Integrals, Series and Products" in a database, so that this information can be accessed on-line by mathematicians and physicists. Many articles have mathematical formulas in their titles, so any program that extracts bibliographic data should be able to handle mathematics as well. This would enable bibliograpic searches on particular formulas or calculations.

An example of the third application would be the extraction and subsequent use in a computer program, written in an ordinary programming language or, for example, in Mathematica[4].

In the publishing environment, authors and publishers would use one standard DTD for scientific papers, which enables them to prepare a primary publication — in paper and (or) in some electronic form — and to store the information in databases for various secondary purposes.

The question now is: what should a DTD for mathematical formulas look like, if it is going to be used for these purposes? There are two choices for a DTD for mathematics:

1. a **P-type DTD** which reflects the presentation or visual structure;

2. an **S-type DTD** which reflects the semantics or logical structure.

Following the spirit of SGML, markup of a formula should describe the logical structure of the formula, rather than the way it is represented on a certain medium, say, the page of a traditional (non-electronic) book. Is descriptive markup of mathematical material possible? If it is possible, who can use it and for which purposes?

In the process of scientific publishing two sorts of information can be exchanged: mathematical material that is structured according to a formal structural specification, and material that is not structured.

22.2 Characteristics of mathematical notation

Mathematical notation is designed to create the correct ideas in the mind of a trained reader. It is therefore *deliberately* ambiguous and incomplete: indeed, it is almost meaningless to all other readers. Or, more technically: the intrinsic information content of any mathematical formula is very low. A formula gets its meaning, that is, its information content, only when used to communicate between two minds that share a large collection of concepts and assumptions, together with an agreed language for communicating the associated ideas.

The ambiguity encountered in mathematical notation can be of two types [5]:

1. A generic notation uses the same symbols to represent similar but different functions; for example, " $+$" or " $-$". In the case of addition this is not really a problem, but multiplication *is* a problem since multiplication of numbers is commutative, whereas matrix multiplication is non-commutative!

2. A more fundamental ambiguity is posed by the same notation being used in different fields in different ways. For example: f' stands for

the first derivative of f in calculus, but can mean "any other entity different from f" in other areas.

More examples of ambiguity are:

- Does $\bar{x}$ represent a mean, a conjugation, or a negation?

- Is i an integer variable — for example, the index of a matrix — or is it $\sqrt{-1}$?

- The other way around: is $\sqrt{-1}$ denoted by i or by j? There are examples of authors writing things like $[L_i, L_j] = \frac{1}{2}L_k$, where the first i is an index, and the second i stands for $\sqrt{-1}$.

- What is the function of the 2 in SU_2, $\log_2 x$, x_2, x^2, T_2^2? In SU_2 it is the number of dimensions of the Lie group; in $\log_2 x$ it is the base of the logarithm; if x is a vector, the $_2$ is an index; the ^{2} in x^2 is an index; the ^{2} in x^2 could be a power, but if T is a tensor, the $_2$ in T_2^2 is a contravariant tensor index.

- Is $|X|$ the absolute value of a real (complex) number X or the polyhedron of a simplicial complex X[6]?

The inverse problem, which is equally common, arises when different typographical constructs have the same mathematical meaning. For example, the meanings of both the following two lines would be coded identically:

$$3 + 4 \,(\mathrm{mod}\, 5)$$
$$3 +_5 4$$

and this would lead to great difficulty if an author wanted to write:
"We shall often write, for example, $3 + 4 \,(\mathrm{mod}\, 5)$ in the shorter form $3 +_5 4$, or even simply $3 + 4$ when this will not lead to confusion."

Of course, natural languages are similarly ambiguous and incomplete, but the difference is that no one is suggesting that in an SGML document each word should be coded so that it reflects the full dictionary definition of the meaning which that particular use of the word is intended to have!

22.3 Who performs the markup of math?

In traditional publishing, the technical editor adds markup signs in the margin of the manuscript, depending on the text and the visual representation that the house style dictates. It is, however, unlikely that a technical editor is capable of identifying the precise function of every part of a mathematical formula, for several reasons, most of which were discussed in the previous section, namely that mathematical notation:

- is not unambiguous;

- is not completely standardized;
- is not a closed system.

Even if the technical editor were capable of identifying every part of a formula, this would be too time-consuming — and therefore too costly.

This leads to the following conclusion. A publisher has no choice but to use a P-type DTD for mathematical material that is submitted in unstructured form or in P-type notation. If S-type markup of a mathematical formula is possible, conversion from P-type to S-type is difficult or even impossible: the tags for S-type markup should not be added by the information gatherer, but by the information providers, that is, the authors, who should be able to identify each part of their formulas.

22.4 Feasibility of S-type notation

In the second scenario, authors would submit papers with mathematical formulas in S-type notation. This would enable the publisher to translate to any mathematics typesetting language (P-type notation). However, the reasoning of above leads us to the following conjecture:

Conjecture.   It is impossible to create an S-type dtd for *all* of mathematics.

Representing the "full meaning" of a mathematical formula, if such a notion exists, will almost certainly lead to attempts to pack more and more unnecessary information into the representation until it becomes useless for any purpose.   This is rather like Russell and Whitehead reducing "simple arithmetic" to logic and taking several pages of symbols to represent the "true meaning of $2 + 2 = 4$."

Even if it were possible to define an S-type DTD for a certain branch of mathematics, this still presents problems.   Supposing an S-type DTD contains an element for a "derivative" of a function. Since the S-type DTD will not contain any presentational attributes, a decision will have to be made to represent the derivative of $f(x)$ on paper as $f'(x)$ or $\frac{df(x)}{dx}$. There are, however, times (such as in this book) that both representations are required for the same semantical object, and that the author will need other notation in addition to that defined by the S-type DTD.

A reason for the belief that an S-type DTD is possible, is that many people in the worlds of document processing or computer science are convinced that each symbol has at most a few possible uses and that mathematical notation is as straightforward to analyze as, for example, a piece of code for a somewhat complicated programming language - the reality is that mathematical notation is more akin to natural language: it is ambiguous and incomplete, as I pointed out earlier.

This does not mean that finding an S-type DTD is not a worthwhile endeavor, or that something less ambitious could not be made: it may be possible to create a limited S-type DTD based on an input language to a mathematical manipulation system (see 22.6).

22.5 Some problems with existing mathematics DTDs

To show that it is not obvious to capture mathematical syntax in a DTD, let alone its syntax, consider the example of a limit

$$\lim_{x \to a} f(x)$$

The syntactical structure of a limit consists of four parts:

1. The limit operator.

2. The part containing the variable and its limit.

3. The expression of which the limit is to be taken.

4. The expression of which the limit is to be taken.

The first part could:

• always be "lim," in which case it is just a part of the presentation of the formula and it should be left out;

• be one of a finite list of alternatives, indicating the type of limit (lim inf, sup, max, etc.), in which case it should be an attribute;

• be any expression;

• be any text.

I think the second possibility comes closest to the syntax of the limit construct. The second and third parts can be any mathematical expression.

There are three DTDs currently in use for describing mathematical formulas:

1. the mathematics DTD in ISO/TR 9573:1988 [7];

2. the "AAP" mathematics DTD recommended by ANSI/NISO Z39.59–1988 [8];

3. the mathematics DTD proposed by the Euromath project [9].

Let's look at the way this formula is coded with the DTDs from ISO/TR 9573:1988, AAP maths and Euromath, respectively. Using the mathematics DTD from ISO/TR 9573:1988 there are three possibilities:

• `lim <sub pos=mid> x &rarr; a </sub> f(x)`

- `<plex><operator>lim</operator><from>x &darr; a`
  `</from><of>f(x)</of></plex>`

- `<mfn name=lim><sub pos=mid>x &rarr; a </sub>`
  `<of>f(x)</of></mfn>`

The AAP maths DTD strongly suggests the following representation:

- `<lim><op><rf>lim</rf></op><ll>x &rarr; a</ll>`
  `<opd>f(x)</opd></lim>`

With the Euromath DTD we would have:

- `<lim.cst><l.part.c limitop=limm><range><relation>x`
  `\&rarr; a</relation></range></l.part.c><r.part.c>`
  `<textual>f(x)</textual>`

The AAP and Euromath expressions are closest to the limit-syntax. The best solution from ISO/TR 9573:1988 involves a more general "plex" construct, which can be used for integrals, sums, products, set unions, limits, and others. When the plex construct contains the actual lower and upper bounds it may even give semantic information. Mathematicians, however, are not completely satisfied with this solution.

The plex operation is probably a notation for an iterated application of a binary operation (e.g., sums and products), while limits are of a different nature. In many cases only the from part will be used, and there the whole range of the bound variable will be indicated, as an interval or a more general set. How does one go about extracting the bound variable?

This supports the conjecture from the previous section, namely that it is very hard to capture the semantics for all mathematics. It also suggests that some redundancy is required to select whichever notation is most appropriate in a certain context.

It also shows that no one of the three existing DTDs for mathematics is suitable for using as an S-type or a P-type DTD, which is not surprising since they were not designed to do so. Their hybrid approach, however, is fraught with ambiguities.

22.6 Re-using mathematical formulas

There are two important uses for a generically coded mathematical formula. The first one is in a mathematical manipulation — or computer algebra — system (MMS), such as Mathematica or Maple [10]. Computer programs for the numerical evaluation of formulas, for example, written in FORTRAN or Modula-2, can also be regarded as mathematical manipulation programs.

The second form of re-usage is in a mathematical typesetting system, for formatting the formula on paper or on screen; examples of this are TₑX and EQN.

For computer algebra systems the notation for the formula should be such that a particular type of manipulation on a particular system is possible, given a "background" of concepts and assumptions that enables the system to interpret the input as a mathematical statement.

The coding of a formula that is adequate for document formatting, for example the TₑX notation `f^{(2)} (x)`, is very unlikely to contain much of the information required for a manipulation system to make use of it. However, for a limited field of discourse it is feasible to use the same coding for both types of system.

Some examples: the square of $\sin x$ is typographically represented as $\sin^2 x$, but a system like Mathematica or Maple would probably prefer something like $(\sin x)^2$ as input. Typesetting the inverse of $\sin x$ as $\sin^{-1} x$, however, could be confusing: does it mean $1/(\sin x)$ or $\arcsin x$?

An MMS would probably require the second derivative of a function f with respect to its argument x to be coded as $(D, x)((D, x), f(x))$, but on paper this would be represented as $f''(x)$, or $f^{(2)}(x)$, or

$$\frac{\mathrm{d}^2 f(x)}{\mathrm{d}x^2}$$

On the output side of a MMS there are other problems since some of the coding necessary for typographically acceptable output cannot be automatically derived by the system from the coding used by the MMS.

A common interface should be designed together with the manufacturer of a MMS. Perhaps an MMS-type DTD will be required.

22.7 The harmonized math effort

I have argued as follows:

1. A logical DTD in the sense of describing the structure of the mathematical meaning is as impossible for maths as it is for natural language, and also it is useless for formatting since the same mathematical structure can be visually represented in many different ways. The correct one for any given occurrence of that structure cannot be determined automatically, but must be specified by the author.

2. What needs to be encoded for formatting purposes is information that enables a particular set of detailed rules for maths typesetting to be applied. This could be described as a "generic-visual encoding" or "encoding the logic of the visual structure."

3. This is different to what needs to be encoded for use in mathematical manipulation software. Since neither of these encodings can be

deduced automatically from the other, a useful database will need to store both. Perhaps a separate DTD will be required to enable this communication.

In 1991, the AAP maths update committee was established. It had as goal the design of a harmonized mathematics DTD that would replace the three existing ones. The result of this committee is the mathematics DTD which is now part of ISO 12083:1993 [11]. The reasoning and conclusions above were an important influence on the design of the harmonized mathematics DTD, which is a pure P-type DTD.

Formulas are considered to be a linear string of objects, with arguments and limits of limits, integrals, sums, and so on, all described by embellishments on a sub-formula. As an example, consider the limit example of above, using the ISO 12083:1993 mathematics DTD:

```
<subform><roman>lim</roman></subform><bottom>x &rarr;
a</bottom> f(x)
```

22.8 Conclusions

Although a pure P-type DTD will enable at least the translation of formulas between different word processors and into Braille, the harmonized math DTD does not solve all problems.

For example, mathematics is by its nature extensible, so there will always be new types of manipulations to be done. Notations are changed or new notations are invented almost every day, figuratively speaking. Normally these new subjects will use existing typographic representations, but the computer algebra system will not know what formatting to use! Occasionally a new typographic convention will be needed. And although there is agreement on the notation for most mathematical concepts, authors of books on mathematics tend to introduce alternative notations: for instance, when they feel this is necessary for didactic reasons. Mathematical notation is not standardized, and it is open — anyone can use it, and add to it, in any way they wish.

This problem, however, may not be a serious one. The collection of style elements is almost a closed set, since the number of fonts, symbols, and ways to combine them is limited. In fact, most notation is not syntactically new, since the limited number of constructs works well as a notation. The multitude of notations is obtained by combinations of fonts, symbols, and positions (left or right subscript, left or right superscript, atop, below, ...), and by giving one notation more than one meaning. This again seems to support the view that only a P-type DTD can be constructed for *all* of mathematics.

Another problem is that an SGML DTD of whatever type doesn't solve the problems of new atomic or composite symbols that occur frequently in mathematics. As with new elements, an author can add entities for these new symbols. There is no method to add the name of a new symbol, whether atomic or composite, to an existing set of entity definitions for symbols, other than to contact the owner of the set and wait for an update. (The DTDs in ISO12083:1993 recommend use of the public entity sets defined in ISO/TR 9573 part 13.)

The idea of viewing a formula as a linear string of encodable objects could be worked out further. Limits and integrals can also be seen as such, and perhaps there are other objects that can be seen as fundamental constructs like a fraction with a denominator and a numerator. (These could be seen as embellishments.) By expanding this idea, one could perhaps arrive at a unification based on structural logic, that is, a single construct for all visual maths properties. Perhaps this logic may then be translated into some other notation that would allow calculation.

Tables and matrices are still a problem. A generalized case for tables could be made by a concatenation and deconcatenation operator in both horizontal and vertical directions. Eventually a matrix will be part of a table logic, not the other way around. This idea will also be expanded later, in the course of the AAP Tables update committee.

Finally, there is the question of two dimensional objects, such as commutative diagrams. This problem is also related to that of tables. SGML is very good at describing tree like objects, but less good at describing things that have more dimensions. One can, for example, map a table into a tree that has rows as its branches and columns as its nodes. You could, however, also map (the same) table into a tree with columns as its branches and cells as its nodes. The user may want both descriptions, and yet SGML forces us to make a choice. This is probably the limit of SGML's applicability.

22.9 Bibliography for Chapter 22

The material from this chapter has been adapted from [1]. I am grateful to my co-authors and EPSIG for being able to use this material.

[1] N.A.F.M. Poppelier, E. van Herwijnen and C.A. Rowley
     Standard DTDs and Scientific Publishing, EPSIG News, Pages 10–19
     September 1992
[2] M. Abramowitz, I. Stegun
     Handbook of Mathematical Functions
     Dover, New York, 1972
[3] I.S. Gradshteyn, I.M. Ryzhik
     Table of integrals, series and products
     Academic Press, New York, 1980

[4]   S. Wolfram
      Mathematica: a system for doing mathematics by computer
      Addison-Wesley, Reading, 1991
[5]   N.M. Soiffer
      The design of a user interface for computer algebra systems
      Ph. D. Thesis, University of California, Berkeley, 1991
[6]   M. Nakahara
      Geometry, Topology and Physics
      Adam Hilger, Bristol, 1990
[7]   ISO
      ISO TR 9573:1988, Techniques for using SGML, chapter 8
      Geneva, 1988
[8]   ANSI/NISO
      ANSI/NISO Z39.59–1988, Standard for Electronic Manuscript
      Preparation and Markup
      Bethesda, 1988
[9]   B.von Sydow
      On the math type in Euromath
      Gothenburg, 1991
[10] B.W. Char, K.O. Geddes, G.H. Gonnet and S.M. Watt
      Maple User's Guide
      WATCOM Publications Ltd, Waterloo, 1985
[11] ISO
      ISO 12083:1993, Information and Documentation — Electronic
      Manuscript Preparation and Markup
      Geneva, 1993

23. Graphics and SGML

In this chapter I discuss how it is possible to use SGML to describe graphics objects. This is of rather academic interest, as the recommended way of including graphics is via NOTATION. SGML is an inefficient language to describe graphics, even if there is an editor. The interest for using SGML to describe graphics could be as an intermediate language for format conversion (see [1]).

D. Chamberlin and C. Goldfarb have presented some graphic applications of SGML [2]. The CGM notation contains primitives which are used to describe any graphical object (e.g. LINE, POLYGON and CIRCLE). It is easy to write down a DTD which includes these primitives as elements.

The Graphical Kernel System(GKS) [3] has primitives which look like those of CGM (POLYLINE, POLYMARKER, TEXT, FILL AREA, CELL AREA, and GENERALIZED DRAWING PRIMITIVES (GDPs)). In the GKS implementation of GTS-GRAL [4] five GDPs exist: CIRCLE, ARC, ELLIPSIS, BEZIER CURVE, ELLIPTICAL ARC and CUBIC CURVE. A DTD for this implementation is shown in the following example:

```
<!ENTITY  % Grafel "Polyline|Polymark|Text|Fillarea|Cellarea|Circle|Arc
                    |Ellipsis|Elliparc|Bezier|Cubic"               >
<!ELEMENT   Figure   - - (Picture, Figcap?)                        >
<!ELEMENT   Figcap   - O (#PCDATA)                                 >
<!ELEMENT   Picture  - - (%Grafel;| Grafgrp)*                      >
<!ATTLIST   Picture      WINDOW      CDATA      '0,0;1000,1000'
                         WIDTH       CDATA      '6In'               >
<!ELEMENT  (Grafdefn|Grafgrp) - - (%Grafel;| Grafgrp)*             >
<!ATTLIST   Grafdefn     id          ID         #REQUIRED          >
<!ATTLIST   Grafgrp      Defn        IDREF      #CONREF            >
<!ELEMENT   Polyline - - (Coor,Nextcoor+)                          >
<!ATTLIST   Polyline     type  (solid|dashed|dotted|dash-dot) solid
                         width       NMTOKEN    #IMPLIED
                         red         NMTOKEN    #IMPLIED
                         blue        NMTOKEN    #IMPLIED
                         green       NMTOKEN    #IMPLIED           >
<!ELEMENT   Polymark - - (Coor,Nextcoor*)                          >
<!ATTLIST   Polymark     type  (Point|Plus|Asterisk|Circle|Cross) Cross
                         size        CDATA      #IMPLIED
                         red         NMTOKEN    #IMPLIED
                         blue        NMTOKEN    #IMPLIED
                         green       NMTOKEN    #IMPLIED           >
<!ELEMENT   Text     - - (Coor,#PCDATA)                            >
<!ATTLIST   Text         font        CDATA      #IMPLIED
                         precision   (string|char|stroke)   #IMPLIED
                         red         NMTOKEN    #IMPLIED
```

```
                        blue            NMTOKEN    #IMPLIED
                        green           NMTOKEN    #IMPLIED
                        height          NMTOKEN    #IMPLIED
                        upvector        CDATA      #IMPLIED
                        expansion       CDATA      #IMPLIED
                        path            (right|up|left|down) right
                        horalign  (hnormal|left|centre|right) #IMPLIED
                        veralign   (vnormal|top|cap|half|base|bottom)
                                                          #IMPLIED
                        spacing         NMTOKEN    "0.0"          >
<!ELEMENT   Fillarea  - - (Coor,Nextcoor,Nextcoor+)                >
<!ATTLIST   Fillarea    istyle   (hollow|solid|pattern|hatch) hollow
                        size            NUMBER     #IMPLIED
                        hstyle          CDATA      #IMPLIED
                        prefpoin        CDATA      #IMPLIED
                        red             NMTOKEN    #IMPLIED
                        blue            NMTOKEN    #IMPLIED
                        green           NMTOKEN    #IMPLIED
                        patarray        CDATA      #IMPLIED        >
<!ELEMENT   Celarray  - - (#PCDATA)                                >
<!ELEMENT   Circle    - O EMPTY                                    >
<!ATTLIST   Circle      center          CDATA      '0,0'
                        radius          NUMBER     '100'           >
<!ELEMENT   Arc       - O EMPTY                                    >
<!ATTLIST   Arc         CENTER          CDATA      '0,0'
                        ip              CDATA      '0,1'
                        mp              CDATA      '1,0'
                        fp              CDATA      '0,-1'          >
<!ELEMENT   Ellipsis  - O EMPTY                                    >
<!ATTLIST   Ellipsis    CENTER          CDATA      '0,0'
                        xlength         CDATA      '10'
                        ylength         CDATA      '100'           >
<!ELEMENT   Elliparc  - O EMPTY                                    >
<!ATTLIST   Elliparc    center          CDATA      '0,0'
                        xlength         CDATA      '10'
                        ylength         CDATA      '100'
                        irad            CDATA      '0'
                        frad            CDATA      '90'
                        rotation        CDATA      '0'             >
<!ELEMENT   Bezier    - O EMPTY                                    >
<!ATTLIST   Bezier      dimension  (2,3,4,5,6,7,8,9,10,11) 2
                        points    CDATA '(.5,.5),(.8,.8)'          >
<!ELEMENT   Cubic     - O EMPTY                                    >
<!ATTLIST   Cubic       dimension       NUMBER     2
                        points    CDATA '(.1,.5),(.3,.8)'          >
<!ELEMENT   Coor      - - (X,Y)                                    >
<!ELEMENT   Nextcoor  - - (X,Y)                                    >
<!ELEMENT   X         - - #PCDATA                                  >
<!ELEMENT   Y         - - #PCDATA                                  >
<!--        entity-name contents                                 -->
```

```
<!ENTITY    MAP1       "<Coor><X><!USEMAP MAP-INX>"                      >
<!ENTITY    MAP2       "</X><Y><!USEMAP MAP-INY>"                        >
<!ENTITY    MAP3       "</Y></Coor><!USEMAP MAP-INPO>"                   >
<!ENTITY    MAP4       "<Nextcoor><X>!USEMAP MAP-INX1>"                  >
<!ENTITY    MAP5       "</X><Y><!USEMAP MAP-INY1>"                       >
<!ENTITY    MAP6       "</Y></Nextcoor><!USEMAP MAP-INPO>"               >
<!--        mapname     delimiter             entity-name             -->
<!SHORTREF MAP-X        "("            MAP1                              >
<!SHORTREF MAP-INX      ","            MAP2                              >
<!SHORTREF MAP-INY      ")"            MAP3                              >
<!SHORTREF MAP-INPO     ","            MAP4                              >
<!SHORTREF MAP-INX1     ","            MAP5                              >
<!SHORTREF MAP-INY1     ")"            MAP6                              >
<!--        mapname     element                                       -->
<!USEMAP    MAP-X       Polyline                                         >
<!USEMAP    MAP-IN      To                                               >
<!USEMAP    MAP-INFR    From                                             >
<!USEMAP    MAP-INPA    P                                                >
<!USEMAP    MAP-INQU    Q                                                >
<!USEMAP    MAP-INCL    Close                                            >
```

Using this DTD, the document instance describing the bicycle in Figure 92 is shown in the example below:

```
<Figure>
<Picture width='2I'>
<Grafdefn ID='BIKE'>
<Polyline>(0.60000005E-1,0.2350001),(0.9900006,0.2350001)
</Polyline>
<Polyline>(0.2150003,0.3550002),(0.2950001,0.5350002),(0.2950001,
0.5650002)
</Polyline>
<Polyline>(0.2950001,0.5450002),(0.5950003,0.5450003),(0.5950003,
0.5450003)
</Polyline>
<Polyline>(0.5450004,0.5650004),(0.5950003,0.5450003),(0.6150002,
0.5450003),
   (0.6150002,0.5650004),(0.5350003,0.5650004)</Polyline>
<Polyline>(0.2950001,0.5650002),(0.2850001,0.5650002),(0.2750002,
0.5750002),
(0.2750002,0.5850003),(0.2850001,0.5950004),(0.2850001,0.5950004),
(0.3050002,0.5950004),(0.3050002,0.5950004),(0.3150002,0.5950004),
(0.3150002,0.5950004)</Polyline>
<Circle center='0.215,0.355' radius='0.12'>
<Circle center='0.655,0.355' radius='0.12'>
<Polyline>(0.4450003,0.3550003),(0.4450003,0.3050003),(0.4550002,
0.3050003),
(0.4350003,0.3050003),(0.4350003,0.3050003)</Polyline>
<Polyline>(0.4450003,0.3550003),(0.4450003,0.4050002),(0.4550002,
0.4050002),
```

```
(0.4350003,0.4050002)</Polyline>
<Polyline>(0.5450004,0.5650004),(0.6150002,0.5650004),(0.6150002,
0.5450003),
(0.5950003,0.5450003),(0.5450004,0.5650004),(0.5450004,0.5650004)
</Polyline>
<Polyline>(0.4450003,0.3550003),(0.2850002,0.5150003)</Polyline>
<Polyline>(0.4450003,0.3550003),(0.6550004,0.3550003),
(0.5850003,0.5450003),(0.4550003,0.3550003)</Polyline>
<Polyline>(0.2750002,0.6050004),(0.2750002,0.5900003),(0.2850002,
0.5900003),
(0.2900002,0.5950004),(0.2850002,0.6050004),(0.2750002,0.6050004),
(0.2750002,0.6050004)</Polyline>
<Polyline>(0.2650001,0.5550003),(0.2650001,0.5250002),(0.2850001,
0.5250002),
(0.2950001,0.5350002),(0.2850001,0.5550003),(0.2650001,0.5550003)
</Polyline>
<Circle center='0.445,0.355' RADIUS='.031'>
</Grafdefn>
</Picture>
<Figcap>Bicycle picture
</Figure>
```

I added some short reference mappings which will enable the parser to do additional checking on the number of coordinates. The ones I added work for the Polymark element but they can be extended analogously for Polymark, Text, and Fillarea. By fully exploiting SGML the structure can be checked in detail before handing the data on to be processed. The x and y elements make it easy to map the elements onto the GKS Fortran routines from [4] with correct arguments. The mapping between elements and the GKS Fortran subroutine calls is shown in Table 44.

Table 44. The mapping from the GKS DTD to GTS-Gral Fortran routines

element/ attribute	name	GKS fortran equivalent

element	polyline	`REAL COORX(n) COORY(n)`
		`COORX(n) = #PCDATA`
		`COORY(n) = #PCDATA`
		`CALL GPL(n,COORX,COORY)`

attribute	type	`CALL GSLN(type)`
	width	`CALL GSLWSC(width)`
	colour	`CALL GSPLCI(colour index)`

element/ attribute	name	GKS fortran equivalent

element	polymark	`REAL PX(n) PY(n)`
		`PX(n) = #PCDATA`
		`PY(n) = #PCDATA`
		`CALL GPL(n,PX,PY)`

attribute	type	`CALL GSMK(type)`
	size	`CALL GSMKSC(size)`
	colour	`CALL GSPLCI(colour index)`

element	text	`CHARACTER*(*) string`
		`COORX = #PCDATA`
		`COORY = #PCDATA`
		`CALL GTX(COORX,COORY,string)`

attribute	font, precision	`CALL GSXFTP(text font, text` `  precision)`
	expansion	`CALL GSCHXP(expansion)`
	colour	`CALL GSTXCI(colour index)`
	spacing	`CALL GSCHSP(spacing)`
	up vector	`CALL GSCHUP(upvect.x,upvect.y)`
	path	`CALL GSTXP(text path)`
	height	`CALL GSCHH(height)`

element	fillarea	`REAL COORX(n) COORY(n)`
		`COORX(n) = #PCDATA`
		`COORY(n) = #PCDATA`
		`CALL GFA(N,COORX,COORY)`

attribute	istyle	`CALL GSFAIS(inernal style)`
	style	`CALL GSFASI(style)`
	colour	`CALL GSFASI(colour index)`

Using this mapping results in the Fortran program shown in the example below. To show how the values of the data are I have filled them through data statements rather than through a loop.

```
      PROGRAM BIKE
C *** Draw POLYLINE/MARKER/TEXT. Use default coordinate system
C      World is a unit square
C *** Fill in correct WKTYP
C *** Choose the LINE/MARKER TYPE/COLOUR you like
```

```
C *** Set up system for VM/CMS at CERN
      INCLUDE (GTSDEV)
      INCLUDE (ENUM)
      INTEGER ERRFIL, WKID, CONID, WKTYP
      PARAMETER( ERRFIL=13, WKID=1, CONID=1)
      INTEGER ASFLIST(13)
      REAL    PXA(2), PYA(2)
      REAL    PXB(3), PYB(3)
      REAL    PXC(3), PYC(3)
      REAL    PXD(5), PYD(5)
      REAL    PXE(10), PYE(10)
      REAL    PXF(5), PYF(5)
      REAL    PXG(4), PYG(4)
      REAL    PXH(2), PYH(2)
      REAL    PXI(4), PYI(4)
      REAL    PXJ(7), PYJ(7)
      REAL    PXK(6), PYK(6)
      CHARACTER*1 STR
C *** set aspect source flags to recommended value
      DATA    ASFLIST /13*GINDIV /
      DATA    PXA / 0.60000005E-1,0.9900006 /
      DATA    PYA / 0.2350001,0.2350001 /
      DATA    PXB / 0.2150003,0.2950001,0.2950001 /
      DATA    PYB / 0.3550002,0.5350002,0.5650002 /
      DATA    PXC / 0.2950001,0.5950003,0.5950003/
      DATA    PYC / 0.5450002,0.5450003,0.5450003 /
      DATA    PXD / 0.5450004,0.5950003,0.6150002,0.6150002,0.5350003 /
      DATA    PYD / 0.5650004,0.5450003,0.5450003,0.5650004,0.5650004 /
      DATA    PXE / 0.2950001,0.2850001,0.2750002,0.2750002,0.2850001,
     +              0.2850001,0.3050002,0.3050002,0.3150002,0.3150002 /
      DATA    PYE / 0.5650002,0.5650002,0.5750002,0.5850003,0.5950004,
     +              0.5950004,0.5950004,0.5950004,0.5950004,0.5950004 /
      DATA    PXF / 0.4450003,0.4450003,0.4550002,0.4350003,0.4350003 /
      DATA    PYF / 0.3550003,0.3050003,0.3050003,0.3050003,0.3050003 /
      DATA    PXG / 0.4450003,0.4450003,0.4550002,0.4350003 /
      DATA    PYG / 0.3550003,0.4050002,0.4050002,0.4050002 /
      DATA    PXH / 0.4450003,0.2850002 /
      DATA    PYH / 0.3550003,0.5150003 /
      DATA    PXI / 0.4450003,0.6550004,0.5850003,0.4550003 /
      DATA    PYI / 0.3550003,0.3550003,0.5450003,0.3550003 /
      DATA    PXJ / 0.2750002,0.2750002,0.2850002,0.2900002,0.2850002,
     +              0.2750002,0.2750002 /
      DATA    PYJ / 0.6050004,0.5900003,0.5900003,0.5950004,0.6050004,
     +              0.6050004,0.6050004 /
      DATA    PXK / 0.2650001,0.2650001,0.2850001,0.2950001,0.2650001,
     +              0.2850001 /
      DATA    PYK / 0.5550003,0.5250002,0.5250002,0.5350002,0.5550003,
     +              0.5550003 /
      WRITE (5,*) 'Workstation type ?'
      READ (5,*) WKTYP
```

```
C *** Initialization
      OPEN( UNIT=ERRFIL,FORM='FORMATTED',STATUS='UNKNOWN')
C *** Open GKS
      CALL GOPKS(ERRFIL,0)
C *** Open the workstation
      CALL GOPWK(WKID,CONID,WKTYP)
C *** Activate the workstation
      CALL GACWK(WKID)
C *** Set aspect source flags
      CALL GSASF(ASFLIST)
C *** Set attributes and draw primitives
C *** line attributes
      CALL GSLN(GSOLI)
      CALL GSPLCI(3)
C *** draw lines
      CALL GPL(2,PXA,PYA)
      CALL GPL(3,PXB,PYB)
      CALL GPL(4,PXC,PYC)
      CALL GPL(5,PXD,PYD)
      CALL GPL(10,PXE,PYE)
      CALL GPL(5,PXF,PYF)
      CALL GPL(4,PXG,PYG)
      CALL GPL(2,PXH,PYH)
      CALL GPL(4,PXI,PYI)
      CALL GPL(7,PXJ,PYJ)
      CALL GPL(6,PXK,PYK)
C *** Draw circles
      CALL GUCIR2(0.215,0.355,0.12)
      CALL GUCIR2(0.655,0.355,0.12)
      CALL GUCIR2(0.445,0.355,0.031)
C *** Hold screen
      CALL GMSG(WKID,'Hit CR to Exit')
C *** request for input
      CALL GRQST(WKID,1,ISTAT,LSTR,STR)
C *** Termination
      CALL GDAWK(WKID)
      CALL GCLWK(WKID)
      CALL GCLKS
      CLOSE(UNIT=ERRFIL)
      END
```

Having the graphical dcata in one (high level) SGML source file enables an easy translation between CGM, GKS, Fortran and PostScript. Another advantage is that the data structure can be checked by an SGML parser.

This demonstrates that translating from SGML into another language can be done.

23.1 Bibiliography for Chapter 23

[1]   S.A. Mamrak, C.S. O'Connell and R.E. Parent
      The Automatic Generation of Translation Software for Graphic
      Objects, IEEE Computer Graphics & Applications, Pages 34–42
      november 1989
[2]   D.D.Chamberlin, C.F.Goldfarb
      Graphic Applications of the Standard Generalized Markup Lan-
      guage (SGML), Computing and Graphics, vol. 1, Pages 343–358
      1987
[3]   ISO
      ISO 7942:1984, Graphical Kernel System
      Geneva, 1984
[4]   GTS-GRAL GmbH
      GKSGRAL User and Reference Manual. Fortran. Fifth Edition
      Darmstadt, 1987

24. Other ISO text processing standards

24.1 SDIF

SDIF (SGML Document Interchange Format) is the standard (ISO 9069:1988) [2] for electronic text interchange.

SGML documents may consist of a number of separate parts such as document type definitions, external entity definitions, external documents, and external data. SGML does not say how to organize these parts. When interchanging documents the sender and receiver must be able to pack and reconstitute an entire document and process it.

The SDIF standard explains how to **pack** the parts associated with an SGML document into a single datastream with **descriptors** indicating how they are related to each other. The datastream is then encoded using the Abstract Syntax Notation 1 (ASN1, ISO 8824). It thus allows SGML to be compatible and used with the OSI layer-model network standards.

For example, if a document contains the declaration of an external entity, this entity is included with a descriptor in the data stream, linking the declaration with the entity text.

At the receiving end, an SDIF **unpacker** can determine from the descriptors which parts were external to the document before it was packed and reconstitutes the various files in a similar configuration to that of the sender. The integrity of the data is taken care of by SGML.

If the system is able to interchange documents by using SDIF, this is indicated by the **SDIF support** parameter in the SGML system declaration (see section 15.7). This parameter has subparameters PACK, UNPACK, NO, YES, and ASN1. To this day no commerically available SDIF packers/unpackers exist. SDIF is probably not a requirement for most in-house SGML implementations.

24.2 DSSSL

24.2.1 Background

Although SGML provides the language for modeling a class of document, the standard does not prescribe any particular model or predefined tag set. The use of SGML to describe a class of document (or tag set) is known as an SGML application and consists of a DTD to describe the document and its supporting documentation. Only within an SGML application do the defined elements have meaning. SGML, however, does not provide a standardized mechanism for describing what to do with (the processing information for) these elements in the document, thus allowing association of various processing semantics. (Note that the SGML LINK feature provides a basic technique for attaching processing information to SGML elements, but does not standardize the meaning of this information, nor is it robust enough to handle complex formatting instructions.)

DSSSL, the Document Style Semantics and Specification Language (ISO DIS 10179:1991 [3]), provides the language for standardizing the specification of this processing information associated with an SGML document, concentrating on formatting information. A DSSSL specification is external to the SGML document to which it applies, and thus multiple specifications can be applied to a given SGML document, allowing for various presentations of the same data. DSSSL achieves this through tree-to-tree transformations. A "complete" package for interchange can be thought of as the document instance (the data themselves), its DTD (the rules for its structure and content), and its DSSSL specification (the rules for how the data is to be processed).

The processing semantics standarized by DSSSL focus on formatting, that is, typography, composition, and layout, but the standard is designed to allow for development of other standardized processing semantics. This is achieved by providing for three distinct areas of standardization:

1. A query language for addressing into an SGML document, known as location models. The language is based on navigation through a hierarchical structure of objects based on object types, object attributes, and relationships of objects within the tree.

2. A model and language for transformation of one SGML document into another SGML document, known as the General Language Transformation Process (GLTP). The GLTP provides transformation functions that are independent of the processing semantics that are to be applied, such as suppression, replication, reordering, and regrouping of objects.

3. A model and language for application of formatting semantics, known as the Semantic-Specific Process (SSP). The SSP provides a means of describing the "final result" for the formatted document without standardizing formatting algorithms.

24.2.2 DSSSL Design Goals

The scope of DSSSL covers the full range of functionality required for all types of publishing applications, from simple word processing, to desktop publishing, to complex book layout and printing, to on-screen presentation. DSSSL models and languages are not biased toward any particular publishing application or national language.

DSSSL is designed to allow for specifications that apply to a class of documents, that is, that are applicable to all the possible document instances in an SGML application as well as specifications that are specific to a particular document instance. DSSSL location models allow for identification of a set of like objects in the tree as well as for identification of a specific object.

Location models provide for access to, and thus control of, all possible marked-up information in the document. In addition, mechanisms for string processing allow for manipulation of non-marked-up data, such as a simple character to be presented at the beginning of the first line of a paragraph, so that no special "markers" for indicating presentation changes are necessary in the source document.

The DSSSL specification language is declarative; it is not a "programming language." DSSSL specifications can be unambiguously parsed and interpreted among heterogenous systems. In addition, DSSSL specifications can be used by existing formatting systems through the use of "front-end" DSSSL processors and translators. DSSSL has no bias toward batch or WYSIWYG formatting systems and does not prescribe any predefined formatting algorithms.

DSSSL provides a mechanism for specifying the use of "external processes" not governed by the DSSSL specification to manipulate data. The nature of these processes is outside the scope of DSSSL but may include typical data management functions, such as indexing, typical composition functions, such as specialized hyphenation algorithms, and graphics or multimedia processes for non-SGML-encoded data.

The standardization of formatting semantics is provided in DSSSL through a set of basic primitives known as properties. Since these properties are intended for programmatic manipulation, they may not reflect what endusers commonly expect to see as formatting specifications. DSSSL provides mechanisms for defining and extending both syntax and semantic constructs so that a DSSSL application designer can construct a DSSSL application in a manner that best reflects his/her idea of a "stylesheet."

24.2.3 DSSSL processing model and specifications

An example of the DSSSL processing model and interaction of specifications is illustrated in Figure 106.

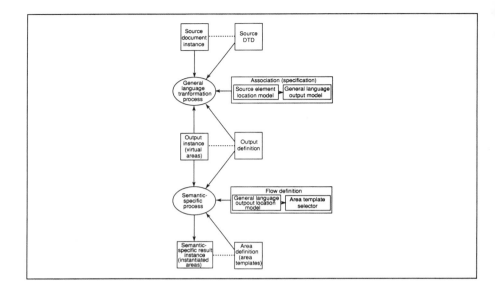

Figure 106. Example of the DSSSL Processing Model and Specifications

A DSSSL specification consists of four major parts:

- output definition;
- association specification;
- area definition;
- flow specification.

24.2.4 *Contents of a DSSSL document*

A DSSSL document contains:

1. The SGML source, corresponding to the structure of the source DTD.

2. The DTD corresponding to the virtual, intermediate document which is the result of the general language transformation.

3. The DSSSL specification, associating to each logical element its semantics according to the DSSSL document architecture.

In addition, there are other supporting parts of the specification that allow, for example, user definition of the concrete syntax to be used in the rest of the specifications.

While the GLTP and SSP are shown as two independent processes, there is no requirement that they be so. It is up to any particular implementation to determine how the various parts of the specification are processed. The key point is that processing specified in the association specification is intended for consumption by the GLTP without requiring any "feedback" from the SSP.

24.2.5 *General language transformation process (GLTP)*

To reiterate, the GLTP transforms the SGML source instance into the output instance, performing operations that do not require knowledge of the SSP (formatter). These operations include suppression, replacement, replication, reordering, regrouping, and annotation of source objects as well as generation of new objects in the output instance. In performing these operations, both the content and the structure of the source document can be modified.

The format of the output instance is not standardized by DSSSL because there is no requirement that it ever be instantiated.

The importance and use of the GLTP will vary based on the SGML application, DSSSL application, capabilities of the SSP (formatter), and implementation. For example, when the order of objects in the source instance lends itself well to the order in which the objects are to be formatted, the GLTP may not be called upon to perform reordering. The GLTP is intended to be used as a tool to prepare the document content for straightforward processing by the SSP.

Inputs to the GLTP include the source instance and its associated DTD, the output definition and the association specification. The output of the GLTP is either an output instance in a form dictated by the implementation, or, if the implementation chooses not to distinguish between the GLTP and SSP, a communication of the results of transformation to the SSP.

The output definition defines the possible objects and structure that can occur in the output instance. It has the same syntax and semantics as an SGML DTD. Results of transformation must comply with the rules for the hierarchy as defined in the output definition. The output definition is used to validate the output instance as you would with any SGML document instance.

The association specification consists of a set of associations. Each association specifies the transformation of a set (possibly one) of like objects in the source instance into a set (possibly one) of objects in the output instance. Key to this transformation is that not only can objects be mapped to a definitive location in the output instance, they can also be mapped to a location dependent on the result of transforming some other source object. In this way, associations are interdependent and allow for use of source instance structure information as input to the transformation. In addition, new objects can be created and objects in the output instance can be annotated with information useful to the SSP.

24.2.6 *Semantic-specific process (SSP)*

The SSP is the process that applies the standardized formatting semantics to the output instance to create the semantic-specific result instance (SSRI), which can be thought of as one possible form of the formatted document. These operations include what are commonly thought of as composition, layout, and style.

The SSP is based on the following concepts:

1. The objects in the SSRI are either areas of glyph areas (see section 24.4).

2. Areas have hierarchical structure, with glyph areas always as a leaf of the tree (a glyph area is a terminal node).

3. Areas in the SSRI have a set of properties and values that completely specify their size, shape, position, and display attributes. These properties are defined by DSSSL.

4. The formatter determines the values of properties based on attributes and values associated with the input objects. Attribute values "constrain" the decisions a formatter can make in determining property values. At the most sophisticated level of conformance for DSSSL, the DSSSL specification designer can provide multiple set of attributes, each weighted, to give the formatter more or less room to make decisions.

The lower levels of conformance are much more like a traditional "stylesheet" approach with style properties and their values as the specification. In this instance the formatter has more control over the results.

The value of attributes can range from known quantities (e.g., 4 picas) to complex expressions involving references to attributes on other input objects and resolved property values on areas created by the formatter.

Inputs to the SSP are the area definition and the flow specification. The format of the SSRI is not standardized by DSSSL, however: in whatever form the formatter decides to instantiate the SSRI, it must represent the optimal resolution of attribute values into property values based on the designer's designated weights. Possible instantiated forms of the SSRI might be an SPDL document or device-specific document suitable for rendering on a laser printer or some sort of file ready for screen presentation.

The area definition provides a "template" for the areas that can occur in the SSRI. It is *not* an SGML DTD, but can describe the desired structure of the formatted document. It describes which areas can occur within other areas and how many times they can be instantiated. In addition, attributes can be attached to areas that must be resolved into properties each time the area is instantiated.

The flow specification describes how objects from the output instance are mapped into areas in the SSRI. The flow specification is a collection of flow rules. Each flow rule specifies the mapping of some set (possibly one) of like objects in the output instance into some area in the SSRI. In conjunction with the area definition, the flow rule specifies the parameters under which the formatter must create new areas. In addition, attributes can be attached to flow rules that must be resolved into properties when the objects are mapped.

This is somewhat analogous to an association, but there is a critical difference. In the GLTP, the DSSSL specification designer can precisely control the structure of the output instance. In the SSP, it is the formatter that makes the final decisions, and the specification designer provides only the information necessary for the formatter to make those decisions.

Areas are rectangular. The properties specified for instantiated areas include the following:

• A coordinate system used to express the locations of points within the area. A z-axis is defined for resolving transparency and opacity for overlaid areas.

• X, Y, and Z coordinates to locate an area within another area.

• The extent of the area in X and Y directions (width and height).

• A set-to shape and clipping mask to determine the allowed areas where glyphs can be placed in the area. This allows for non-rectangular placement of content.

• Font (uses font referencing as defined by ISO/IEC 9541).

• Parameters for determining the mapping of a character to its proper glyph.

• Character display attributes, such as upper case or small caps.

• Background and foreground color and opacity.

• Parameters for specifying screens and tints.

Attributes used within DSSSL specifications are defined in terms of how they affect the resolution of property values. All properties are also attributes, and their effect is a one-to-one assignment of value. Attributes are defined to allow specifying the effect on multiple properties with a single attribute specification. A set of attributes is defined in ISO 10179 such as width (to affect x-extent), alignment (to affect positioning), and quadding (to affect positioning). In addition, DSSSL allows for user-definition of attributes that can be defined in terms of their affect on properties. Thus, for example, a DSSSL specification designer can define the meaning of "indent" for a given DSSSL application in terms of its effect on positioning.

24.2.7 Specification language tools

There are several constructs used throughout the DSSSL specification language. A general purpose computational language called Scheme [4] as defined by the IEEE language standard, provides typical mathematical and string-processing operations. In addition, special purpose functions specifically designed for use in a DSSSL specification have been added to the base language.

The query language is based on the conceptual model of a parsed SGML document represented as a tree structure. Within the tree, allowed node, or object, types are defined as well as attributes associated with each object. The baseline set of object types is element, attribute (SGML source attribute), data entity (non-SGML-encoded data), processing instruction, and character. Elements, attributes, and entities have an object attribute of "name." Other object types and object attributes are defined for other SGML constructs. Object relationship are defined in terms of preorder traversal of the tree and include ancestor/parent, descendant/child, and preceding and following siblings. The query language allows full addressing into the tree through specification of desired object type, object attribute values, and relationships.

Dynamic mapping of characters to glyphs is provided through the definition of two tables specifying the mapping of character bit codes to generic characters and generic characters to glyphs. These tables can be associated with objects in the output instance or SSRI.

24.3 SPDL

24.3.1 Objectives

SPDL - the standard page description language defines "a language for the specification of electronic documents, comprised of black and white, gray scale, or full color text, images, and geometric graphics, in a form suitable for presentation (printing or displaying of other suitable media)." It is a final form document format, providing facilities for the efficient representation of the decisions made by the composition and layout process.

SPDL has much in common with PostScript [6] and its predecessor Interpress[7]. In fact, Adobe and Xerox have dominated the standardization effort that resulted in SPDL. It defines a machine-independent means of describing documents comprised of text and graphical material, for presentation on paper or other media.

SPDL currently has the status of a draft international standard [5].

24.3.2 Structure

An SPDL document has *document structure* and *document content.* The SPDL document structure is hierarchical, the highest level being a **document**. A document may contain **pagesets** and **pages**. A page may contain **pictures** and **tokensequences**. A description of this structure in the form of an SGML DTD is provided with the draft standard.

The SPDL document structure is shown in Figure 107.

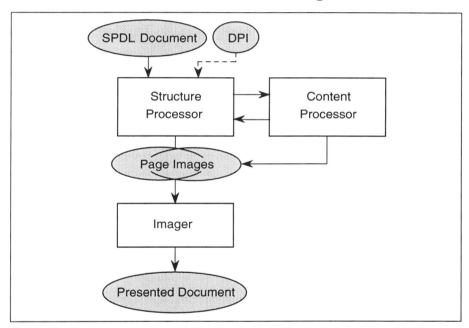

Figure 107. The SPDL Document Structure

The document content of an SPDL document is the data contained in tokensequence structures. Tokensequences have substructures that allow for rendering text, raster graphics and geometric graphics. The process of token interpretation is implemented via virtual state machines. Imaging activities are defined in terms of an imaging model that includes coordinate systems, inks, and a clipping region.

24.3.3 Processing

SPDL document processing is shown in Figure 108.

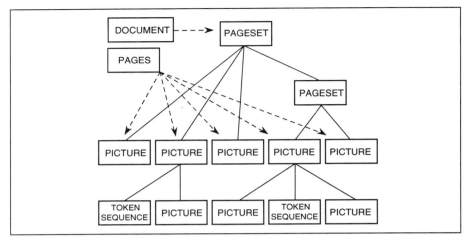

Figure 108. SPDL document processing

All formatting and page composition decisions are made by the layout and composition process, which could be a DSSSL formatter. This includes selection of fonts, positioning of characters on paper, rendering of graphics.

The presentation process is supposed to take the document in SPDL form and to render it within the constraints of the presentation medium so as to provide the best approximation to the description provided by the layout and composition process.

24.4 FONTS

24.4.1 *Founts*

A fount is a set of all characters in a particular typeface (and point size in hot metal; e.g., the font 10 point Times Roman belongs to the serif typeface Times, and the font 11 point Helvetica Italic belongs to the sans-serif typeface Helvetica).

In his book about "Methods of Book Design" Hugh Williamson [8] writes:

*To the printer, an alphabet is a set of twenty-six letters of a certain design and body, together with a few additional combinations of letters. A **fount** is usually made up of a set of alphabets of one size and based on one design. It may consist of one alphabet only, if no more alphabets exist in that design and size. Usually however a text fount will comprise five alphabets — roman and italic upper and lower-case, and small capitals.*

*A **series** is a set of founts closely related to each other in design, and usually very similar to each other, but graded in size. If only one* *alphabet has been made in a certain design, that alphabet alone may be a series. A **family** is a group of series compatible for composition, but loosely related in design. A family may include excerpts from more than one series.*

Nowadays the word **fount** (in American called **font**) is very often used in a more restricted sense, namely one physical series of characters of a given design (e.g 10 point Times Roman, as opposed to 10 point Times Roman Italic or Times Roman Bold). The same restricted definition is also used in the ISO 9541 font interchange standard. Historically it would be more correct to talk about the Times-Roman font (fount), consisting of all the different variants. To limit confusion in the following I shall use the name "fount" in this broader sense.

24.4.2 Glyphs

Over the centuries several schemes have been proposed to classify typefaces and founts. To facilitate this classification, one often speaks about **glyphs**. A glyph is a format independent representation of a shape into which a character has been transformed by the formatter.

A standard font resource architecture and a standard font interchange format are required to enable document interchange. The Font Information Interchange standard "defines a method of naming glyphs and glyph collections, independent of any document encoding technique; it assumes that one or more methods of associating document encoding techniques with glyph identifiers used in font resources will be provided by text processing systems." SPDL uses the structured names and font resource architecture as described by ISO 9541.

24.4.3 ISO 9541

In part 1 "Architecture" of ISO 9541 [9] a typeface design grouping scheme is proposed. Typefaces with similar appearance or common characteristics are grouped together using three levels: class, subclass and specific group. Part 2 of the standard defines the "interchange format" and Part 3 the "glyph shape representation."

24.5 HyTime

An example of SGML's openness is its application to hypertext. Hypertext makes accessing information that is referred to easier. For example, in a system comprising pieces of text, images, and other data you can jump from one place to another. These jumps, which may go outside a document, can be activated by **buttons**, and the connections between and within parts of documents are called **links**. SGML was not developed for hypertext, but turns out to be convenient for making documents into hyper-objects and to describe these links.

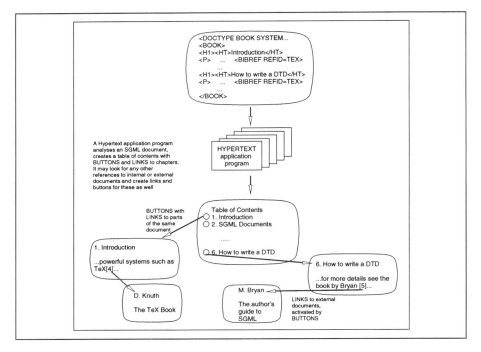

Figure 109. SGML and Hypertext

Making SGML files into hyper-objects can be done with *Dyna*Text [10], for example. *Dyna*Text is a hypertext product that 'eats' SGML, understands its logical structure (what are titles, what are figures, etc.) and has a powerful full-text indexing facility and query language. The SGML Tutorial [11] is an example of a *Dyna*text electronic book based on Practical SGML.

Early systems combined descriptive markup with hypertext. In the eighties, a standard way of describing hyperdocuments was required, and SGML seemed to be a good tool for the job. At the same time, a project was started to create the Standard Music Description Language (SMDL), an attempt to describe musical, time-based structures with SGML. The hypertext parts in SMDL were split off in a new ISO project called **Hytime**.

HyTime has now become ISO 10744:1992, and is the ISO standard [12] for structured representation of hypermedia and time-based information. A document is seen as a set of concurrent time-dependent events (audio, video, dance, music, etc.). Events are connected by webs of 'hyper-links' (see Figure 109.) Hyper-links are described by special addressing (objects outside the documents). HyTime uses SGML as the syntax for representing links. The data which is being linked, however, may exist in any format desired.

An excellent introductory book on HyTime is [13]. For more information on HyTime, contact the SIGhyper, the SGML User's group Special Interest Group on hypertext[14]. Some introductory literature may be found in the articles [15] and [16].

HyTime does not specify a single "HyTime document type definition" or a "HyTime document architecture." HyTime is defined as a set of rules, called architectural forms, that application designers can apply in their DTDs.

HyTime consists of several "modules" that may be used more or less arbitrarily depending on the facilities that are required. For example, there are modules which tell you how to define HyTime compatible elements in a DTD (via **architectural forms**), how to indicate the position of an object (**coordinates** and **markers**), and how to link various parts of a HyTime structure (**hyperlinks**). HyTime also has a query language, which permits you to create dynamic links to objects that change in time.

The following sections give an introduction on how to apply some simple HyTime constructs to your DTD.

24.5.1 *APPINFO parameter of SGML declaration*

The starting point of an interconnected system must be an SGML document using HyTime constructs, called the hub document. Conformance of a document to HyTime, and thus the ability of a document to become a hub is indicated by a parameter of the APPINFO parameter of the SGML declaration. Its format is:

```
APPINFO HyTime
```

All documents created with a HyTime DTD can become a hub by setting the APPINFO parameter to HyTime in the SGML declaration.

24.5.2 *Architectural forms*

HyTime facilities are integrated into SGML DTDs via the technique of architectural forms. An architectural form describes in abstract terms what an element should do, without specifically giving the element a name. It defines the rules for creating and processing elements (just as document architectures are rules for creating and processing documents). By giving the element an attribute with the name HyTime, with values that are specified by the HyTime standard, a HyTime system knows what action it should take.

As an example, consider four types of architectural forms, to indicate what the highest level in the element structure of a HyTime document is, to create links to internal parts of the document, links to external (non-machine readable) bibliography references, and links to external documents:

1. Usually, the highest level in the element structure of a HyTime document is the element which has the name of the document type. This element should conform to the **HyDoc** architectural form. This can be done by giving the HyTime attribute a fixed value HyDoc on the element. It requires the presence of the base module of HyTime.

2. For internal links, you could use existing elements for cross-references defined by your DTD. This can be done, for example, by adding the HyTime fixed attribute **clink**. Now all the cross reference elements conform to the contextual links (clink) architectural form. By adding unique identifier attributes (ID) to all elements that could be used as the end of a link (internal or external), you enable the creation of robust pointers thus making your documents accessible. These links require the presence of the base module and the hyperlinks module of HyTime.

3. A citation element, which describes a bibliographic entry, can be made to conform to **bibloc**. This is done by adding the HyTime fixed attribute bibloc. The references that they present are not expected to be accessed automatically, since they probably do not exist on a computer that is accessible. This requires the presence of the location address module.

4. HyTime provides a way of linking to anything that can be named as an entity or via an ID. This is accomplished by using the **nameloc** architectural form. The nameloc architectural form requires the presence of the location address module.

24.5.3 Location addresses and the nameloc architectural form

There are three broad ways in which objects can be addressed by a HyTime document:

1. By the name of an entity or a unique identifier (a "name"). These are name space locations.

2. By a coordinate position. These are coordinate locations. These positions require the presence of the measurement module.

3. By a semantic construct. These are semantic locations. These are for the description of information objects to which access can not be automated (the citation element uses the bibliographic location address).

To come back to point 1, name space locations are locations addressed by a name. They can consist of the following:

- entities;

- elements in another document with an ID;

- elements of this or another document without an ID;

- elements in this document that are not a location address, but that have an ID (that is why it is a good idea to give many elements unique identifier attributes, even if you are not (yet) thinking of using HyTime).

The nameloc element type form associates a local ID with the objects in the list above (entities, elements in other documents with IDs, elements without IDs). The content of the nameloc element is an unlimited number of namelist elements. The nameloc element has an ID attribute that is required. The content of a namelist element is #PCDATA, and it may contain entity or element names.

Imagine an SGML document called "manual.sgm" that you want to refer to from another document. You would add the following entity definition to your document:

```
<!ENTITY manual SYSTEM "manual.sgm">
```

This file would be included by adding the entity reference **&manual;** to your article. Defining the named location address for this entity would be achieved as follows:

```
<nameloc id=manlink>
<nmlist>
manual
</nmlist>
</nameloc>
```

Linking to this object is then achieved via any element of form clink (citeref in this example) with a reference to a unique identifier attribute (**rid** in this example):

```
<citeref rid=manlink>
```

If you want to define a named location address for elements which have a unique identifier, you can do this by giving the nametype attribute on the **nmlist** element the value "element". The following example defines a location name address for an element which has unique identifier **ID=chap1** in the same document:

```
<nameloc id=chaplink>
<nmlist nametype=element>
chap1
```

```
</nmlist>
</nameloc>
```

Again, linking to this element would be achieved via any element of form clink (the secref element in this example):

```
<secref rid=chaplink>
```

By giving the attribute **obnames** on the nmlist element the value obnames the addressed objects are treated as names, and the value of the nameloc is the entire element with ID=chap1. The default value is "nobnames" meaning that the content of the nameloc is the string "chap1".

You can go a step further and define location name addresses for objects that have unique identifiers inside manual.sgm. Suppose that the element with ID=chap1 exists inside manual.sgm, and you want to define a named location address for it. This is done by defining two consecutive name locations, one acting as a **source** for the other. This is done by using the **locsrc** attribute on the **nmlist** element as follows:

```
<nameloc id=chaplink>
<nmlist nametype=element obnames=obnames locsrc=source>
chap1
</nmlist>
</nameloc>
<nameloc id=source>
<nmlist nametype=entity obnames=obnames>
manual
</nmlist>
</nameloc>
```

This named location address can be linked to by a clink element (such as **citeref** in this example):

```
<citeref rid=chaplink>
```

The link is established as follows. The IDREF with value chaplink defines the end of the link to be the location address with unique id chaplink. This one, in turn, has its source in the nameloc with id source. This second nameloc contains an entity that is defined as manual.sgm. Since obnames is given, the entire document is returned. Then, in the first nameloc, the address is defined as the element with id chap1, which is found in the document manual.sgm. Since obnames is given, the entire chapter is returned to the citeref element for further processing.

24.5.4 HyTime conformance

To create **minimal hyperlinking** HyTime documents, the HyTime declarations corresponding to a minimal hyperlinking HyTime document should be added to your DTD:

```
<?HyTime VERSION "ISO/IEC 10744:1992" HYQNT=32>
<?HyTime MODULE base>
<?HyTime MODULE locs multiloc>
<?HyTime MODULE links>
```

24.6 Conclusions

When completed, SGML, DSSSL, SPDL, and FONTS will provide:

1. a standard way (SGML) to specify the logical structure of a class of documents, as well as a way to encode a document that is an instance of that class;

2. a standard way (DSSSL) to specify how documents in a given SGML class are to be represented visually;

3. a standard way (SPDL) to represent in the computer the concrete visualization of a specific document;

4. a standard way (FONTS) of referring to a font resource architecture and interchange format.

The way these standards interact is shown in Figure 110. See [17] for a more detailed description of their relationship. DSSSL is not yet a full international standard, and the complexity of a DSSSL specification prohibits its manual creation. DSSSL will therefore only be used when the appropriate formatters are available. At the time of the writing of this book, these systems seem still to be several years away.

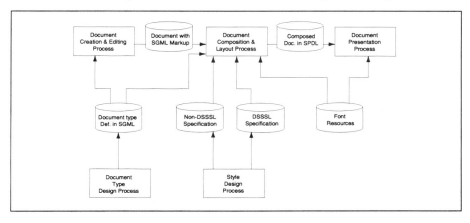

Figure 110. Text processing Model

Due to its close resemblance to existing page description languages, however, practical implementations of SPDL may appear on the market rather sooner than those of DSSSL. The font interchange standard is referred to by other standards such as DSSSL and SPDL.

In the meantime, this does *not* mean that SGML is unusable. It simply means that the way SGML is applied is not standard: all SGML products have their own system for translating the tags into a particular text formatter. Today, SGML users may already profit from the advantages in the area of portability, generic codes, independence of external appearance, and multiple uses of a single source document.

The HyTime standard is somewhat independent of the general text processing standards. It provides the basis for the construction of standardized hypertext systems, consisting of documents that apply the standards described above.

24.7 Bibliography for Chapter 24

The section on DSSSL was adapted from the article (N1427) written by Paula Angerstein for ISO/IEC JTC1/SC18/WG8 [1]. I am grateful to her for being able to use this material and to Sharon Adler for bringing it up to date.

[1]   P. Angerstein
      Summary of the Document Style Semantics and Specification
      Language (DSSSL), Draft International Standard 10179
      1991
[2]   ISO
      ISO 9069:1988, Information processing — SGML support facili-
      ties — SGML Document Interchange Format (SDIF)
      Geneva, 1988
[3]   ISO
      ISO DIS 10179, Information technology — Text and office sys-
      tems — Document Style Semantics and Specification Language
      (DSSSL)
      Geneva, 1991
[4]   C. Hanson
      MIT Scheme Reference Manual for Scheme Rel. 7.1.3
      Cambridge, November, 1991
[5]   ISO
      ISO DIS 10180, Information processing — Text Composition —
      Standard Page Description Language (SPDL)
      Geneva, 1991

[6] Adobe Systems Incorporated
PostScript Language Reference Manual, Second Edition
Addison-Wesley, Reading, 1990

[7] S.J. Harrington, R.R. Buckley
Interpress, the Source Book
a Brady Book, New York, 1988

[8] Hugh Williamson
Methods of Book Design, Third Edition
Yale University Press, New Haven, 1985

[9] ISO
ISO 9541–1:, Information technology — Font information interchange — Part 1: Architecture
Geneva, 1991

[10] Electronic Book Technologies
DynaText Tutorial, Release 2.0 for UNIX
Providence, 1993

[11] Eric van Herwijnen for Electronic Book Technologies
The SGML Tutorial
Providence, 1993

[12] ISO
ISO 10744:1992, Information technology — Hypermedia/Time-based Structuring Language (HyTime)
Geneva, 1992

[13] Steven J. DeRose, David G. Durand
Making HyperMedia work: A users' guide to HyTime
Kluwer Academic, Boston, 1994

[14] Steven R. Newcomb, c/o Technoteacher Inc.
SigHyper
Tallahassee, Florida 32303-4408, 1993

[15] Charles F. Goldfarb
Hytime: A standard for structured hypermedia interchange, IEEE computer magazine
August 1991

[16] Steven R. Newcomb et al.
Hytime: The Hypermedia/Time-based Document Structuring Language, CACM 34/11, Pages 67–83
November 1991

[17] Joan Smith
SGML and Related Standards
Ellis Horwood, Chichester, 1992

A. Solutions to the exercises

A.1 Answers 1.1.2

1. The header "M E M O R A N D U M" is a visual aspect. It is printed by the system on top of each memorandum, left justified, in capital letters with a blank between each letter and underlined.

2. A blank line follows the header.

3. The word "TO:" is printed by the system in capital letters, left justified.

4. The name of the person who the memo is addressed to is printed at tab position 6.

5. A blank line follows the name of the person receiving the memo.

6. The word "FROM:" is printed by the system in capital letters, left justified.

7. The name of the person who wrote the memo is printed at tab position 6.

8. A blank line follows the name of the author of the memo.

9. Text paragraphs are left right justified.

10.Quotations start with "... and end with ..."

11.A blank line follows the body of the text.

12.The author's signature appears at tab position 24.

A.2 Answers 1.1.5

1. The command \noindent stops the formation of a new paragraph.

2. The command \settabs places tab stops at columns of 6 characters.

3. The command \+ starts a new line.

4. The command & skips to a tab stop.

5. The command \cr gives a carriage return plus line feed.

6. The command \it puts text in italic characters.

A.3 Answers 1.2.2

1. The following are the parts of the logical structure of the memo:

- The memo itself.
- The recipient of the memo.
- The author of the memo.
- The text body of the memo.
- Some paragraphs.
- A quotation.
- A signature.

2. The following is a representation of the memo that is independent of its appearance and permits the recognition of its logical parts:

```
--start of memo--
--memo's recipient-- Comrade Napoleon --end memo's recipient--
--memo's author- Snowball --end memo's author--
--start of memo's main text--
--start of first paragraph--
In Animal Farm, George Orwell says:
--start of quotation-- the pigs had to
expend enormous labour every day upon mysterious things
called files, reports, minutes and memoranda. These were
large sheets of paper which had to be closely covered with
writing, and as soon as they were so covered, they were burnt
in the furnace
--end of quotation--
--end of first paragraph
--start of second paragraph --
Do you think SGML would have helped the pigs?
--end of second paragraph--
--end of memo's main text--
--signature-- Comrade Snowball --end of signature--
--end of memo--
```

A.4 Answers 1.6

1. SGML is not a text-formatting system. It is a description of a document that is independent of any software process or hardware system.

2. WYSIWYG is not incompatible with SGML since SGML does not specify anything about the user interface that should be used to create conforming documents. There are several WYSIWYG SGML editors commercially available.

3. A text processing application includes facilities for document interchange, formatting, filing, storage, and retrieval.

4. The difference between SGML and PostScript is that SGML describes documents independent of the way they are formatted while PostScript describes the pages of a document in a way that can be understood by a printer, or a screen previewer.

5. SGML achieves the separation between structure and appearance by concentrating 100% on a documents logical structure.

A.5 Answers 2.5

1. Specific markup contains directives for the physical appearance of a document while generic markup describes the logical structure.

2. Specific markup makes a document less portable because the specific commands are only understood by one processor.

A.6 Answers 4.1

1. Both documents are SGML documents.

2. The first document belongs to the document class "memos". The hierarchy of this class of documents is:

a. The memo element that contains all the other elements.

b. The to element that contains the name of the person the memo is addressed to.

c. The from element that contains the name of the person the memo is from.

d. The body element that contains the main text of the memo. It may contain paragraphs, or quotations.

e. The close element which contains the signature of the person who sent the memo.

The elements should appear in this order, with the exception of the to and from elements.

The second document belongs to the document class "letters". The hierarchy of this class of documents is:

a. The letter element that contains all other elements.

b. The to element that contains the name and address of the person who the letter is sent to. It contains the name element followed by the address element.

c. The from element that contains the name and address of the person who sent the letter. It contains the name element followed by the address element.

d. The subject element that contains the subject of the letter.

e. The salut element that contains the opening salutation of the letter.

f. The body element that contains the main text of the letter. It contains paragraphs.

g. The close element that contains the closing salutation of the letter.

The elements should appear in this order, with the exception of the to and from elements. The two documents are completely different since their logical structure is not the same, and consequently one needs different markup languages for each document.

3. You need a system that can generate many different markup languages, one containing the tags required for memos, another containing the tags for letters, and so on. The language should be able to describe the nesting of the document's logical elements, their frequency, their sequence, and optionality. SGML achieves this by the mechanism of a document type definition.

A.7 Answers 4.3

1. The definitions are contained in the lines delimited by `<!`. These are called "markup declarations."

```
<!ELEMENT      - markup declaration for an element
<!ATTLIST      - markup declaration for an attribute
<!ENTITY       - markup declaration for an entity
```

Writing and understanding these declarations is the topic of Part II of this book.

2. The logical elements of the letter are:

a. The letter element, containing the whole letter.

b. The to element, containing the name and address elements.

c. The name element, containing the name of a person.

d. The address element, containing the address of the person named previously.

e. The from element, containing the name and address elements.

f. The subject element, containing the subject of the letter.

g. The salut element, containing the opening salutation of the letter.

h. The body element, containing paragraph elements.

i. The paragraph elements, containing text.

j. The close element, containing the closing salutation of the letter.

A.8 Answer 4.5

You could do two things:

1. Create two DTDs: one for personal letters, another for business letters.

2. Use a parameter on the tag, indicating that the letter is personal or for business.

The first option is good only if the structure of personal letters differs from that of business letters. This is unlikely — both types of letters have the same logical elements, although they may appear different on paper. The second option is called an "attribute" in SGML.

A.9 Answer 4.7

First, you need to think of a name for the special symbol, in this case an e with an acute accent. You could think of eacute, for example. This name only contains ASCII characters. You then need an "escape" character to tell the system (the parser in the case of SGML) that you are describing a symbol, and another one when you come to the symbol name's end. In SGML, the former is an ampersand (&) and the latter a semi-colon (;), so that a reference to the e with acute accent would become: é.

How would you represent the capital E with acute accent?

A.10 Answer 7.7

The tree diagram for the class of letters is shown in Figure 111.

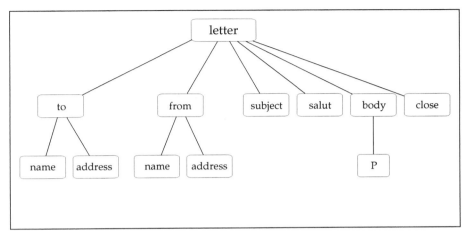

Figure 111. Letter Tree Structure

A.11 Answer 8.3

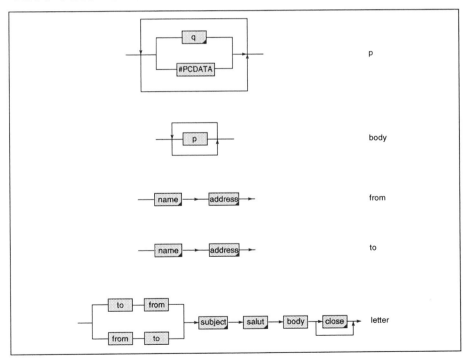

Figure 112. Letter Structure Diagrams

The structure diagram for the class of letters is shown in Figure 112.

A.12 Answers 9.11

1. Figure 113 shows the structure diagrams of (a | b?) and (a | b)?.

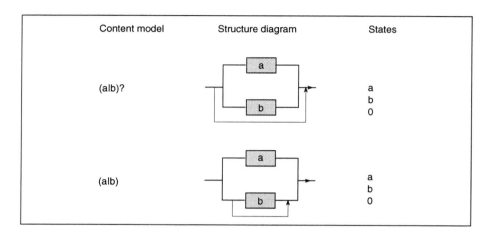

Figure 113. Structure Diagrams for (a | b)? and (a | b?)

2. Figure 114 shows the structure diagram of (A*, (B|C)?.

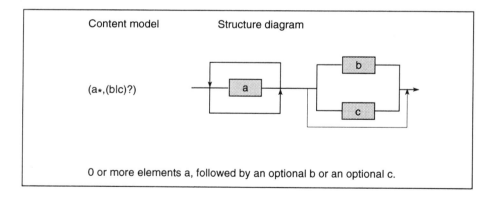

Figure 114. Structure Diagram for (a*,(b | c)?)

3. Figure 115 shows the model group and structure diagram for 0 or many elements A, followed by 0 or 1 elements B, followed by one A.

Content model   Structure diagram

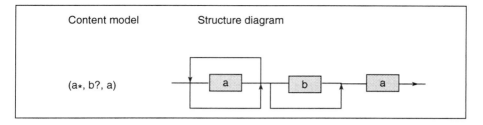

(a*, b?, a)

Figure 115. Structure Diagram for (a*, b?, a)

A.13 Answers 10.8

1. Removing the #P from #PCDATA, but leaving the parentheses, creates a valid model group with an element CDATA. The parser cannot find any element declaration for this element. To correct the error, the parentheses must be removed. In that case, the element **TO** will have CDATA declared content. Since it must be possible to put #PCDATA inside a model group, we need to distinguish it from an element PCDATA by putting the reserved name indicator in front.

2. A letter DTD plus marked-up letter are shown in the Figure 116.

```
<!DOCTYPE LETTER [
<!-- DTD for simple letters                                        -->
<!--          ELEMENTS    MIN   CONTENT              (EXCEPTIONS)   -->
<!ELEMENT  LETTER       - -   ((TO & FROM),SUBJECT,SALUT,BODY,CLOSE?)  >
<!ELEMENT  TO           - O   (NAME, ADDRESS)                       >
<!ELEMENT  FROM         - O   (NAME, ADDRESS)                       >
<!ELEMENT  BODY         - O   (P)*                                  >
<!ELEMENT  P            - O   (#PCDATA)*                            >
<!ELEMENT  (NAME|ADDRESS|CLOSE|SUBJECT|SALUT)       - O   (#PCDATA) >]>
<LETTER>
<TO>
<NAME>Henry Ford</NAME>
<ADDRESS>Motor way, Detroit, U.S.A</ADDRESS>
</TO>
<FROM>
<NAME>Eric van Herwijnen</NAME>
<ADDRESS>Geneva, Switzerland</ADDRESS>
<SUBJECT>thief-proof cars</SUBJECT>
<SALUT>Dear Henry,</SALUT>
<BODY>
<P>Wouldn't it be nice if you could design me a thief-proof car?</P>
</BODY>
<CLOSE>Sincerely yours,</CLOSE>
</LETTER>
```

Figure 116. The Element Declarations for a Letter

3. Figure 117 shows a file with some markup in a text.

```
<!DOCTYPE wywa [
<!-- DTD for a while-you-were-away note                       -->
<!ENTITY %   doctype "wywa" --document type generic identifier -->
<!--         ELEMENTS   MIN  CONTENT (EXCEPTIONS)              -->
<!ELEMENT    wywa       - -   ((To & From & Of), Phone?, Notes?)  >
<!ELEMENT    To         - O   (#PCDATA)                        >
<!ELEMENT    From       - O   (#PCDATA)                        >
<!ELEMENT    Of         - O   (#PCDATA)                        >
<!ELEMENT    Phone      - O   (#PCDATA)                        >
<!ELEMENT    Notes      - O   CDATA                            >
<!--         ELEMENTS   NAME     VALUE          DEFAULT   -->
<!ATTLIST    From       seeme    (seeme)        #IMPLIED   >
<!ATTLIST    Of         called   (called)       #IMPLIED
                        phoned   (phoned)       #IMPLIED
                        came     (came)         #IMPLIED
                        replied  (replied)      #IMPLIED
                        wantsyou (wantsyou)     #IMPLIED >] >
<wywa>
<To>The big pig</To>
<From>The small pig</From>
<Of called>The middle pig
<Phone>767 5087
<Notes>Please call back about a pile of burnt memo's. This is an
example of some markup in the middle of the text: supposing a<b.
</Notes>
</wywa>
```

Figure 117. Using CDATA to Suppress Markup Recognition

A.14 Answers 11.2

1. Figure 118 shows ID and IDREF attribute declarations.

```
<!DOCTYPE article [
<!--        ELEMENT       MIN  CONTENT              (EXCEPTIONS) -->
<!ELEMENT article         - -   (aug)                          >
<!ELEMENT aug             O O   (au/aff)*                      >
<!ELEMENT au              - O   (#PCDATA)                      >
<!ELEMENT aff             - O   (#PCDATA)                      >
<!--        ELEMENTS      NAME     VALUE    DEFAULT       -->
<!ATTLIST author          rid      IDREFS   #IMPLIED       >
<!ATTLIST authloc         id       ID       #REQUIRED     >] >
<article>
<aug>
<au rid=a1>Eric van Herwijnen</au>
<au rid=a2>Lou Reynolds</au>
<aff id=a1>CERN, Geneva, Switzerland</aff>
<aff id=a2>EBT, Providence, USA</aff>
</aug>
</article>
```

Figure 118. Unique ID Attribute and a IDREF to a Unique Identifier Attribute

2. The attribute declaration that allows you to indicate whether a letter is a private or a business letter is shown in Figure 119.

```
<!ATTLIST letter type (private|business) private>
```

Figure 119. Private or Business Letters

A.15 Answers 14.4

1. The DTD and document instance for the WYWA note are shown in Figure 120.

```
<!DOCTYPE wywa [
<!-- DTD for a while-you-were-away note                            -->
<!ENTITY %  doctype "wywa"      --document type generic identifier  -->
<!--          ELEMENTS    MIN   CONTENT (EXCEPTIONS)                 -->
<!ELEMENT  wywa         - -  ((To & From & Of), Phone?, Notes?)     >
<!ELEMENT  To           - O   (#PCDATA)                             >
<!ELEMENT  From         - O   (#PCDATA)                             >
<!ELEMENT  Of           - O   (#PCDATA)                             >
<!ELEMENT  Phone        - O   (#PCDATA)                             >
<!ELEMENT  Notes        - O   (#PCDATA)                             >
<!--          ELEMENTS    NAME      VALUE          DEFAULT          -->
<!ATTLIST  From         seeme     (seeme)         #IMPLIED          >
<!ATTLIST  Of           called    (called)        #IMPLIED
                        phoned    (phoned)        #IMPLIED
                        came      (came)          #IMPLIED
                        replied   (replied)       #IMPLIED
                        wantsyou  (wantsyou)      #IMPLIED       >]>
<wywa>
<To>The big pig</To>
<From>The small pig</From>
<Of called>The middle pig
<Phone>767 5087
<Notes>Please call back about a pile of burnt memo's.
</wywa>
```

Figure 120. DTD and Instance of a WYWA Note

2. A DTD for the first page of the article is shown in Figure 121.

```
<!ENTITY % ISOpub PUBLIC
 "ISO 8879-1986//ENTITIES Publishing//EN">
%ISOpub;
<!ENTITY % ISOlat1 PUBLIC
 "ISO 8879-1986//ENTITIES Added Latin 1//EN">
%ISOlat1;
<!-- ENTITIES for maths -->
<!ENTITY % sp.pos "vsp|hsp" >
<!ENTITY % f-cs   "g|bg|%sp.pos|rm">
<!ENTITY % f-cstxt "#PCDATA|%f-cs">
<!ENTITY % f-bu   "fen">
<!ENTITY % f-ph   "sup|inf">
<!ENTITY % f-butxt "fen|%f-cstxt|%f-ph;>
<!ENTITY % f-post "par|sqb|lsqb|rrsqb|cub|ceil|fl|ang|sol|vb|uc|dc">
<!ENTITY % f-style "s|d|t|da|dot|b|bl|in">
<!-- ELEMENTS for text -->
<!ELEMENT article - - (front) >
<!ELEMENT front   - - (titlep?, preface*)>
<!ELEMENT titlep - O (title, subtitle?, (author, authloc?)*, publishr?)>
<!ELEMENT (title|author|authloc|publishr|par)
                      - O (#PCDATA|ieqn|rm)* >
<!ATTLIST author rid IDREFS #IMPLIED >
<!ATTLIST authloc id ID #REQUIRED >
<!ELEMENT preface - O (prefhead?, par*) >
<!ELEMENT ieqn   - - (f)? >
<!-- ELEMENT for math -->
<!ELEMENT f   - - (%f-butxt)* >
<!ELEMENT (g|bg|rm) - - (#PCDATA)* >
<!ELEMENT fen   - - (%f-butxt|cp|rp)* >
<!ATTLIST fen   lp   (%f-post;)  vp
   style   (%f-style;) s >
<!ELEMENT (cp|rp) - O EMPTY >
<!ATTLIST (cp|rp) post     (%f-post;) vb
     style   (%f-style;) s >
<!ELEMENT (sup|inf) - - (%f-butxt;)* >
<!ATTLIST (sup|inf) loc     CDATA       #IMPLIED >
<!ELEMENT (hsp|vsp) - O EMPTY >
<!ATTLIST (hsp|vsp) sp      CDATA       #IMPLIED >
```

Figure 121. A DTD for the First Page of Articles

The first page of the article, marked up according to this DTD, is shown in Figure 122.

```
<!DOCTYPE article SYSTEM "\advanced\article.dtd">
<article>
<front>
<title-page>
<title><ieqn><f>ZZ'</f></ieqn>Mixing and Radiative Corrections at LEP I
</title>
<author>A. Leike</author>
<author>S. Riemann</author>
<authloc>DESY &mdash; Institute f&uuml;r Hochenergiephysik, O-1615
Zeuthen, Germany</authloc>
<author>T. Riemann</author>
<authloc>Theory Division, CERN, CH-1211 Geneva, Switzerland
</authloc>
<publisher>CERN-TH.6545/92</publisher>
</title-page>
<preface><prefhead>Abstract</prefhead>
<par>
We present a method for a common treatment of <ieqn><f>Z'</f></ieqn>
exchange,QED corrections, and weak loops in <ieqn><f>e<sup>+</sup>e<sup>
-</sup></f></ieqn>annihilation. QED corrections are taken into account
by convoluting a hard scattering cross section containing <ieqn><f><g>g
</g>,Z</f></ieqn>, and <ieqn><f>Z'</f></ieqn> exchange. Weak corrections
and <ieqn><f>ZZ'</f></ieqn> mixing are treated simultaneously by a
generalization of weak form factors. Using the properly extended
Standard Model program for the <ieqn><f>Z</f></ieqn> line shape,
<ieqn><f><hsp sp="0.167"><inf>ZF</inf>I<sup>T</sup>T<inf>ER</inf></f>
</ieqn>, we perform and compare two different analysis of the 1990
LEP I data in terms of theories based on the
<ieqn><f><rm>E<inf>6</inf></rm></f></ieqn>&mdash;group and in terms of
LR-symmetric models. From the LEP I data alone, the <ieqn><f>ZZ'</f>
</ieqn> mixing angle may be limited to <ieqn><f><fen lp="vb"><g>q</g>
<inf>M</inf><rp post="vb"></fen>&le;0.01</f></ieqn> and the
<ieqn><f>Z'</f></ieqn> mass to <ieqn><f>M<inf>2</inf>&gt;118-148</f>
</ieqn> GeV, depending on the model (95% CL).</par>
</preface>
</front>
</article>
```

Figure 122. SGML for the First Page of the Article

A.16 Answer 15.3

1. Running the sgmls parser on the WYWA note with the —c option gives the result shown in Figure 123.

```
TOTALCAP    244/35000
 ENTCAP       8/35000
ENTCHCAP      4/35000
 ELEMCAP     48/35000
  GRPCAP     88/35000
  ATTCAP     48/35000
AVGRPCAP     48/35000
```

Figure 123. The Capacity of the WYWA Note

2. Figure 124 explains why GRPCAP has value 88.

```
There are 11 content tokens, each counting for 8 point:

(To & From & Of)
Phone?
Notes?
To
From
Of
5 times (#PCDATA)

((To & From & Of), Phone?, Notes?) is a content model group,
not a content token.
```

Figure 124. GRPCAP Value Explanation

A.17 Answer 15.5.9

The modified SGML declaration for NAMES longer than eight characters is shown in Figure 125.

```
<!SGML "ISO 8879:1986"
                          CHARSET
 BASESET   "ISO 646:1983//CHARSET
           International Reference Version (IRV)//ESC 2/5 4/0"
 DESCSET   0    9 UNUSED --the first 9 characters starting at 0 are not
                         used--
           9    2 9       --the next two, 9 and 10, map onto 9 and 10 of the
                          baseset--
          11    2 UNUSED --11 and 12 are not used--
          13    1 13      --13 is mapped onto 13 of the baseset--
          14   18 UNUSED --the next 18, starting with 14, are unused--
          32   95 32      --the next 95, starting with 32, are mapped
                          onto 32-126 of the baseset--
         127    1 UNUSED --the character 127 is unused--
 CAPACITY PUBLIC "ISO 8879:1986//CAPACITY Reference//EN"
 SCOPE     DOCUMENT
 SYNTAX
 SHUNCHAR CONTROLS 0 1 2 3 4 5 6 7 8 9 10 11 12 13 14 15 16 17
           18 19 20 21 22 23 24 25 26 27 28 29 30 31 127
 BASESET   "ISO 646:1983//CHARSET
           International Reference Version (IRV)//ESC 2/5 4/0"
 DESCSET   0 128 0
 FUNCTION RE                13
          RS                10
          SPACE             32
          TAB       SEPCHAR  9
 NAMING   LCNMSTRT ""
          UCNMSTRT ""
          LCNMCHAR "-."      -- Lower-case hyphen, period are --
          UCNMCHAR "-."      -- same as upper-case (45 46).   --
          NAMECASE GENERAL  YES
                   ENTITY   NO
 DELIM    GENERAL  SGMLREF
          SHORTREF SGMLREF
 NAMES    SGMLREF
 QUANTITY SGMLREF
          NAMELEN 20
                          FEATURES
 MINIMIZE DATATAG NO  OMITTAG  YES  RANK    NO  SHORTTAG YES
 LINK     SIMPLE  NO  IMPLICIT NO   EXPLICIT NO
 OTHER    CONCUR  NO  SUBDOC   NO   FORMAL   NO
                          APPINFO NONE>
```

Figure 125. SGML Declaration with NAMELEN 20

An example of the WYWA note containing an element name of more than 8 characters is shown in Figure 126.

```
<wywa>
<To>The big pig</To>
<From>The small pig</From>
<Concerning called>The middle pig
<Phone>767 5087
<Notes>Please call back about a pile of burnt memo's.
</wywa>
<!DOCTYPE wywa [
<!-- DTD for a while-you-were-away note                          -->
<!ENTITY %  doctype "wywa"      --document type generic identifier  -->
<!--        ELEMENTS   MIN  CONTENT (EXCEPTIONS)                  -->
<!ELEMENT   wywa       - -  ((To & From & Concerning), Phone?,
                                                    Notes?)       >
<!ELEMENT   To         - O  (#PCDATA)                             >
<!ELEMENT   From       - O  (#PCDATA)                             >
<!ELEMENT   Concerning - O  (#PCDATA)                             >
<!ELEMENT   Phone      - O  (#PCDATA)                             >
<!ELEMENT   Notes      - O  (#PCDATA)                             >
<!--        ELEMENTS   NAME     VALUE            DEFAULT          -->
<!ATTLIST   From       seeme    (seeme)          #IMPLIED          >
<!ATTLIST   Concerning called   (called)         #IMPLIED
                       phoned   (phoned)         #IMPLIED
                       came     (came)           #IMPLIED
                       replied  (replied)        #IMPLIED
                       wantsyou (wantsyou)       #IMPLIED        >]>
<wywa>
<To>The big pig</To>
<From>The small pig</From>
<Concerning called>The middle pig
<Phone>767 5087
<Notes>Please call back about a pile of burnt memo's.
</wywa>
```

Figure 126. WYWA note with Element Name Longer than Eight Characters

An sgml parser that is able to read the SGML declaration will parse the above example without errors.

A.18 Answer 16.2

The following minimizations are made:

1. The to start-tag is incorrectly omitted.
2. The from start-tag is incorrectly omitted.
3. The from end-tag is correctly omitted.
4. The called attribute name on the of tag is correctly omitted.

5. The of end-tag is correctly omitted.

6. The phone end-tag is correctly omitted.

7. The notes end-tag is correctly omitted.

A.19 Answer 17.4

```
<!NOTATION PS SYSTEM "" --PostScript Notation -->
<!ENTITY bike SYSTEM "bike.ps" CDATA PS>
......
&bike;
```

A.20 Answer 19.5

Replacing the element declaration for the memo element by the following one will achieve the desired result:

```
<!ELEMENT MEMO   O O ((TO & FROM), BODY, CLOSE?)        >
```

All the short reference maps stay the same.

B. The sgmls parser

There are several versions of the SGML User's Group parser material. Depending on which version you require, you may need the help of a system programmer to install it on your system. The examples in this book refer to sgmls version 1.1 [1].

Using this parser to parse the memo example gives the output in Figure 127:

```
ASTATUS TOKEN PUBLIC
(MEMO
(TO
-Comrade Napoleon
)TO
(FROM
-Snowball
)FROM
(BODY
AID IMPLIED
(P
-In Animal Farm, George Orwell says:
(Q
-...the pigs had to\nexpend enormous labour every day upon mysterious
things called files,\nreports, minutes and memoranda. These were
large sheets of paper which\nhad to be closely covered with writing,
and as soon as they were so\ncovered, they were burnt in the furnace...
)Q
-\nDo you think SGML would have helped the pigs?
)P
)BODY
(CLOSE
-Comrade Snowball
)CLOSE
)MEMO
```

Figure 127. Output of sgmls Processing the Memo

The output from the parser means the following:

1. The capital A indicates that the attribute with name (see section4.6) STATUS has as value TOKEN (see Table 11) PUBLIC, indicated by the capital A.

2. The logical element (see section 4.4) MEMO is opened, indicated by the opening parenthesis.

3. The To element is opened.

4. The data "Comrade Napoleon" are found, indicated by the hyphen.

5. The To element is closed, indicated by the closing parenthesis.

6. And so on.

7. The symbol \n means a new line was found in the data.

An SGML parser need only report markup errors in the document instance, or in the DTD. In general, it does not need to do anything with the content of the elements. The sgmls output is unique to the sgmls parser.

The output of a parser is not standardized. Instead of obtaining tagnames between parenthesis, we could get the parser to print TEX, RTF, or other text formatter commands. To resume, you can use sgmls to:

1. Verify that your SGML document instance and DTD are correct.

2. Replace the SGML tags by word-processor or database loader commands. You can also complete any minimized markup.

Note that the output of an SGML parser is not a fundamental part of SGML.

Public domain SGML parsers play an important role. They allow people to work and experiment with SGML at low cost, and permit developers to share their ideas which will ultimately result in better products. It also serves to attract the attention of the academic world which is good for the evolution of SGML or similar systems.

B.1 Bibliography for Appendix B

[1]   J.Clark
      sgmls README file, version 1.0
      1993

C. The ISO 646:1983 character set

Table 45 shows the ISO 646:1983 IRV (International Reference Version) character set. The difference between ISO 646:1983 IRV and ASCII is that the currency sign ("¤") is replaced by the dollar ("$") in the latter set. Whenever I mention ISO 646:1983 in this book, I mean ISO 646:1983 IRV.

Table 45. The ISO 646:1983 IRV character set

	0-	1-	2-	3-	4-	5-	6-	7-
-0	NUL	DLE	SP	0	@	P	`	p
-1	SOH	DC1	!	1	A	Q	a	q
-2	STX	DC2	"	2	B	R	b	r
-3	ETX	DC3	#	3	C	S	c	s
-4	EOT	DC4	¤	4	D	T	d	t
-5	ENQ	NAK	%	5	E	U	e	u
-6	ACK	SYN	&	6	F	V	f	v
-7	BEL	ETB	'	7	G	W	g	w
-8	BS	CAN	(	8	H	X	h	x
-9	HT	EM	)	9	I	Y	i	y
-A	LF	SUB	*	:	J	Z	j	z
-B	VT	ESC	+	;	K	[	k	]
-C	FF	FS	,	<	L	\	l		
-D	CR	GS	-	=	M	]	m	}
-E	SO	RS	.	>	N	^	n	~
-F	SI	US	/	?	O	_	o	DEL

To find the two-figure code of a symbol (e.g. the number "5"), look up to find the first figure ("3"), and look right to find the second ("5"). This yields "35".

D. How to read ISO 8879

The SGML standard is difficult to read and from this section you will get an idea why this is so. The likelihood that you will ever have to read the standard is small. Unless you intend writing an SGML parser, you should not need to do so. If you do, here are some tips that may help you. See also [1], that contains the integral text of the SGML standard as well as annotations.

D.1 Structure of the SGML standard

The standard is organized in chapters (headings numbered 1, 2, 3, etc.) which are called clauses. Sections (headings numbered 1.1, 1.2, etc.) are sub-clauses and sub-sections (headings numbered 1.1.1, 1.1.2, etc.) sub-sub-clauses.

Clauses 0-3 contain an Introduction, Scope, Field of Application and a list of References. Clause 4 gives the definition (in readable English) of various objects that apply to the standard. These definitions are not part of the formal language definition, but they help to understand it. Some of them have been adapted for use in the glossary in this book. Clause 5 explains the notation (see the next section for a summary) and clauses 6-15 define the SGML language.

An amendment to the standard was issued in 1988 (Amendment 1). Although most systems nowadays comply to Amendment 1 of SGML, it is worth checking this to make sure that you are using the up-to-date SGML.

D.2 Notation used in the SGML standard

The SGML language is defined using a special notation. Each SGML concept has a syntactic variable associated to it. For example, start-tag, end-tag, element, content, but also minimized start-tag and declared content are SGML syntactic variables. A formal definition of an SGML syntactic variable is given in a syntax production. Table 46 shows how a production is made.

Table 46. SGML syntax production definition

Example: [146] notation = "NOTATION",*ps+,name group*		
Order	**Parameter or Symbol**	**Explanation**
1	[146]	production number
2	notation	syntactic variable
3	=	equals sign
4	"NOTATION",*ps+,name group*	the expression containing the definition

The definitions are in terms of syntactic tokens. These may be variables that are defined elsewhere (they are given in italic print e.g. *name group*), reserved names within quotes (e.g. "NOTATION", called syntactic literals), delimiters (e.g. *ps+* which means one or more parameter separators) and other character strings.

To explain syntax productions in more detail is not necessary here; the designer of an SGML parser should understand them but the implementer of an SGML application should not.

A problem with the standard is that the definitions are nested. It is difficult to find the exact definition of quantities. To give an idea of the complexity of the standard, let us suppose you want to find out how an element is defined, you need to know which production you have to look at. If you know it is number 13, you can find that it is defined as:

[13] element = *start-tag?, content, end-tag*

Unless you know what the definitions of start-tag, end-tag and content are, you are none the wiser. There is also some text and a note which for the moment you ignore since you want to concentrate on one thing at a time. You must also check in Amendment 1 that nothing was changed to this clause, which it was not.

To proceed, you need to know the production numbers of these three syntactic variables. For this purpose [2] is useful to find your way through the standard. It provides a complete index and an alphabetical list of the definitions of all the variables used in the standard.

Now that you have the index, you can look up the production numbers you need: start-tag has number 14, end-tag number 19 and content number 24. Table 47 shows the contents of these productions.

Table 47. Productions for understanding the element definition

Production
[14] start-tag = (stago, *document type specification, generic identifier specification, attribute specification list, s**, tagc)	*minimized start-tag*
[19] end-tag = (etago, *document type specification, generic identifier specification, s**, tagc)	*minimized end-tag*
[24] content = *mixed content*	*element content*	*replaceable character data*	*character data*

You subsequently look up the productions corresponding to the new unknown syntactic variables. In practice, if you have read this book, you will understand the meaning of most syntactic variables.

The standard has nine Annexes of a more "tutorial" character which are not part of the standard itself. A good way to start to "attack" the SGML standard is to first read the Annexes A-D. From then on, the standard should be consulted as a reference work, using [2] as an index.

D.3 Bibliography for Appendix D

[1]   C.F. Goldfarb
      The SGML Handbook
      Clarendon Press, Oxford, 1990
[2]   J.M. Smith, R. Stutely
      SGML: The user's guide to ISO 8879
      Ellis Horwood, Chichester, 1988

Glossary

This glossary includes terms and definitions that are mentioned in the text. Some definitions were taken from the SGML standard. The definitions are intended as a compact reminder rather than an exhaustive list; their formulation may vary slightly from that given in the main text, thus helping the reader to obtain a more complete view of the topic. For complete definitions, however, the reader should consult the main text or any reference given with the definition.

AAP Association of American Publishers. An organization representing the interests of the American Publishing industry.

ANSI American National Standards Institute. The American organization for developing and distributing national standards on miscellaneous subjects.

application Defined by ISO 8879 as a "Text processing application": the related set of processes performed on documents of related types. For example: publication, creation, revision, office correspondence. See also SGML application.

ASCII American Standard Code for Information Interchange. A way of representing characters that are used in texts as a sequence of 0s and 1s. ASCII is a convention developed by the American National Standards Institute. It contains 7-bit characters (8-bits including parity check).

attribute A qualifier indicating a property of an element, other than its type (which is done by a generic identifier) or its content (which is delimited by start-tags and end-tags). Attributes are only found on start-tags, and can indicate reference identifiers, confidentiality, formatting information, and so on.

Author/ Editor A WYSIWYG SGML input system running on PC Windows, Macintosh and SUN made by SoftQuad Inc.

base character set The character set which is used for the characters in the document instance. In the reference concrete syntax, this is ISO 646:1983, known as the International Reference Version.

batch text formatter A text-formatter that is run in batch mode, i.e. non-interactively. Examples are Script, TeX, nroff. They usually run on large multi-user computers.

CALS Computer-aided Acquisition and Logistics Support. The U.S. Department of Defense's program to electronically acquire and manage technical information on weapon systems. Four standards are part of this initiative: SGML, CGM, IGES, and FAX Group IV.

canonical document An SGML document that has been parsed without errors, where all omitted tags have been added, all abbreviated tags are completed, all entity references are expanded, all implied attributes are added, all short references are expanded, and all marked sections are ignored or included. They are sometimes called complete or normalized documents and are used as the starting point for processing by an application. Minimal documents do not require entity references to be expanded.

CAP Computer-Assisted Publishing. An environment where any part of the publishing process is done on a computer. For example, the manuscript may be prepared with the help of a word processor.

CCITT Comité Consultatif International de Téléphones et Télécommunications. A standards body concerned with telecommunications. CCITT FAX group IV is one of the CALS standards.

CDA Digital Equipment Corporation's Compound Document Architecture, an enhancement of the ODA standard (ISO 8613).

CDATA Declared data type for an element that contains no markup. Any characters that would normally signify markup are treated as literal data.

CGM Computer Graphics Metafile for the storage and transfer of picture description information. The ISO standard (ISO 8632) for storage and description of complete pictures. It is expected to become adopted as the picture interchange standard used between all graphics standards.

code page A definition of a set of characters in terms of their hexadecimal values. Normally a code page is represented by a square table, with 16 (0-F) rows and columns and with one character in each cell. The hexadecimal digits of a character are then found by looking up first the column of a given cell and then placing its row immediately behind it. The two hexadecimal characters thus found translate into binary (the first character into the first four bits, the second character into the second four bits).

complete document See canonical document.

compound document architecture See CDA.

content model A group in an element declaration that defines the allowed content of the element.

connector A symbol that is used inside a model group to indicate the relative order in which subelements may occur in an element: (",","&" and "|").

database A computer system whose purpose is to record and maintain information in a structured way. In a relational database the data are presented in a tabular form.

database publishing Publishing of any material with a database structure, such as encyclopaedia, journals, dictionaries, and so on.

DBMS Data Base Management System. A database plus various application tools such as a query language, a report writer, a form generator for formulating queries through full screen menus, etc.

DCF See SCRIPT.

declaration The SGML declaration defines which characters are used in a document instance, which syntax the DTD is written in, which SGML features are used, and so on. It is supposed to accompany each SGML document, although a default to the one described in the standard may be assumed.

declared content The alternative to a content model in an element declaration, when the element cannot contain sub-elements.

descriptive markup Markup that uses tag names that are related to the purpose or function of elements, rather than procedures that are formatting related.

Desk Top Publishing A publishing system using a desktop computer such as a PC or Macintosh.

document A collection of textual information possibly augmented with graphics, tabular, and numeric data. These items may be gathered dynamically and are assumed in this book to be present on a computer. In terms of SGML, a document is a logical construct that contains a document element, that is at the root of a tree of elements which form its content.

dpi

Dots per inch. The unit used to describe the resolution of a screen or a printer. A measure of quality of a laserprinter. Most printers manage 300 dpi; good ones manage 600 dpi; sophisticated ones go up to 1000 dpi. The amount of data is proportional to the resolution and inversely proportional to the speed of such devices. Traditional photo typesetter devices used for books and magazines go over 2500 dpi. Although the rules applying to fonts, lines, and halftones differ, one may say roughly (see [1] that the human eye distinguishes a resolution of up to 1200 dpi.

DSSSL

Document Style Semantics and Specification Language, ISO DIS 10179. An ISO standard under preparation. DSSSL addresses the need for detailed, typographically sophisticated, specification of layout and composition, in a manner that is independent of particular formatting systems or processes.

DTD

Document type definition. The definition of the markup rules for a given class of documents. A DTD or a reference to one should be contained in any SGML conforming document.

EBCDIC

Extended Binary Coded Decimal Interchange Code. A way of representing the characters that are used in texts as a sequence of 0s and 1s. EBCDIC is a convention developed and used by IBM. Many different (national language) versions exist.

EDI

Electronic Data Interchange. Information that is interchanged between suppliers and customers in a way that permits direct input into corporate database applications.

EDIFACT

A set of syntax rules developed by the United Nations Economic Commission for Europe (UN/ECE) for EDI messages for the fields of Administration, Commerce and Transport. The hierarchical structure of these messages makes it possible to use SGML to create and process them.

electronic mail

The computerized exchange of unstructured information between users of the same computer or between users of different computers linked by a network. The content part of a mail message is free format and therefore cannot be used as input to a program. The content is enveloped in a header containing the electronic mail address of the recipient and the sender, the subject and other information. This is described (see [2]) in the X400 standard for electronic mail.

electronic publishing A publishing process that takes place entirely on computers. Documents are available electronically and can be inspected on the screen.

element A part of a document that is a logical entity such as a chapter, a section, a title, a paragraph, and so on.

EMPTY Declared content type meaning that this element may not have any content or sub-elements and that it is not permitted to have an end-tag.

entity A unit of information that may be referred to by a symbol in a DTD or in a document instance. Entities may be used for character strings, characters that cannot be keyed in on a keyboard, or for separate files that may or may not contain SGML data.

EPS Encapsulated PostScript. A special form of PostScript that contains information on the size of the laid-out page. This enables such files to be imbedded in documents that are processed by a text formatter.

EQN The mathematics processor developed for the UNIX troff system. Its syntax is widely used by other mathematics formatters such as IBM's Script Mathematical Formula Formatter.

exclusion exception A group containing element names in an element declaration prefixed by a minus ("-"). This specifies elements that are not allowed to occur anywhere inside the element (or any of its sub-elements) being declared.

file A unit of information to be used by a computer. A file can be a document, a program, or other data. Files can be stored in a computer's memory, on disk, or other peripherals such as magnetic tape.

flush A typesetter's term for text with no indentation.

font A finite set of signs that are represented by a given output device as specific graphic elements. Fonts usually contain signs that all share the same typeface. In UK English this word is spelled "fount."

formatter A system which takes as input a text file, marked up with commands it understands, and produces as output a fully laid-out file in a language that a printer understands (for example, PostScript).

FQGI	Fully qualified generic identifier. A sequence of element names, starting with the document type itself and continuing down to the element of interest. For example, the FQGI of a paragraph in a memo could be <u>memo/ body/p</u>.
general entity	An entity defined for use within a document instance.
generalized markup	Codes that describe the logical purpose of the various elements inside a document, such as chapters, paragraphs, and so on.
generic identifier	The name of an element or "tag-name."
GKS	Graphics Kernel System. The ISO Standard (ISO 7942) that defines a common interface to interactive computer graphics for application programs.
Glyph	A format independent representation of a shape into which a character has been transformed by the text formatter.
GML	Generalized Markup Language. A generic markup language developed by IBM and marketed as a product with DCF, the Document Composition Facility.
heterogeneous computer network	A set of computers using different character encoding schemes such as EBCDIC and ASCII connected together via a network. In the absence of a network, we assume that contact is made via a magnetic tape or a diskette.
hypertext	A database of linked documents with a powerful user-interface permitting the user to "walk" through the database by activating references formed by links to external or internal parts of documents. These references are often activated by pointing to areas on a screen called "buttons". The links may be dynamic or preplanned.
HyTime	ISO 10744:1992, the International Standard for Hypermedia and Time based systems.
icon	A symbol used on computers with a graphical user interface. They represent programs and documents and are executed or read by pointing a mouse to them.
IEC	International Electrotechnical Commission. An organization involved in electrotechnical standardization and closely collaborates with ISO on these matters. ISO and IEC frequently have joint technical committees.
inclusion exception	A group of elements in an element declaration, preceded by a "+." This specifies elements that are allowed to

occur anywhere inside the element (or any of its sub-elements) being declared.

instance   The document instance is the part of an SGML document that contains the marked up textual data.

IEEE   The Institute of Electrical and Electronic Engineers, Inc. A professional body which also publishes a number of magazines in the computing field.

IGES   Initial Graphics Exchange Specification. An encoding for engineering drawings.

inter-change   The transportation of documents to a different computer or to a different application (from a text formatter to a database, for example).

IRV   International Reference Version (of the ISO 646:1983 character set). See also baseset.

IS   International Standard. A standard approved by ISO.

ISO   International Organization for Standardization. An organization based in Geneva that concerns itself with the development and distribution of internationally accepted standards on miscellaneous subjects.

justification   The process of arranging characters in a line of text to achieve a specific length of the line. Usually this is achieved by varying the space between words and sometimes between characters.

keyword   A parameter with a reserved name for use inside markup declarations. Reserved names are defined by the reference concrete syntax. The reserved name indicator ("#") is placed before the reserved name in those cases where a name defined by an application may also appear.

laser-printer   A printer that is able to produce a wide range of typefaces and composes text and pictures by printing small dots using laser technology. The resolution of such printers (measured in dots per inch) is an indication of their quality. See dpi.

LaTeX   A generic macro system designed by L. Lamport, based on TeX (see [3] and also [4]).

LEXX/LPEX   The Live Parsing Editor. A context-sensitive editor for VM/CMS and OS/2 from IBM. For more information, see your IBM sales representative.

Macintosh   A range of personal computers manufactured by Apple Computer.

macro   A collection of commands. In the context of this book, the commands are usually formatting commands.

marked section   A part of a document instance that is tagged for conditional processing, that is, it may be ignored or included depending on the value of a flag.

markup   The process of adding formatting or other processing commands to a text.

markup declaration   An SGML instruction in a DTD or a document instance, or in the words of the SGML standard "Markup that controls how other markup of a document is to be interpreted."

meta-language   A language that can describe itself. SGML is often quoted as a meta-language. It means that SGML is capable of abstractly describing itself, as well as any other concrete generalized markup language.

MIL-M-28001   Markup Requirements and Generic Style Specification for Electronic Printed Output and Exchange of Text. Contains the DTD and output specifications for CALS technical manuals.

minimal SGML document   A document instance that uses no minimization features, but has all start-tags and end-tags specified, and uses the reference concrete syntax.

minimiza-tion   Sometimes the context of a textual element implies how it should be marked up. In such cases tags (usually end-tags) may be omitted. This process is called markup minimization.

MIS   Management Information Systems. The computerization of all information that is relevant to the management of an organization. It comprises corporate databases, office automation, publishing, etc.

mixed content   An element has "mixed content" when both sub-elements and #PCDATA portions can co-occur. These can cause ambiguities and should be avoided. Only use in conjunction with the "|" (or) connector.

model group   The part of a content model that specifies the order and occurrence of subelements and character strings within an element. Model groups are found in element markup declarations.

mouse   A hand-held device attached to a computer which has a graphical user interface. It is used to point at icons, select parts of texts and to execute commands.

ms	A generic markup language written in troff, available on UNIX systems.
NDATA	Non-SGML data. Used for SGML entities that are in representations or notations other than SGML, such as bitmaps and other multimedia objects.
notation	A way of indicating parts of a document that follow markup rules other than those defined by SGML, such as Encapsulated PostScript, etc.
nroff	A text formatting language for line printer quality output devices that runs on the UNIX operating system.
occurrence indicator	A symbol used in a model group to indicate how often a sub-element may occur in an element: ("*","&"and "?").
OCR	Optical Character Recognition. Special software normally used in conjunction with a scanner that is capable of recognizing letters, thus enabling the conversion of paper documents to ASCII text rather than to the bits in a scanned image.
ODA	Office Document Architecture (ISO 8613). A text interchange standard for office documents with the emphasis on transmitting the external form of the document rather than its logical contents.
ODIF	Office Document Interchange Format (ISO 8613). An encoding of formatted documents for representing ODA documents in a publishing environment.
ODL	Office Document Language. An SGML-based language for representing ODA documents in a publishing environment.
operating system	A special program that manages the flow of information and the use of hardware inside a computer. An operating system can be multi-user (e.g., VM/CMS, UNIX, VMS) or single-user (DOS).
ORACLE	The manufacturer of a relational database management system that runs on a wide variety of computers. The first commercially available system using SQL.
parameter entity	An entity defined for use in a DTD, not within a document instance.
parsed character data (PC-DATA)	Data characters that occur in marked up text that are not recognized as markup during parsing.
parser	See SGML parser.

PC	Personal Computer. A computer that is used by a single user and is small enough to be situated on the desk of that user. In this book the term PC is used to describe IBM compatible PCs as well as Macintoshes.
PCDATA	See parsed character data.
PDL	Page Description Language. See PostScriptand also SPDL.
point	A unit used to indicate the size of a typeface. Equal to 1/72 inches.
PostScript	A language describing a fully laid-out page in terms of fonts, lines, grey scales, and so on, in a way that is interpretable by a printer. The language was developed by Adobe Systems.
proof	A version of a document that has been prepared specifically for the purpose of reviewing it prior to its final reproduction.
proper subelement	An element that is permitted in the content because it was defined so in a content model rather than by an inclusion exception.
query language	A high-level language for adding data to and retrieving data from databases. An example is SQL, the Structured Query Language.
RCDATA	Replaceable character data. The declared content type for elements that may contain text and entity references but no sub-elements.
reference concrete syntax	The concrete syntax defined in the SGML standard. It defines the names, characters, delimiters, and notation that are suggested for use in defining concrete markup languages.
relational database	A database in which the data have a tabular structure. Rows and columns have data values. A two-dimensional tabular structure is the most general data representation. Tree (or hierarchical) and network models for example can be represented as tables. To be able to operate on the data, a query language is part of the database system.
re-portwriter	A tool provided with a database management system to make reports. It formats the results of a retrieval query and has commands for presenting the output in a readable form. The Oracle reportwriter is called Reportwriter.

reserved name

Defined by the SGML standard as "A name defined by the concrete syntax, rather than by an application, such as a markup declaration name."

reserved name indicator

A symbol ("#") indicating that a reserved name is used, rather than a name defined by an application.

REXX

A procedural language that allows programs and algorithms to be written in a clear and structured way. Interpreters exist for VM/CMS, DOS, MVS/TSO, OS/2.

RPT

See report writer.

Script

A text formatter that exists in at least two flavors, one from IBM (also referred to as Script/VS) and another from Watcom Inc. Both have their origins in CP-67/CMS Script. IBM Script is part of the Document Composition Facility (DCF) product.

SDATA

Specific character data. A type of entity whose data should not be parsed as SGML data but passed directly to the application program.

SDIF

Standard Document Interchange Format (ISO 9069). A standard describing the interchange for documents enclosed with SGML.

SGML

The Standard Generalized Markup Language, ISO 8879. Defined by the standard as "A language for document representation that formalizes markup and frees it of system and processing dependencies." An abstract language, with which an arbitrary number of markup languages may be defined.

SGML application

Defined by the SGML standard as "Rules that apply SGML to a text processing application". It will contain a DTD and it may contain definitions of application procedures in a programming or text processing language. An SGML application exists independently of any implementation.

SGML implementation

A collection of SGML application procedures that are written in a programming language or a text formatting language. They provide the mapping from the structure defined by a given SGML application to a concrete system such as a textformatter or a database.

SGML parser

Defined by the SGML standard as "A program (or portion of a program or a combination of programs) that recognizes markup in SGML conforming documents." In terms of programming language processors, an SGML parser performs the functions of both a lexical analyser and a parser with respect to SGML documents. A parser that is able to read a DTD and to check whether markup errors exist and report them if they do, is called a **validating SGML parser**.

sgmls
A popular sgml parser available from the public domain. Some commercial products are based on it. This parser is based on the ARCSGML parser donated by an anonymous donor to the SGML User's Group for free distribution.

SMFF
The Script Mathematical Formula Formatter. IBM's mathematical formula formatter which is intended for use with the IBM Script VS product. It uses a subset of the EQN syntax.

SPDL
Standard Page Description Language. A proposed ISO standard language to describe images to output devices, similar to PostScript.

specific markup
Markup that contain instructions that are concerned with the physical appearance of a document. They are either hand written (in the traditional publishing process) or formulated in terms of a text formatting language.

SQL
Structured Query Language. The ANSI (and now also ISO) standard ANSI, Database Language SQL (ANSI X3.135-1986) query language for relational database management systems. Commercial implementations include those from Oracle and IBM (SQL/DS).

strong typing
A feature of programming languages to declare variables as integer, real, logical, etc.

stylesheet
A collection of formatting instructions for a given text element (a style) or a group of text elements.

Syspub
A generic markup language from Watcom Products, written in Script.

tag
A symbol delimiting a logical element inside a document. Defined by the SGML standard as "descriptive markup." There are start-tags and end-tags.

template
A set of commands that will help a user create documents of a certain type.

TEX
Tau Epsilon Xi. An elegant text formatter developed by Donald Knuth with a powerful and intuitive way of describing mathematical formulas. It is very popular in the scientific world because it is portable and available in the public domain (see [5]).

text	Data which are composed of characters and words. In this book we assume these data are available electronically on a computer.
text for-matter	See formatter.
troff	A text formatting system for high quality printers which runs on the UNIX operating system.
typeface	A typeface is a collection of groups of letters (fonts) with certain general characteristics. There are two groups: serif (e.g., Times) and sans-serif (e.g., Helvetica).
typesize	The size of a typeface is defined as the distance from one line of text to the next and is usually measured in points (1/72"). A typesize of 10 points is the most agreeable [1] size for reading at an average distance of 40 cm.
UNIX	An interactive operating system for all-size computers developed by AT&T. Its great advantage is its portability.
validating SGML parser	See SGML parser.
variant concrete syntax	A concrete syntax that differs from the reference concrete syntax. Must be defined if the characters that are used in the document instance do not correspond to those in ISO 646:1983, or if any of the reference concrete syntax delimiters are changed.
VM/CMS	Virtual Machine/Conversational Monitor System. An interactive operating system in use on IBM middle to large size computers.
VMS	An operating system from Digital Equipment Corporation that runs on their popular VAX computers.
Waterloo	A modern university in Waterloo, Canada, with a strong computer science department that runs the Watcom group.
window	Computers that have a graphical user interface and are capable of splitting the screen into several windows. Inside each window, the computer may be used to do a different task. If the windows are made on a computer that runs a multi-tasking operating system (such as UNIX or OS/2), these tasks will run at the same time. An example of a windowing system for UNIX is X Windows[6].
word pro-cessor	An interactive system for editing and formatting text (e.g., Wang systems). Can be described as an electronic typewriter with a screen and memory.

WYSIWYG   What You See Is What You Get. A term used to describe a computer system where each user action is immediately displayed on the screen in a way that closely resembles the formatted document on paper. This term should be used with care since it raises user expectations in a way that often cannot be fulfilled, since the resolution of a screen rarely corresponds to that of a printer.

[1]   R.A. Morris
Image Processing Aspects of Type, in Document Manipulation and Typography
Cambridge University Press, Cambridge, 1988
[2]   CCITT
Red Book Vol.-FASCILE VIII.7, Recomm. X.400-X.430
Geneva, 1985
[3]   L. Lamport
LaTeX, A Document Preparation System
Addison-Wesley, Reading, 1986
[4]   M. Goossens, F. Mittelbach and A. Samarin
The LaTeX companion
Addison-Wesley, Reading, 1994
[5]   Donald E. Knuth
The TeX book
Addison-Wesley, Reading, 1986
[6]   R.W. Scheiffer, J. Gettys
The X Window system, ACM Transactions on Graphics,
April, 1986

Index

N